Language Handbook

Key Thinkers on Key Topics

edited by Dan Clayton,
with a Foreword by Professor Ronald Carter

*We would like to dedicate this 2nd edition to the memory
of the life and work of Ron Carter 1947-2018.*

Acknowledgements

Editor: Dan Clayton

Cover image: Rebecca Scamber, 2018 using 'Faces with letter speech bubbles' © Alamy Ltd

Published by: The English and Media Centre © 2018
18 Compton Terrace, London, N1 2UN
www.englishandmedia.co.uk

ISBN: 978-1-906101-62-6

Printed and bound by Stephens and George Ltd

Typeset in Adobe Garamond Pro and Humanist BT

Thanks to the British Library for permission to reproduce three cartoons from *Punch*: 'I beg your Pardon, Ma'am, but I think you dropped this?' *Punch*, October 1855; 'The Airship Menace' *Punch*, 1915; 'Thrift' *Punch*, 5th December 1868. Thanks to Getty for licensing images: © Said Khatib/Agence France-Presse/Getty Images; © Mahmud Hams/Agence france-Presse/Getty Images; © Jack Guez/Agence France-Presse/Getty Images

CONTENTS

Foreword – Professor Ronald Carter		4
Introduction to the 2nd Edition – Dan Clayton		6
A Note on the Text		9
1.	Gender and Communication Professor Deborah Cameron	10
2.	Language Variation 1 – Social Factors: Class and Ethnicity Professor Paul Kerswill	22
3.	Language Variation 2 – Patterns of Accent Variation in British English Dr Kevin Watson	42
4.	English Around the World Professor Jane Setter	56
5.	American English Professor Lynne Murphy	70
6.	Urban Youth Language Dr Rob Drummond	83
7.	Spoken Language Dr Sue Fox	97
8.	Language Change Dr Graeme Trousdale	112
9.	Attitudes to Language Change Dan Clayton	122
10.	Language and Technology Professor Angela Goddard	135
11.	Child Language Acquisition Dr Paul Ibbotson	148
12.	Critical Discourse Analysis Professor Christopher Hart	163
13.	Textual Analysis and Stylistics Professor Peter Stockwell	181
14.	Forensic Linguistics Dr Nicci MacLeod	193
Glossary		206
The Contributors		216
Index		220

FOREWORD

Over the past forty years or so, the study of language, especially the English language, has changed in striking ways. In the 1970s and 1980s, and especially in secondary schools, language study was still a relatively new discipline and a relatively new area of research and teaching.

As with many new disciplines, the first steps involve defining core terms of reference, producing a stable metalanguage and describing what actually constitutes the field. In any such process of disciplinary definition there is, in the early years, an inevitable element of idealisation of the core data of the subject involved. In the case of language study this entailed a practice of inventing examples or drawing on language data without reference to who was involved in the communication or to where, when and for what purpose the communication was taking place.

So it's not surprising really that language was described and defined in a generally context-free way and that the modes of study of the subject matched this lack of context by inviting students mainly to define and describe the central forms of the language: the sound system, the grammar, semantics and vocabulary structures that make up the core of the language. Very obviously invented examples were not uncommon and students could be asked to describe the grammar of sentences that are very obviously written and unlikely to be commonly spoken. Who can parse 'It was the alienated philosopher who tried to pull the very strong jaw of the hen that couldn't stop clucking?'

There were, of course, grand exceptions that ran in parallel such as the *Language in Use* series (part of a 1970s Schools Council project) produced under the overall direction of Michael Halliday where the emphasis was on language as it is actually used and produced in a variety of different spoken and written contexts[1]; but such an approach was an exception at that time, however influential it subsequently came to be. It's also not surprising either that English language study in its earliest days had a relatively limited appeal and such appeal that it *did* have was mainly confined to those who are interested in the more atomistic components of things and who accept that such approaches inevitably entail more mechanistic and narrowly analytical practices.

Since this time the field of English language study has grown at a remarkable rate in both range and scope and it is now a standardised part of the university and school curriculum with a growing number of students taking A Level or degree courses in English with a main focus on linguistic study. As the field has produced richer and ever more detailed accounts of how language works and of the systems by which the forms of language are organised (still the heart and core of the discipline), so increasing attention has been given to language use and to language in context. This book reflects many of the most exciting and important developments in this direction while also, as in the case of a topic such as world Englishes, pointing to challenging futures[2].

Foreword

The chapters in the *Language Handbook* chart the changes and current practices in the discipline, underlining the importance of how language works in, and adjusts to, different social contexts, privileging in theory and methodological practice the need for real and evidenced data over concocted examples, evidencing the significance of world English use, showing the many interfaces between language and literature, linking the cognitive and the social and illustrating how technology and the internet are, among other factors, driving forces in the ever more complex and controversial processes of language change and standardisation. At the same time (and this is probably a topic for another volume), corpus linguistics is, as a number of contributors highlight, redrawing the map of how we might describe language. Access to corpora such as the BNC (British National Corpus) (now vastly more accessible than even five years ago) is changing how we do research in and with language, as well as what is investigated and how, and why classroom language study might look the way it does over the next twenty years. And the ubiquitous nature of language in both our everyday social and cognitive life, and as constitutive of other disciplines, points further to interdisciplinary study as a rich future.

The move to examination of 'real' naturally-occurring (as opposed to invented) language data has changed the way English language is studied in classrooms and has led to more empirical data collection and investigation, as well as to more student-centred research tasks and projects. The engagement with data collection (spoken and written) by means of, for example, interviews, media forms, corpus sources, laboratory experiments and the multi-billion word data bank of the internet has involved students actively in English language study and this has been reinforced by curricula which continue to assess not only the capacity for formal analysis but also the additional skills of language research. The simple use of digital recorders to collect examples of spoken language has in itself shown the limitations of too narrow a focus on written language and also challenged students of language at all levels to explore the differences and distinctions between speech and writing, leading in turn to new descriptive accounts of language in use.

I started by reflecting back to some of the origins of English language study in the 1970s and 80s. The English and Media Centre, the editor of the *Language Handbook*, Dan Clayton, and the distinguished cast list of contributors are to be congratulated on having produced a richly nuanced and wonderfully accessible volume, a volume, in fact, that is very much for our time.

Professor Ronald Carter

[1] For example: Doughty, P., J. Pearce & G. Thornton, G., 1971. *Language in Use*. Schools Council Project London: Edward Arnold, London.
[2] For a valuable contribution to current directions in English language study particularly from the point of view of the student see also Goddard, A., 2012. *Doing English Language*. London: Routledge.

INTRODUCTION TO THE 2ND EDITION

When we put together the first edition of the EMC *Language Handbook* in 2012, we had a clear idea in mind. We wanted to provide something for both students and teachers of A Level English Language. For students, we wanted to offer some of the most up to date and well-informed perspectives on key areas of study for their course, contextualised within a wider framework that allowed them to see how the different areas related to each other. For teachers, it was a similar aim. We wanted to offer the chance to refresh their subject knowledge, stimulate their intellectual curiosity and to have ready access to material that they could use with students who wanted to read around the course and stretch themselves.

To achieve this, we approached leading linguists to write chapters that would give an accessible overview of their field, lead into the research and thinking that's gone on in the past, before bringing us up to date with some insights into more recent developments. At the heart of the first edition was a desire to go beyond the usual territory and open up new areas of thinking for both audiences, areas that they could then explore and pursue. And we'd like to think the first edition of the *Language Handbook* went some way towards doing these things.

Now, six years on, with new A Level specifications and new content for students and teachers to think about, we have taken the opportunity to update the Language Handbook with four new chapters: forensic linguistics, critical discourse analysis, American English and urban youth language and an updated chapter on language and technology.

As we said in the introduction to the first edition, this is not an exam board-approved textbook or revision guide, so you won't find constant references to where topics fit in to particular components and specifications, discussions about assessment objectives, or explanations about how to impress the examiner marking your paper. Instead, what you'll find are plenty of ideas, examples and new approaches, all of which have been carefully chosen because they are relevant to most advanced level study, as well as being useful for those beginning university study.

By its nature some of what you find in here will be challenging and new. That's the point. A certain degree of previous study is assumed, so we would expect you to have at least covered the basics of grammar and textual analysis, and to have looked at some of the key topics – child language development, language change, language variation and diversity – with your teachers or lecturers. However, there is an extensive glossary which does offer some basic definitions if you need to go back and refresh your memory.

An overview of the chapters

Each of the fourteen chapters in the handbook has been put together with a common structure. They each begin with a quick introduction and look at why the topic is interesting to study, then offer an overview of some of the key work done in the field so far, before moving on to consider current thinking, debates and directions. Each chapter also offers a summary of key ideas and suggestions for further reading.

Deborah Cameron's chapter on gender and communication looks at competing arguments and models about how women and men communicate, and takes issue with generalisations about gender. Placing the study of spoken language and gender in its historical context, she moves on to look at new approaches that deconstruct simplified notions of gender, foregrounding the local and the individual.

Both **Paul Kerswill's** and **Kevin Watson's** chapters look at language variation. Kerswill's focus is on variation linked to class and ethnicity and Watson's on regional variation, with both drawing on their own research and that of others to bring us right up-to-date with the changing picture in the UK.

Sue Fox, whose chapter draws on data from studies of changing London English, offers an overview of many of the features of spoken English before moving on to some of the most recent work on what are called discourse-pragmatic markers, considering the changing functions of features of spoken language.

Graeme Trousdale's chapter on language change foregrounds social context and overarching patterns of change, but draws too on the link between diachronic and synchronic variation to make the point that change is rarely a regular and consistent process, but one that has links to age, class, region and identity too.

My chapter on attitudes to language change considers the different complaints there have been about how language changes, the development of Standard English and forms that kick against it. The chapter looks too at what lies beyond the basic 'prescriptive versus descriptive' continuum of attitudes to language change, offering alternative models and ideas.

Jane Setter's chapter on English around the world addresses one of the most contentious areas of language study at the moment: the spread of English around the world and its varying uses and forms. Do *the English ... have as much control over English as the Italians have over pizza and Indians over chicken korma* – as one anonymous *Daily Telegraph* contributor put it – or is there still an umbilical link between England and English? Moving into arguments about English, Englishes and English as a lingua franca, Setter opens up the topic for further discussion and debate.

Lynne Murphy's new chapter on American English looks at one of the most successful varieties of English around the world and charts its rise to prominence. Considering not just what it is but how it is viewed, Murphy examines some of the differences and similarities between the English of the UK and USA but also the various social and regional variations used within the USA.

The new chapter on urban youth language by **Rob Drummond** considers the innovations in language that have come from young people. Looking at ideas around how language can be used to perform different identities and the various influences on these identities – music, culture, social and ethnic background and age among them – Drummond examines the features and uses of different forms of language in the UK and beyond.

Angela Goddard's updated chapter on language and technology considers the bigger picture of the technologies we use to communicate, but has at its heart issues of identity and interaction. Goddard examines some of the ways in which the web has changed how we communicate and takes us through some of the most recent research into online communication and how it can be analysed.

Paul Ibbotson's chapter on child language development offers us a world beyond the rather reductive (and outdated) Skinner versus Chomsky debates that have come to dominate A Level English Language. Looking at work on cognitive-functionalism and constructions in speech, he charts the fascinating development of new ideas about how and why children acquire language and offers fresh approaches to the topic.

The new chapter on critical discourse analysis by **Christopher Hart** reflects a trend in some of the new A Levels towards a more discourse-analysis based approach. Hart looks at how language helps to construct versions of the world around us, shaping our perceptions and revealing underlying ideologies. Through detailed discussion of a range of telling examples, Hart focuses on the power of language but also the power students of language have to make sense of the world around them.

Peter Stockwell's chapter on textual analysis and stylistics complements the previous chapter and offers an overview of thinking about textual analysis and a wealth of original examples and different models for looking at different text types, moving into the literary and creative. Both of these chapters open up ways of looking at language that lead directly into undergraduate study – critical linguistics and stylistics – but which also underpin much analysis at A Level. Here Hart and Stockwell reveal a bit more about why we study language in the way we do, the kind of texts that are often most revealing for analysis and what benefits these different approaches can bring.

The final chapter, another new one, rounds off the second edition by focusing on forensic linguistics. In this chapter **Nicci MacLeod** takes students well beyond the A Level course into a field where language study overlaps with the law and policing. Covering a range of cases and offering some fascinating insights into the ways linguists work to solve crimes, MacLeod explains some of the key principles of the forensic linguist and shows the ways that language study can be applied practically.

Dan Clayton, Editor

A NOTE ON THE TEXT

Use of phonetic and phonemic symbols

Phonetics is the study of sounds made by human beings across all languages. Phonology is the study of how these sounds are used systematically in specific human languages (e.g., English, French, Hindi) and how the phonemes – meaningful units of sound in those languages – are used to create changes in meaning.

We have followed linguistic convention in using the following system when representing sounds:

- phonetic transcriptions are shown in square brackets [sound]
- phonemic transcriptions are shown in slant lines /sound/.

Where a single letter rather than sound is indicated we have used 'letter'.

Phonological terms

Some of the chapters in the handbook (particularly those exploring accent and dialect) use specialist phonological terms such as ***alveolar***, ***vowel centralisation*** and ***diphthong***. These terms are best understood when they are heard, as well as defined in words. The following websites offering audio illustrations of key phonetic terms are recommended as good starting points for students looking to develop their understanding of phonetics:

> http://www.phonetics.ucla.edu/course/chapter1/chapter1.html
> (University of California, Los Angeles, A Course in Phonetics)

> http://www.uiowa.edu/~acadtech/phonetics/
> (University of Iowa, The Sounds of Spoken English)

> http://www.bbc.co.uk/worldservice/learningenglish/grammar/pron/sounds/
> (BBC Learning English, Pronunciation Tips)

Words in bold in the text

Rather than embolden all linguistic terms in every chapter, we have chosen to embolden only those words which are key to the topic under discussion.

Glossary

The glossary includes an extensive list of linguistic terms, going beyond those specifically discussed in the chapters, as a basic reference for students at an early stage of their specialist language study.

1 GENDER & COMMUNICATION

Professor Deborah Cameron

1. Introduction

The study of gender and communication is often thought of as a field of inquiry which investigates differences in the way language is used either by or about the two sexes. But many researchers today would question that definition, which implies that we can make general statements about the verbal behaviour of two groups that each comprise half the world's population. Generalisations of this kind (e.g., 'women talk more than men', or 'men communicate more directly than women') are a staple ingredient of popular writing. But academic research confirms what is also obvious to common sense, if you give it a moment's thought: both 'men' and 'women' are internally diverse groups, and how they communicate is bound to differ considerably depending on who and where they are. It is not obvious that Tamil-speaking farmers in rural south India will exhibit the same gendered speech patterns as English-speaking car mechanics in Swindon; the mechanics' own patterns may be different from those observed in a Catholic monastery a few miles down the road.

With that diversity in mind, most contemporary researchers prefer a more open-ended definition of what they study than just 'differences between men and women'. When people ask me what my research is about, I say it's about the relationship between language and gender – how gender influences language-use and how language-use may influence our perceptions of gender. This definition acknowledges that there is a relationship, but it avoids implying that the nature of that relationship is always and everywhere the same, a simple matter of 'men talk like this and women talk like that'.

2. Why study gender and communication?

There is more than one reason why gender is of interest to linguistic researchers. One area of linguistic inquiry with a longstanding interest in the subject is **sociolinguistics**, the study of language variation and change. All living languages show variability (i.e. they are not used in a completely uniform way by all speakers in all contexts), and the variation linguists have documented is structured rather than random, reflecting (among other things) the social differences that exist among language users. Gender divisions, along with regional, class and ethnic differences, have been found to influence language-use in many speech communities. Although there are no distinctively male and female speech varieties analogous to regional varieties like Yorkshire dialect, ethnic varieties like African American English or social class varieties like Received Pronunciation, most studies of variation have found that there are statistically measurable differences in men's and women's ways of speaking.

Gender appears to play an especially important role in one kind of variation that many sociolinguists are interested in: variation over time, or, in other words, linguistic change. Where some aspect of a language is changing, it is common for researchers to find that women are ahead of men in adopting the newer form. In British English, for example, we are currently seeing a change in the pronunciation of the vowel in words like *goose*, which is becoming more fronted (produced further forward in the mouth). The leaders of this change – those who produce the highest proportion of fronted /u/ sounds and/or the most extreme fronting – tend to be young women. It is not surprising to find that younger speakers are more innovative than older ones: young people are also at the forefront of change in other spheres, like fashion or the adoption of new technologies. But it is less obvious why women should be more innovative linguistically than men. To understand why this is a common pattern, linguists must consider how gender works as a social system. One explanation which has been suggested is to do with the gender segregation of the job market. Many typically female jobs (e.g., nursing, serving in shops or working in call centres) involve talking to a wide range of people from outside your own immediate social network; this means that women are well-placed to pick up linguistic innovations. Another theory is that the cultural tendency to judge women by 'symbolic' criteria (how they appear as opposed to what they do) leads them to pay close attention to the fine details of speech, and to be more extreme than men in their use of the linguistic features that symbolise group membership.

The sociolinguists whose work I have just been discussing are interested in gender because of the light it sheds on more general phenomena like language change. But for other researchers, including anthropologists, sociologists and psychologists as well as linguists, the angle of approach is the opposite: language offers a lens through which to examine the workings of gender in society. That, in fact, was how language and gender studies originally emerged as a distinct area of inquiry.

3. Language, gender and feminism: a brief history

The modern field of language and gender studies emerged first in north America (though it was soon taken up in other places, like Australia, Britain and Western Europe) in the 1970s – the peak period of what is often labelled the 'second wave' of feminism. The 'first wave' had occurred in the nineteenth and early twentieth centuries: its key political achievement was to win full citizenship rights for women by securing their right to vote. But as the feminists who became active in the Women's Liberation Movement of the 1970s pointed out, women were still in many ways second-class citizens. They continued to face discrimination in education and at work; married women were still treated as subordinate to their husbands (for instance, they needed their husband's permission to take out a loan, even if they had an independent income); wife-beating, sexual harassment and even rape were not taken seriously as crimes; and popular culture routinely stereotyped women in ways that ranged from the patronising (the ditzy housewives and empty-headed 'chicks' who appeared in advertisements and sitcoms) to the outright misogynist (the domineering mothers found in contemporary novels and the disposable sex-objects of hardcore pornography). It was second-wave feminists who invented the term 'sexism' to describe this cultural phenomenon. And in their efforts to analyse it systematically, they paid attention to the role that language played in it.

The study of language and gender as we know it today developed from this feminist interest in connecting language, not simply to differences between men and women, but to the social system of gender which made the sexes both different and unequal. I stress this point because it is important to recognise that there is nothing inherently feminist about simply studying sex-differences. On the contrary, this can be and often has been an anti-feminist enterprise, undertaken to prove women's inferiority and so justify their unequal treatment. When feminists of the 1970s began their own examination of language, there was already a long tradition of commentary of this sort on the supposed linguistic differences between men and women. Much of this was anecdotal – rather like the popular writing I mentioned earlier – but some of it did purport to be based on scientific research. Anthropologists had published articles about traditional societies in which, they alleged, men and women either spoke entirely different languages, or followed systematically different rules for the use of a shared language. Psychologists had reported linguistic experiments with male and female subjects in European societies whose results they interpreted as evidence of women's inferiority. For example, men's superior intellects were said to be reflected in their larger and more varied vocabularies, and their more frequent use of complex sentences with embedded (subordinate) clauses.

The feminists who turned to this topic in the 1970s criticised the male bias of this earlier research tradition, but they did not reject its emphasis on male-female differences in language, nor its habit of treating men's language as the default mode from which women's language deviated. What was distinctive about the new wave of feminist studies was the way they interpreted the differences they discussed, as evidence not of women's natural deficiencies, but of their social subordination in male-dominated societies.

3.1 The 'dominance' approach

Probably the best-known example of this **dominance approach** is Robin Lakoff's pioneering 1975 essay 'Language and woman's place'. What Lakoff set out to show was how conventional language use had the effect of putting and keeping women in their place. One aspect of this was what we now call 'sexist language'. Women were often referred to using words and phrases which foregrounded their physical attributes (e.g., ***blonde***) and/or their relationships to men (***the wife***), and which were not paralleled by similar expressions for men. Alternatively they were left out of the picture altogether through the use of masculine terms as generics (e.g., ***man*** as the name for the human species, and ***he*** as the only 'correct' pronoun for referring to 'the child', 'the poet', 'the scientist', etc.). This was a common concern for feminists in the 1970s, and Lakoff was not the first to raise it. What was original about 'Language and woman's place', and what it is mainly remembered for today, was Lakoff's suggestion that women are not just kept in their place by the way they are spoken or written about, but also by the way they use language themselves.

Beginning when they are little girls, Lakoff argued, women are socialised to use a kind of language that makes its users sound trivial, silly and powerless. The hallmarks of this 'women's language' included 'super-politeness' (e.g., making requests very indirectly and avoiding 'strong' swear-words), using empty and trivial vocabulary (words like *** lovely*** and ***aquamarine***, rather than just 'blue'), phrasing statements as tag-questions, as if soliciting others' approval for one's own opinions (*** that's a lovely scooter, isn't it?***) and hedging propositions to make them sound less forceful (*** I'm just going to the shop***, *** I'm a little bit worried about Susie***). Lakoff acknowledged that women could choose to avoid these ways of talking, but if they did, she observed, they risked being criticised as 'unfeminine'. If they used 'women's language', on the other hand, they would be criticised for lacking competence and seriousness.

Other researchers in the 1970s set out to show how everyday conversational patterns both reflected and reproduced the social hierarchy in which males outranked females. Many studies found that men tended to dominate the **conversational floor** (that is, take more of the talking time) in formal and public settings such as school classrooms, academic seminars, business meetings and political or media discussions. Some reported that even women with high status, like doctors and other professionals, were constantly liable to be interrupted by men. At the same time it was women who were most often expected to do the conversational support-work in social and domestic settings – making small-talk to put people at their ease, responding enthusiastically to others' contributions, and asking questions whose function was to give others the floor. Women made the effort, and men reaped the benefits.

This research tradition had strong links to the feminist movement of the time: for many researchers, the point was not just to produce knowledge for its own sake, but to raise awareness about the role of language in reproducing gender inequality so that women (and fair-minded men) could take practical measures to change things. If teachers understood that they were unconsciously giving the boys in their classes more talking time than the girls, they could make a conscious effort to treat the two groups equally. If women realised that they habitually spoke in a way that made them sound powerless, they could try to adopt a more assertive style. And if men who in theory supported gender equality realised that in practice they were dominating women, they could make a decision to do less talking and more listening.

3.2 The 'difference' approach

But there was another strand in second-wave feminism which focused less on identifying and treating the symptoms of male dominance and more on giving greater visibility and value to the cultural contributions of women. As feminists of this persuasion saw it, the fact that women did things differently was not, in itself, a problem; the problem was rather that women's ways of doing things were not valued in the same way as men's. In relation to language, this view produced what has come to be called the **difference approach**: a body of research on male and (especially) female speech styles which emphasised that they were different *but equal*. Some research of this kind was produced in the 1970s, when 'dominance' and 'difference' were generally seen as two sides of a single coin. But the 'difference' approach became more prominent in the 1980s, when it also began to be presented more explicitly as an alternative to 'dominance'.

Whereas 'dominance' researchers had tended to focus on verbal interactions involving both sexes, 'difference' researchers were more interested in describing the talk that took place between same-sex peers – for instance, friends, playmates, school classmates and work colleagues. As these researchers pointed out, there is a strong tendency for our core friendship groups, the people we spend most time with and feel closest to, especially in childhood and adolescence, to be made up of individuals of our own gender. These are the people who have most influence on our own ways of speaking, and the result will tend to be differences in the speech-styles which are typical of men and women. One claim that was made frequently was that all-female groups tend to favour a co-operative and egalitarian style of speech, whereas all-male ones are more competitive and hierarchical. Girls and women use talking to share their experiences and feelings; they are good at supporting others and avoiding or defusing conflict. Boys and men, by contrast, use talking to assert themselves and vie with each other for status. Boasting, insults and direct orders are common moves in all-male conversation, whereas all-female conversation puts more emphasis on complimenting, seeking agreement, and making suggestions for what 'we' should do.

Some 'difference' researchers – most notably Deborah Tannen in her bestselling book *You Just Don't Understand* (1990) – added a further step to this argument. Tannen suggested that many of the problems which had been attributed to the workings of male dominance were better explained as cases of male-female miscommunication. If men and women have different styles of speaking, acquired in their single-sex peer-groups, then it is logical to suppose that they will approach mixed-sex conversations with different assumptions and expectations, and that consequently they will have a tendency to misinterpret one another's intentions. For instance, a man who expects orders to be direct (because that's how things are done in all-male peer groups) may take the indirect request made by his female boss as merely a suggestion, and not the definite instruction she intended to convey. According to this account, the man is not simply a sexist who resents having to take orders from a woman: he genuinely does not understand that his boss is giving him an order. Tannen compares this to the kind of problem an English business traveller might encounter in dealing with a colleague from another culture, like Finland or Japan. The solution is not for either sex to change the way they speak (if the two styles are 'different but equal', why should anyone have to give up their own style?). Rather men and women should be aware of their differences and learn to make allowances for them. Popularised by Tannen, this argument was repeated in John Gray's even more successful *Men are from Mars, Women are from Venus* (1992), and many other self-help books published in the 1990s which had no connection with either feminist politics or academic debates about language and gender. The latter, in fact, were soon to go in a very different direction.

4. New directions: looking locally

Many language and gender researchers in the early 1990s were dismayed by the popular success of *You Just Don't Understand*. Those who subscribed to the 'dominance' view of language and gender felt that Tannen downplayed the role of power and inequality in producing the differences she discussed. They also disputed her argument that male-female differences are like cultural differences, and lead to similar problems of miscommunication. The male and female members of one society may spend a lot of time in single-sex peer groups, but unlike people from different cultures, such as the US and Japan, they also have extensive experience of interacting with one another (most families are mixed-sex groups), and a shared language system in which to interact.

But these 'dominance'-based objections were not the only reason why many researchers were troubled by Tannen's approach. By the early 1990s there was a growing feeling of dissatisfaction among linguists with the kinds of generalisations that underpinned both 'dominance' and 'difference'. Right from the start, there had been disputes about the empirical validity of general statements like 'men's style is competitive, women's is co-operative' (a 'difference' claim), 'men dominate the floor and women do conversational support work' (a 'dominance' claim), or the more specific proposals made by Lakoff about 'women's language' (e.g., women make more use than men of tag-questions, hedging and elaborate colour terms). Numerous studies were carried out to test these hypotheses, but the results had a tendency to be mixed and inconclusive. Even patterns for which the evidence was fairly solid (such as the tendency, mentioned above, for women to be leaders of linguistic change) were not without exceptions; and typically it was only some men and women, not all of them, whose behaviour exemplified the pattern (which is a problem if your explanation for the pattern relies on the idea that 'men-in-general are like this and women-in-general are like that'). In sum, the more evidence researchers gathered, the harder it became to maintain the idea that some core set of linguistic practices (like speaking more or less co-operatively, or politely, or 'correctly') consistently distinguished male from female language-users. While gender differences of some sort were found more or less universally, the actual linguistic patterns which differentiated men and women were not the same ones in every case, and the differences were rarely as clear-cut as 'all the men do one thing, and all the women do another'.

In 1990 the sociolinguist Penelope Eckert published a now-famous article to which she gave the title 'The whole woman'. In it she made two related criticisms of the way most linguists had approached gender. First, she pointed out that although they used the term 'gender', their actual procedures for studying its influence on speech – simply categorising informants as either women or men and comparing the two groups – conflated gender with biological sex. Feminists and social theorists make a distinction between the two. Sex is a matter of chromosomes and reproductive organs, which do not vary across cultures and through time; gender is a matter of social roles and identities, which are far more variable. Though some aspects of language-use are related to biological sex (for instance, biology accounts for most, though not all, of the difference in average male and female voice-pitch), the variations sociolinguists study are more directly related to social conditions (e.g., the jobs men and women do, their education, who they socialise with). Simply categorising speakers by sex and looking for differences between the two sexes may both obscure the actual extent of gender-related variation, and fail to tell you much about the reasons for it.

Eckert's other, related criticism was that linguists had implicitly treated gender (or sex) as a discrete variable, something whose influence on speech could be studied in isolation from every other influence. This, she argued, showed a lack of understanding of what gender is and how it works. In reality gender does not exist, or influence behaviour, in isolation, but interacts with other aspects of identity and social location, like ethnicity, age and class. It is true that someone's status as either a man or a woman will in most cases have a significant influence on the way that person lives their life; but what it actually means to live your life as a man or a woman is clearly going to be affected by whether you are Chinese or Polish, white or black, working class or middle class, a teenager or a pensioner (and many other factors as well, from education to religious beliefs). No one is, or thinks of him/herself as, just a generic 'man' or 'woman': they think of themselves as specific kinds of men and women, and the way gender is expressed in their behaviour (including their use of language) is shaped by those more specific identities.

Anyone who has ever seen the reality TV show *Ladette to Lady* will understand what Eckert was getting at. The show sets out to transform individuals who have one way of being a woman – the modern 'ladette' way which is associated with being young and working class – by explicitly teaching them a different kind of femininity, the kind associated with the traditional upper-class 'lady'. This provides a dramatic illustration of how large the gap can be between different versions of the same gender; it also shows that language (both accent and style) plays an important role in marking the differences.

If gender is not reducible to biological sex, and if women and men come in many varieties, not just one, then the goal of language and gender studies cannot be to make universal statements or large-scale generalisations about men's speech and women's speech: these will always be over-generalisations. In 1992 Eckert and her collaborator Sally McConnell-Ginet summarised what they thought researchers should be doing instead in the injunction 'think practically and look locally'. In other words, 'don't start from global propositions about 'men' and 'women'; go into some specific community, look closely at the way gender works in that community, and try to relate the way men and women use language to their local conditions' (Eckert & McConnell-Ginet 1992). Researchers who follow this advice are still studying the influence of gender on language, but their investigations no longer automatically revolve around the traditional quest for male-female differences. They are just as interested in the possibility that local conditions might produce a high degree of similarity between men and women; and they are very interested in differences among men or among women, since the 'look locally' approach begins from the assumption that such differences are normal, and suggests that they can tell us interesting things about the way gender is understood and lived out in different communities, or subgroups within communities.

Since the 1990s, a lot of the most interesting language and gender research has focused on the diversity of the gender identities which language can be used to perform in different local contexts. There have been studies of the language used by, for instance, African-American drag queens, white college fraternity brothers, female footballers and male rugby players, high school girls in Bolton, male and female managers in New Zealand, nerd girls in California, phone-sex workers, and women MPs in the British House of Commons. Research of this kind has confirmed that gendered performances vary considerably in different communities and contexts (some of the studies just mentioned found the same individuals performing gender in strikingly different ways depending what they were doing and who they were talking to). It has also underlined the need to pay attention to small local distinctions within one gender-group: often these nuances turn out to be extremely important to the speakers themselves. In their study of Bolton high school girls, for instance, Emma Moore and

Robert Podesva found that the same linguistic variable (the tag question, as in *that's a lovely scooter, isn't it?*) was used to differing extents, and for different purposes, by girls who belonged to different cliques. Though on all the basic demographic criteria these girls were far more similar than different – they were all in the same year at the same school – their ways of using language reflected the significance they attached to the differences between rebellious 'townies', mainstream 'populars', girly 'Eden village girls' and academic 'geeks'. Identity is not just about who you *are*, but just as much about who you feel you are *not*, and wouldn't want to be confused with.

5. Performing gender

In the last paragraph you may have noticed that I used the terms 'perform' and 'performance'. This reflects the influence, since the 1990s, of the idea that gender, and identity more generally, is constructed through the repeated performance of certain culturally meaningful acts – including, of course, linguistic acts. This contrasts with the earlier view, exemplified in the work of people like Lakoff and Tannen, that gendered identities and ways of speaking are acquired once and for all in childhood. That view implies that identities are fixed; the **performative** view, by contrast, suggests that identity is unstable, and that speakers must continually reaffirm their status as a particular sort of person by repeating the acts their culture associates with that sort of person. This also implies that in principle speakers can choose to perform identity in different or unexpected ways – they are not simply pre-programmed to do the same thing in the same way forever.

Of course there are limits on our freedom to perform identity: we are susceptible to social pressure to present ourselves in particular ways, and in relation to gender that pressure can be very strong. Some versions of masculinity and femininity are stigmatised as 'deviant', and are therefore avoided by those who are anxious to be seen as 'normal' (it is common, for instance, for school-age boys to avoid any way of speaking or acting that carries the cultural label 'gay'). At the same time, it can be argued that the recent popularity of the 'performative' approach is a response to the relaxation of the traditional, very rigid gender divisions which were taken for granted in the past. The idea that gender is a performance rather than a natural condition makes more sense to us now, because of the greater diversity of the gender-performances we are familiar with. An obvious illustration is the much greater visibility, and acceptability, of non-heterosexual masculinities and femininities. But we also recognise a more diverse array of heterosexual gender identities – witness the proliferation of category-labels which draw a contrast between, say, 'lads' and 'metrosexuals', or 'ladettes' and 'girly girls'. Even the idea that there is an absolute dividing line between men and women has been challenged by the emergence of a category of 'transgendered' people who deliberately cross the line, taking on a gender identity which does not match their biological sex. Some trans people perform their self-chosen gender in very conventional ways, but others see themselves as deliberately subverting the two-gender system by performing identities which do not fit neatly into the traditional categories. And, of course, the very idea that one can change or choose one's gender is itself a challenge to conventional understandings of gender identity as something determined by, if not reducible to, sex.

Why, you might ask, are we seeing this proliferation of gender identities and performances? We are not, it should be acknowledged, seeing it to the same extent everywhere in the world; but for people living in affluent and cosmopolitan societies, it has been suggested that the conditions of twenty-first century life make us more intensely concerned than our ancestors were about questions of identity in general. It used to be common (and in some places still is) for people to spend their whole lives in the same small and relatively closed communities, whose members were tightly linked by kinship and shared tradition. In this kind of community, where most of the people you encounter will have known you since birth, there is little scope for negotiating or redefining your individual identity. But in today's highly mobile and fluid societies, where it is not rare for people to change their locations, jobs and partners, and where interaction with others who do not already know them is an everyday occurrence, they have both more choice about what kind of person to be, and more need to put thought and effort into managing their self-presentation.

One contemporary practice which provides a striking illustration of this point is online social networking. Dedicated users of sites like Facebook perform their online identities by carefully designing and then refining their profiles, and by producing an ongoing narrative about themselves in the status updates, comments and other items they regularly post. (Some academic theorists of identity have pointed out how heavily it depends on maintaining a narrative of the self, a chronological account of important life-events; the people behind Facebook evidently recognise this too, since they are now inviting users to integrate the various items they post – reports on what they have been doing, reading, listening to, etc. – into what they have named a 'timeline'.)

Gender is an important element in the identities Facebook-users construct, not only because it has to be specified in their profiles, but also because it is linked to other markers of individual identity, like preferred leisure activities, musical tastes, and involvement or interest in sexual relationships. And language is also of central importance for the process of online identity construction. Though some of the resources Facebook users have to work with are visual (e.g., photos), it is (written) language which provides the most nuanced and versatile medium for telling the story of the self.

6. What's next?

The linguistic performance of gender in online social networks is one topic we might expect to generate more research in future. But we may also hear more about some issues which were originally raised by the 'dominance' researchers of the 1970s. Since the 1990s, concerns about gender inequality have been overshadowed by the newer interest in identity and performance, but there are signs that they are now moving back up the research agenda. Some of the inequalities noted by early feminist commentators have proved remarkably persistent: women are still under-represented as speakers in public forums, from political assemblies to TV game shows, and assertive female speakers are still disparaged as 'strident' or 'unfeminine'. Current popular culture has enthusiastically re-embraced some of the sexist linguistic representations of women which 1970s feminists hoped to banish forever ('chicks' are back, but this time if you complain you will be told that it's ironic in a cool, postmodern kind of way).

Meanwhile, 'Mars and Venus'-style self-help literature has popularised a new stereotype of men and boys as inarticulate, emotionally illiterate blunderers whose brains are not designed for such complicated tasks as listening or reading a book. This too is sexist – not only because it patronises men, but also because it reinforces the tendency to make women responsible for all the conversational support-work. A lot of current popular writing represents male-female linguistic differences as 'natural' in the sense of 'biological' (or in today's fashionable terminology, 'hard wired'). This idea has a long history of being used to justify gender inequality, by suggesting that it is inevitable (you can't change the laws of nature). Its return to favour is another sign that the task which earlier language and gender researchers set themselves – critically analysing the part language plays in maintaining gender inequality – has not become irrelevant. Researchers who take up that task in future can learn much from the debates of the last 35 years; but it will be for them to come up with new analyses and insights which engage with new social and linguistic realities.

7. Key ideas to consider and further reading

- Gender is not the same thing as biological sex: gendered patterns of language use are more about the speaker's sense of identity and group membership than they are about the biological differences between males and females.

- It is common for cultures to have strong beliefs about gender-differences in the use of language, though these are not the same beliefs in every culture, and the evidence of linguistic research often shows them to be exaggerated or untrue. What beliefs on this subject are widely held by the people you know? Why do you think those beliefs are prevalent?

- Studying the relationship between gender and language-use is not just a question of finding differences between male and female speakers – gender always interacts with other social differences, for example of age, ethnicity and social class, and this means there are also significant and interesting differences *among* women or men. What different ways of 'doing gender' with language are you aware of in your own community (e.g., between your own generation and older people, or between young people who identify with different cultures and subcultures)?

- Gender differences in language have been interpreted and explained in different ways: some linguists have related them to power and inequality between the sexes, while others have argued they are more like cultural differences, which arise because there is still a lot of separation between the worlds of boys/men and girls/women. Today, most researchers think 'dominance' and 'difference' are not mutually exclusive, and that the best explanation will be 'local' rather than 'global' – in other words, the nature of and reasons for gender differences in language will be closely related to the social conditions particular groups of men and women live in.

- Two books about language and gender are Cameron (2007) *The Myth of Mars and Venus*, which is short and accessible, and Coates and Pichler (2011) *Language and Gender: A Reader*, which contains a wide selection of articles on different aspects of the subject and is a good resource to dip into.

References

ECKERT, P., 1990. The whole woman: sex and gender differences in variation. *Language Variation and Change* 1: 245-67.

ECKERT, P. & S. McConnell-Ginet, 1992. Think practically and look locally: language and gender as community-based practice. *Annual Review of Anthropology* 21: 461-90.

GRAY, J., 1992. *Men are from Mars, women are from Venus*. New York: HarperCollins.

LAKOFF, R., 1975. *Language and woman's place*. New York: Harper and Row.

MOORE, E. & R. Podesva, 2009. Style, indexicality and the social meaning of tag-questions. *Language in Society* 38. 4.

TANNEN, D., 1990. *You just don't understand!*. New York: Morrow.

2 LANGUAGE VARIATION 1

Social Factors: Class and Ethnicity

Professor Paul Kerswill

1. Introduction

In this chapter, we explore two of the main social factors which influence the way we speak: social class and ethnicity. The third major social factor is sex, or gender – a topic which is discussed separately in Chapter 1, but which is connected both to class and ethnicity in ways we will touch on. A fourth factor, age, is equally important, though people pass naturally from one age group to another in a way that is not true of any of the other factors. Class and ethnicity (and, of course, gender and age) are large-scale factors serving to both differentiate and unite human beings. To take class first: somebody might have a particular income and have a particular type of job. These are just two of the factors which will feed into a sociologist's analysis of that person's social rank or class. At the same time, a British person might be, for instance, of English, Welsh, Pakistani or Caribbean origin. This category is often loosely referred to as that person's ethnicity. Unlike class, there is no implicit hierarchy or ranking between ethnicities. As we will see, class and ethnicity are more complex and controversial than their portrayal in everyday discourse – that is, the way in which they are talked about in the media and the ways people generally think about them.

We'll be looking at how class and ethnicity shape the way we speak. You will learn about some of the major research from the past 50 years that has looked into these effects, starting with one of the founders of **sociolinguistics** (the study of language and society), William Labov. We will come to realise that what I referred to as 'effects' are, in fact, not just people's passive, automatic responses to their 'objective' social class position and ethnicity, but rather the result of their active engagement with their own social identities. In other words, we may feel a certain pride in our own backgrounds, whatever they are. One of the most important ways in which we signal our social identities is through language.

Although our backgrounds might differ widely in terms of social advantage and disadvantage, we still try to project these identities. It is in our teenage years, particularly, that we do this, not only through things like dress and

2. Language Variation 1 – Social Factors: Class and Ethnicity

music, but also the way we speak – slang and pronunciation being the areas where young people are especially creative, and also susceptible to influence. It is not coincidental, therefore, that so much sociolinguistic research is on youth language – and this will be reflected in this chapter.

2. What is the link between class, ethnicity and language?

In the Preface to the play *Pygmalion* (1912), George Bernard Shaw wrote:

> It is impossible for an Englishman to open his mouth without making some other Englishman hate or despise him.

What did Shaw mean by this? This oft-cited quote sums up a situation 100 or more years ago in which **accent** and **dialect** were tremendously important for the way people assessed each other socially: your accent betrayed not just your regional origin, but also your social class. Victorian and early twentieth-century Britain was a society dominated by the effects of the Industrial Revolution of 100 years earlier, during which new industrial towns and cities had emerged and, with them, local urban dialects, which had developed out of the melting pot of people who had moved into the new urban areas to find work. These dialects were spoken by people who became the backbone of the industrial working class, while the language of the factory owners, teachers, clergymen and others with access to literacy was much closer to **Standard English**.

Language became, then, strongly associated with social standing. We can catch a glimpse of middle-class Victorian and early twentieth-century attitudes to the kind of language that was associated with the working class in the two *Punch* cartoons shown in Figures 1 and 2, from 1855 and 1915, respectively. Figure 1 plays upon the social stigma which was heaped on people who 'dropped their aitches' (who probably constituted the majority of the population!) while Figure 2 associates the use of *ain't* with people living in modest houses, contrasted with the splendour of the British Museum.

In the next section, we will ask whether the sorts of attitudes to social-class based dialects which are

Figure 1. 'I beg your Pardon, Ma'am, but I think you dropped this?' *Punch*, October 1855
© The British Library

Figure 2. The Airship Menace. *Punch*, 1915 © The British Library

implicit in these cartoons persist in the present day. We will also introduce some of the studies which first showed that the way we actually use language is correlated with our social backgrounds.

Speech differences based on ethnicity also exist, but in rather more subtle ways: people of any ethnicity can and do speak with a British regional accent, or indeed **Received Pronunciation**, in a way that reflects their social class. Yet there have always been ethnically-based ways of speaking. If, as many people do, we count the different UK nations as constituting ethnicities, then regional accents and dialects are in a sense also 'ethnic': Welsh, English, Scottish and Northern Irish accents can be a badge of national identity. However, for its entire human history the island of Great Britain has seen immigrants arrive from many places, bringing with them a vast array of languages. Generally, the children and grandchildren of immigrants learn the local accent or dialect of the language of the majority – English, in our case. Often, though, these children also acquire a distinctive, ethnically-based way of speaking, and this is likely to be used alongside the local accent.

In terms of ethnicity-based speech differences, it is largely only those relating to the United Kingdom nations which appear in the early *Punch* cartoons. Figure 3, from 1868, plays on a well-known stereotype, using a representation of a Scottish dialect for the dialogue.

2. Language Variation 1 – Social Factors: Class and Ethnicity

Figure 3. Thrift.
Peebles Body (to Townsman who was supposed to be in London on a visit). 'E-eh, Mac, ye're surehame again.'
Mac: 'E-eh. It's just a ruinous place, that! Mun a had na' been the'erre abune twa hoours when – bang – went saxpence!!!'
Punch, 5th December 1868 © The British Library

The language of immigrants and their descendants is hardly, if ever, depicted, and the media are generally hesitant about talking about this at all – with two significant exceptions: the language of Jews in the nineteenth century and **Multicultural London English** in the present day (though, as we shall see, the latter is not exclusive to ethnic minorities). This lack of media portrayal is surprising, given the public awareness of immigration. That said, a good deal of research has been conducted on 'ethnic' varieties, particularly British Asian English, London Jamaican – and Multicultural London English. We will return to these in Section 5.2.

3. The origins of research on language, class and ethnicity – with a side glance at gender

3.1 Class

The first large-scale survey of language and social class was conducted in New York City by William Labov in the early 1960s (Labov 1966). Labov was interested in pronunciation features, not grammar or vocabulary, because he believed that pronunciation is a more fine-grained indicator of social differences. Partly this is due to the fact that individual vowels and consonants occur far more frequently in the flow of speech than do particular grammatical constructions or words (indeed, we can't say anything at all without them). Labov argued that it was important to obtain a representative sample of speakers from the town or city under investigation, in order to be sure of revealing any systematic relationships between the use of language and social factors, particularly class, gender and ethnicity. He also devised the **sociolinguistic interview**, incorporating sections where the interviewee will be as relaxed as possible and others where they are asked to read sentences and word lists, forcing them to pay attention to their speech as much as possible. He termed these **styles**.

We will not say more about Labov's study here, but instead focus on his immediate successor in the UK, Peter Trudgill. Trudgill adopted Labov's methodology in a study of his home city of Norwich in a survey he conducted in 1968 (see Trudgill 1974). Ethnically Norwich was a largely homogeneous place at that time, with relatively few incomers generally. He constructed a sample of speakers stratified by age, gender and social class – using, for the last of these, a composite index covering occupational status, father's occupation, education, income, housing type and district. One of the features Trudgill examined was the use of different pronunciations of the verbal suffix *-ing*, as in *going* or *running*, which alternates between the standard velar consonant [ŋ] (spelt 'ng') and the nonstandard alveolar [n]. This alternation is, in fact, found in almost the entire English-speaking world, and has been in existence for some centuries. It is often referred to, somewhat inaccurately, as 'dropping your g's'. Here, of course, it is only the 'g' in the spelling that is being dropped, since the pronunciation substitutes one distinct sound for another. Figure 4, below, shows how the feature is pronounced in Norwich by people of different classes and in different styles.

Trudgill divides his sample into 'lower', 'middle' and 'upper' working classes and 'lower' and 'middle' middle classes. His styles are: 'word list', 'reading

2. Language Variation 1 – Social Factors: Class and Ethnicity

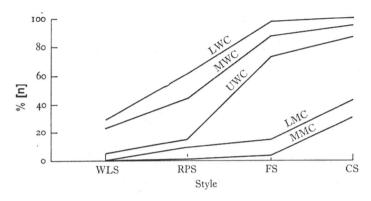

Figure 4. Variable -ing (as in going) by class and style (Trudgill 1974: 92).

passage', 'formal' and 'casual'. The figure shows that, as expected, the social classes are differentiated by this feature, and that there are the familiar style differences, with an increase in the nonstandard [n] in informal styles. Trudgill makes the point that the large gap between all the working-class and middle-class groups, especially in the two free-speech styles FS (formal style) and CS (casual style), may well reflect a polarised class structure in Britain.

A disadvantage of lumping together all the data from different speakers like this is that any variation within a social-class group is hidden from view. Can it really be the case that all speakers sound the same? Everyday experience tells us this isn't the case. One way of looking at this, while still combining data from different speakers, is to look at the crucial variable of gender. Trudgill breaks down his data on -ing by gender as shown in Table 1.

	Male	Female
Middle middle class	4	0
Lower middle class	27	3
Upper working class	81	68
Middle working class	91	81
Lower working class	100	97

Table 1. The suffix -ing in Norwich: percent use of nonstandard [n], formal style (from Trudgill 1974: 94)

In each class, women lead the men in their use of the standard form [ŋ] by an amount which varies from 3 to 24 percentage points. This pattern is one of the most robust findings of sociolinguistic studies of this kind: where there is an obviously standard form set against a nonstandard one, women use the standard more often than the men. A number of explanations have been suggested for this. One is the notion that women are more oriented towards high-prestige and supposedly 'correct' linguistic forms – another instance is the use of /h/ in words spelt with 'h', as we saw in Figure 1. However, this is not an explanation, but a mere observation. Trudgill himself suggests that working-class speech is tied in with a male-oriented working-class culture, whereas others have pointed to differences in upbringing and in gender roles in both the family and in the workplace. There are complex reasons for the so-called sociolinguistic gender pattern, including the likelihood that men and women might respond differently to the same interviewer. We will not pursue these here: you are recommended to read Chapter One for further discussion of this important area.

3.2 Ethnicity

In Britain, the investigation of language and ethnicity has tended to focus on working-class young people living in the inner city, and to take much greater care in creating more natural contexts for the recordings. The first large-scale study was that by Viv Edwards (1986), who recorded young people of Jamaican descent in Dudley in the West Midlands. At that time, a form of Jamaican creole, locally known as Patois, was used by many of the Afro-Caribbean population, including those born in Britain. Edwards expanded Labov's and Trudgill's interview design by having people speak in a group rather than on their own, and by varying the interviewer by age (young or older) and ethnicity (black or white). There were five situations, three of which are as follows (Swann & Sinka 2007: 232):

1. Formal interview with white researcher	Group interviewed about education by older white researcher, smartly dressed and referred to as 'Mr Sutcliffe' by other researchers.
4. Discussion by black peer group	Group left alone to talk about questionnaire they will be asked to complete later. Questions cover attitudes to mainstream white society; treatment of young black people by police etc.
5. Informal conversation with black fieldworker	Group with black fieldworker in conversation over biscuits and drinks towards the end of the session.

The boundary between English and Patois is not always easy to determine, since the languages share much of their vocabulary and a good deal of their pronunciation and grammar – unlike, say Russian and English. To determine the extent to which someone was speaking Patois or English, Edwards examined the use of eleven features which differentiate them. Here are five (Swann & Sinka 2007: 233, based on Edwards 1986: 80):

1. **Dentals**
   English variants: /θ/, /ð/ as in /θɪk/ (*thick*), /ðɛn/ (*then*)
   Patois variants: /t/, /d/ as in /tɪk/ (*thick*), /dɛn/ (*then*)

2. **Vowels**
   English variants: /ʌ/ (Received Pronunciation), /ʊ/ (Midlands and north of England) as in /rʌn/, /rʊn/ (*run*)
   Patois variant: /o/ as in /ron/ (*run*)

3. **Third person singular present tense verbs**
   English variant: John *swims* fast; Kevin *eats* a lot
   Patois variant: John *swim* fast; Kevin *eat* a lot

4. **Plurals**
   English variant: six *cars*; all the ***books***
   Patois variant: six *car*; all di ***book***

7. **First person singular pronoun**
   English variant: *I* feel happy
   Patois variant: *me* feel happy

For each portion of the recording sessions, Edwards calculated what she called a 'Patois index', which was an aggregate of the use of Patois vs. English forms by all participants. Here are the indexes for the three situations above:

Situation	1	4	5
Average score	5.57	43.29	30.11

Table 2. Average scores for Patois/English variants in Dudley (adapted from Edwards 1986: 81)
Note: Scores are expressed as a percentage, where a score of 100 means use of only Patois forms and a score of 0 means use of only English forms. I have reversed these scores from Edwards's original, so that they represent the use of Patois rather than English.

Overall, the use of Patois features falls well below 50 percent, even in the contexts in which its use is most expected (Situation 4). Clearly, the use of Patois is sensitive to both the ethnicity and the age of the interviewer. Topic also plays a part.

These results are to be expected, but we need to delve deeper to understand fully what these numbers mean. If they are comparable with the use of [n] in *-ing*, or a glottal stop [ʔ] for /t/ in words like *water*, then we would expect a fairly even distribution across the stream of speech, with some fluctuation according to topic, seriousness, etc. This, it turns out, is not usually what happens. Mark Sebba (1993), in his own research (also in the early 1980s) on what he calls 'London Jamaican', points out that what is happening is a form of **code-switching**, where one language (with its vocabulary, grammar and pronunciation) is used for one portion of a conversation, for example a speaker's turn, with another language replacing it in the next portion. Using alternating chunks of language like this is a routine, often unnoticed, matter for many bilingual speakers, particularly those who belong to minority linguistic communities. Here is a section from a conversation recorded by Sebba (1993):

Errol: 'ey, did you go out yet?

Patrick: oh let me get a drink

Wayne: yeah, dis mornin'

Daryl: get me some wa- get me ...

Patrick: **naa, me na get not'in f'you**

Lee: get me a drink Patrick

Patrick: **not ... a get not'ing f'you** 'cause

?: a ha ha ha

Wayne: this mornin'

The bold sections are Patois in pronunciation and grammar, the remainder in a London accent. Patrick seems to use Patois in a teasing mode, while also signalling in-group solidarity – both achieving a reduction in the threat posed by his refusal to provide water by keeping the tone light-hearted. Functions such as these are characteristic of code-switching. Sebba, as we can see, uses an interpretive approach to the study of language variation, achieving this through the close analysis of conversation. This complements the quantitative approach of sociolinguists such as Labov, Trudgill and (in her Dudley research) Edwards, too. They are two sides of the same coin.

4. Addressing limitations of the standard sociolinguistic approach: exploring fluid communities, complex identities

At the end of the previous section, we saw Sebba's critique of a purely quantitative approach to the study of how language varies within a person's repertoire of ways of speaking. In particular, he shows that it is not appropriate to the study of bilingual communities, since 'social meaning' seems to be attached to the alternating use of different languages. Now we need to pose the same question in relation to a 'speech community' which is almost entirely monolingual, such as Norwich in the 1960s, where English was spoken but in different ways connected to social class and gender. Can a similar approach to Sebba's be applied to such a community? We address this in the next section. We will also explore more recent approaches to language and ethnicity in British sociolinguistics.

5. New approaches to accent/dialect, class and ethnicity

In this section, we first look at how social-class associations feed into the social meaning of a particular linguistic feature and how speakers make use of this in conversation. Second, we will look at two very different studies dealing with variation in ethnic minority speech in London.

5.1 Possessive 'me' in Teesside

A widespread feature of English, particularly in England, is the alternation of the forms *my* and *me* in expressions of possession, such as:

Where's <u>my/me</u> coat?

I've hurt <u>my/me</u> leg.

Here, the *my* form can be pronounced with a full diphthong, giving [maɪ], or else as the reduced form [ma]. Alternatively, the form [mi] may be used, sounding like 'me'. In what follows, I shall refer to this as **possessive 'me'**. Julia Snell, a native of Teesside, researched this feature among 9- and 10-year-old primary school children in two schools in Middlesbrough and Stockton, the first having a largely working-class catchment, the second a more middle-class one (Snell 2010). Before embarking on her recordings of informal situations using radio microphones, Snell spent seven months in the role of a classroom assistant, becoming a trusted adult who was not a teacher and who spoke in a familiar accent. Table 3 (below) is a quantitative analysis of the use of possessive 'me', as well as 'my' and other reduced forms.

	Ironstone Primary (mainly working class)		Murrayfield Primary (mainly middle class)	
Variant	N	%	N	%
maɪ	99	23.4	61	24.7
ma	265	62.6	168	68.0
mi	30	7.1	3	1.2
mə	29	6.9	15	6.1
Total	423	100	247	100

Table 3. Frequency of first person possessive singular *me* pronunciation variants in Teesside (From Snell 2010: 636, Table 1)

In this table, only the form [mi] counts as possessive 'me', so we need to look at the frequency of this form, comparing it with [maɪ] and its reduced form [ma], which is often found in fast speech. Differences between the schools are small and the use of [mi] occurs in between just 1.2 to 7.1 percent of the cases. So far this tells us rather little: there is a social class difference in the use of [mi], but its infrequency would lead us to dismiss it. Snell argues that we shouldn't, firstly because this is a widespread dialectal feature in much of the country, and because it is stigmatised as the use of the 'wrong' pronoun, *me*, in the possessive. Studies of older speakers in the north of England show a much higher use of possessive 'me'. For example, in oral history interviews with elderly people in Lancashire the frequency is around 50 percent (Hollmann & Siewierska 2007: 413). Snell argues that the feature is currently being lost. She goes on to analyse the few occasions where [mi] is used by the Teesside children, to see if its use (in place of one of the other forms) can be seen as a matter of choice and, if so, what they are trying to achieve in making that choice. In one particular conversation with Snell, a child, Andrew, uses the form 'my' (pronounced [maɪ]) when talking about how his arm feels when touching a hot battery (*my arm*), but when Snell teases him by saying it is his arm that is hot, Andrew contradicts her with mock indignation, saying, **me arm's cold!**. Snell interprets this use of 'me arm' as re-establishing a teacher-pupil relationship, its power to do this deriving from the fact that it is a non-standard feature associated with working-class speakers. She finds the children more generally using the 'me' form to signal a slightly confrontational attitude.

This is just one way in which the quantitative approach to large-scale patterns, in this case establishing what the correlation is between a feature and social class, sheds light on the workings of minute-by-minute interaction – and vice versa.

5.2 Ethnic and multiethnic language in London

For two centuries or more, London has been a magnet for people from overseas; currently, 40 percent of all overseas-born people residing in the UK live there. 32 percent of people within Greater London were born outside the UK, compared to seven percent for the rest of the UK. In the inner London boroughs, the proportion rises to 39 percent (Annual Population Survey 2006). Since these figures do not include people born in Britain to foreign parents, this is an underestimate of the minority ethnic population as a whole. The first, large group of migrant workers to arrive in the post-Second World War period came from the Caribbean, followed by people from India, Pakistan and Bangladesh. There are, of course, many more immigrant groups in London, including West Africans, Greeks, Cypriots, Chinese, Turks and Somalis, as well as people from other European countries and the USA. We saw at the beginning of the chapter that the children of immigrants almost always acquire the local vernacular, while sometimes retaining, or indeed creating, linguistic features from their parents' languages. What is the evidence for this, and what are the processes by which various ethnicities assimilate or remain distinct linguistically? We will look first at a single ethnic minority group, the Indians of West London, followed by a discussion of the emerging new Multicultural London English, in which some of the ethnic divides appear to have been erased.

Devyani Sharma and Lavanya Sankaran investigated the English of three age groups of Punjabi-speaking Indians in the West London district of Southall, where people of Indian descent now constitute a majority (Sharma 2011 and Sharma & Sankaran 2011). The oldest age group were the first generation – the immigrants themselves, who arrived as adults over a long period from the 1950s onwards. The second and third groups were the children of immigrants, divided into those whose parents were among the early immigrants and those who migrated later. A straightforward Labov-style investigation, involving an interview with a single interviewer, might not be very revealing, as we saw for the Afro-Caribbeans. There are at least three reasons for this, I think. First, people who are part of communities such as these have a wide range of social contacts, including older relatives in the ancestral country, their parents, who may have been immigrants who speak English with a non-native accent, their own siblings and friends, and the local host-language community (here, the white British). The range of speech styles has the potential to be correspondingly wide. Secondly, in addition to being part of a complex immigrant community, they also slot into a position in the local social-class hierarchy, depending on the kinds of factors we have already seen. And thirdly, many are likely to be bilingual.

It is obvious, then, that sampling their speech in an interview is likely to be limiting. To get round this, Sharma and Sankaran arranged for their participants to make recordings of themselves talking to a wide range of different people.

These should be people they were routinely in contact with. The researchers' next problem was how to define the different linguistic features. They did this by dividing them into typical Asian and typical London pronunciations. These are the main features they looked at:

Asian features

1. Retroflex /t/: [ṭ] ('retro t', a typical Indian pronunciation with the tongue pulled back further along the roof of the mouth (hard palate) than in English)
2. Monophthongal *face* vowel ('mono e', as in northern England or Scotland, but also in Indian English)
3. Monophthongal *goat* vowel ('mono o', again as in northern England or Scotland, but also in Indian English)
4. Light /l/: [l] (a clear 'l' at the end of a syllable, as in *full* or *milk*, rather than the London vocalised version).

British features

5. Alveolar /t/: [t] ('alveo t', or standard British English /t/, but also including the glottal stop [ʔ])
6. Diphthongal *face* ('diph e', the southern England pronunciation, including RP and Cockney)
7. Diphthongal *goat* ('diph o', the southern England pronunciation)
8. Dark /l/: [ɫ] (the 'dark', or velarised pronunciation; also the vocalised pronunciation typical of London).

As you can see, the Asian and British features are in fact paired, so that feature 5 is in fact the 'British' equivalent of feature 1, and so on. In order to find out more about how an immigrant community integrates linguistically over time, the researchers carried out a case study of a small number of British-born individuals, divided between those who grew up in the 60s and 70s and those who did so in the 80s and 90s. Anwar, aged 41, made six self-recordings, as shown in Figure 5 (page 35, below).

Figure 5 shows the percentage use of Indian vs. British variant forms. It is easy to see that Anwar varies greatly across the six conversation partners, from close to 100 percent Indian forms when talking to the maid to 100 percent British forms when talking to the 'Cockney mechanic'. The figure does not show it, but in the context with the 'posh British Asian lawyer', Anwar uses many RP forms, contrasting with the Cockney forms in the conversation with the mechanic. This, then, is a speaker with a wide linguistic repertoire – even without counting Punjabi, which he also speaks.

2. Language Variation 1 – Social Factors: Class and Ethnicity

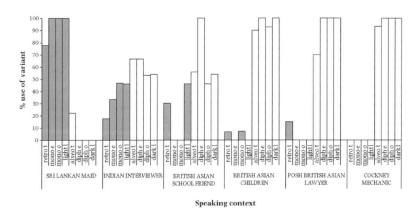

Figure 5. Use by older man (Anwar) of Indian and British and British variants across speaking situations. ■ = Indian variants □ = British variants (from Sharma 2011: 475).

Contrast this with a much younger man, Ravinder, aged 20, part of whose speech repertoire is shown in Figure 6, below.

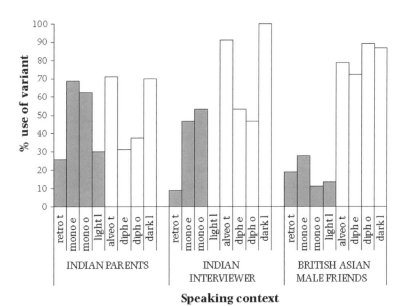

Figure 6. Use by younger man (Ravinder) of Indian and British variants across speaking situations ■ = Indian variants □ = British variants (from Sharma 2011: 478).

With each conversation partner, Ravinder seems to vary his usage only slightly, with a greater preponderance of British forms with his immediate peer group, but (almost) never an exclusive use of one or other form for any of the features. This is in sharp contrast to Anwar, who spans the entire range.

Why is there this contrast? Sharma (2011: 481-3) suggests that, for the older group represented by Anwar, people needed to find ways of integrating linguistically when faced with the hostile, anti-immigrant environment which lasted until the early 1980s. At the same time, the community maintained strong ties with India, with men entering the family business. By the next generation, born 20 or so years later, hostility had greatly reduced, and the neighbourhoods were more ethnically mixed with the British Asians often in a majority. Young men socialised in mainly Asian groups, but their employment and entertainment were local. Sharma believes there was much less need to switch between speech styles to the same extent. The result is, for the young men, a fairly uniform style of speaking, with little style shifting, but with a distinct London Asian flavour.

We have not specifically looked at women's speech here: it turns out that the older women have a narrower repertoire than the men, reflecting the fact, according to Sharma (2011: 485), that they are more home-bound. The younger women, on the other hand, have a broader repertoire than their male counterparts. Sharma argues that this represents a British working-class pattern in which women have a greater range of social contacts than men. In this respect, they have made the transition from a set of traditional, Indian family roles to a British one. This is, I would argue, a form of integration, and their language reflects this to the extent that their repertoires are more like those of their white neighbours, while still retaining Indian traits.

I have referred to the more 'British' way of talking of the young West London Indian speakers. How do these young people fit in linguistically with the remainder of London's youth? The Indians' Punjabi is just one of some 300 languages spoken in the city's primary schools (Baker & Eversley 2000), with over 100 spoken in many of its boroughs. Is there a distinct way of speaking English associated with each and every one of these potential ethnicities? A prominent young speaker of London Asian English is the rapper Shizzio: to what extent is his accent similar to those of other young people in the capital?

To begin to get some answers, we now turn to sociolinguistic research carried out with a wide range of working-class people, mostly young and mainly in the East End. Jenny Cheshire, Paul Kerswill, Sue Fox and Eivind Torgersen were interested, first, in whether new linguistic features identified in projects carried out in the New Town of Milton Keynes (Kerswill 1996, Kerswill & Williams 2000a, 2000b, 2005) in fact emanated from London. Second, they wanted to find out whether the factor of ethnicity made any difference to pronunciation and grammatical features. Third, they wanted to see if young people of Afro-Caribbean origin continued to code-switch between Patois and London English as Sebba had found 25 years before. In order to address these questions, the researchers used sociolinguistic interviews with the participants in pairs, as well as some self-recordings, to get at a portion of their linguistic repertoires (Cheshire, Kerswill, Fox & Torgersen 2011, Cheshire & Fox 2010).

2. Language Variation 1 – Social Factors: Class and Ethnicity

Young people were selected on the basis of their gender and their ethnicity. Unlike in previous studies, the researchers did not focus just on one ethnicity, but made sure the people chosen represented the breadth of ethnic backgrounds in the East End.

What kind of results did they get? In answer to the first question, they found that most of the pronunciation features in south-eastern towns like Milton Keynes and Reading did not originate in London, but rather in the Home Counties surrounding London as part of **regional dialect levelling** (for more detail see Watson this volume, Chapter Three).

The second question relates to whether there is a new, pan-ethnic way of speaking. There is some evidence for this, since a number of features seemed to be shared across all the young speaker groups, including:

- A new quotative for reported speech, as in ***This is me**: you're having a laugh!*
- Use of *a* instead of *an* before vowels, as in: *I had **a** apple*.
- In English, the definite article *the* has two forms, one (roughly) *thuh* before consonants as in ***the** pears*, the other *thee* before vowels, as ***the** apples*. Young Londoners of all ethnicities tend to use *thuh* before vowels as well.
- Young Londoners tend to use more what is called syllable timing, giving a more staccato impression.
- The vowels of *face* and *goat* both tend to be monophthongs or narrow diphthongs, giving *fehs* ([feɪs] or [feːs]) for 'face' and *goht* ([goʊt] or [goːt]) for 'goat', rather than the diphthongs of Cockney and the south-east generally: *fice* ([fæɪs]) and *gowt* ([gʌʊt]) or even *gate* ([gəʏt]), which is the pronunciation favoured by many young people in the south-east.

The researchers conclude that these forms are used in varying degrees by all groups of young people, but especially those living in the inner city (for instance, in Hackney) rather than the suburbs, as well as people of non-white British backgrounds, and young males. Notice that the two vowel features, *face* and *goat*, are identical with those used by the West London Indians. By contrast with the British Asians' use of the retroflex [ʈ], none of these features is limited to just one ethnicity. This suggests that there is, in fact, a wider, new youth accent which is used, to different degrees, by young working-class people across the capital. To make this more concrete, it is worth listening to the spoken accents of the three London-based rappers Dizzee Rascal, Plan B and Shizzio, who have very different ethnic backgrounds: their speech has a lot in common, and none speaks traditional Cockney or even with a general south-east accent.

The researchers call this new accent Multicultural London English (MLE). The print media, however, have dubbed it 'Jafaican', a rather inappropriate term since it is clearly not 'Jamaican'. Nor is it 'fake' in any way!

The third question concerns the linguistic repertoire of young Londoners. Sharma noted that the West London Indians seemed to have moved from a wide-ranging to a narrower, less flexible repertoire in the space of a generation. Sebba noted a similarly wide repertoire among London Jamaicans in the 1980s. The question is whether young Londoners, and Afro-Caribbeans in particular, have also narrowed their linguistic range. There is, today, very limited evidence of the sustained use of London Jamaican among young people, unless they have direct links with the Caribbean. This is not surprising, given the much slower rate of immigration from Jamaica (and the Caribbean generally) than was the case 20 or 30 years ago. Young speakers are likely to be second or third generation, and to have wide contacts with the white British community and other groups, too. Instead, the young Caribbeans buy into MLE, and in fact use its features more strongly than most other groups. It is this strength of use that might make people of Caribbean origin linguistically distinctive, rather than any wider use of Patois. The Caribbeans' experience is, then, parallel to, but not identical with, that of the West London Indians. What is clear is that all these speakers, of whatever ethnicity including white British, have converged in the space of one or two generations on the use of one set of language features, while still retaining some distinctiveness along ethnic lines.

6. Looking to the future

Regional accents and dialects continue to fascinate (see Watson this volume, Chapter Three). This is increasingly true of researchers' interest in what motivates social differences in speech. In this chapter, we have looked specifically at social class and ethnicity, with a glance at gender, too. We have seen that these three factors are closely intertwined. There is still much need, however, for further research on this relationship. For example, why there is a gender difference in the use of 'ethnic' features, and why the two sexes appear to have different repertoires. Is the nature of these differences the same across ethnic groups? Indications are that they are not. What of the relationship between class and ethnicity? It is well known that immigrants tend to take a 'cut' in social class after they arrive: thus, a qualified teacher may find herself working as a shop assistant or cleaner. What are the linguistic consequences of that? One is that the second generation may regain the social status their parents lost, giving rise to greater social mobility among immigrants than among the indigenous population. And finally, to what extent is ethnically-marked speech, including MLE and similar language forms elsewhere, exclusive to the less privileged, or is it also characteristic of middle-class young people? Does it spread to other places, and do adolescent speakers of it continue to use it into their 20s and on into middle age? The future for sociolinguistic research on accents and dialects looks bright.

7. Key ideas to consider and further reading

7.1 Key ideas

- Social class is part of British people's everyday understanding of society. To what extent does it inform how you see society? To what extent do you think the idea of class is now redundant?

- Try to think of some non-linguistic (i.e. social) factors which differentiate people by class. Then think of some linguistic features. When making these lists, did you resort to stereotypes about how different classes live and speak?

- Why do you think women in every social class tend to speak slightly more standardly than men in the same class?

- Ethnicity is not just about race. It may well encompass where you were born, what language you and your parents speak, your religion, and how you celebrate festivals. Some of these factors are permanent and unchanging, like race or your birthplace. Other factors become important through the way you relate to the society around you; for example, your experience of being 'white English' or 'black British' in the UK changes if you move, say, to the USA. Consider the case of African Americans who travel to West Africa: in Ghana local people might label them *obruni*, or 'white man' – to their surprise and sometimes dismay. It is not the case that the Ghanaians are denying that the Americans have the same phenotype, or physical appearance, as themselves, but they are instead emphasising their foreignness.

- Often, the term 'ethnic' is reserved for members of minorities. Is this reasonable? Can majorities be 'ethnic' as well?

- In this chapter, we have looked at cases where minority ethnic people have a distinct accent. In your experience, is this always the case?

7.2 Further reading

Linguistics Research Digest blog: http://linguistics-research-digest.blogspot.co.uk/. This site summarises recent journal articles on linguistics, with a focus on English. The London projects are also covered in four digests on this site, with the titles 'Multicultural London English' 1-4.

For an excellent, scholarly account of the rise of attitudes to class-based varieties of English, particularly in the Victorian period, see Mugglestone (2003). For a more detailed account of language and social class, see Kerswill (2009). A more detailed account of language and ethnicity can be found in Khan (2009).

The rise of Standard English and attitudes to varieties of English is treated in Kerswill and Culpeper (2009). The Milton Keynes projects are described in Kerswill (1996/2007), Kerswill and Williams (2000a, 2000b/2010, 2005), Williams and Kerswill (1999). For further discussion of Julia Snell's research, see http://linguistics-research-digest.blogspot.co.uk/2011/10/me-pencils-up-me-jumper.html.

Robert Lawson has done extensive research on the language of young working-class males in Glasgow. This is presented in Lawson (2011).

References

BAKER, P. & J. Eversley, eds. 2000. *Multilingual capital: the languages of London's schoolchildren and their relevance to economic, social and educational policies.* London: Battlebridge.

CHESHIRE, J. & S. Fox, 2009. Was/were variation: a perspective from London. *Language Variation and Change* 21: 1-38.

CHESHIRE, J., P. Kerswill, S. Fox, & E. Torgersen, 2011. Contact, the feature pool and the speech community: The emergence of Multicultural London English. *Journal of Sociolinguistics* 15/2: 151-196.

EDWARDS, V., 1986. *Language in a black community.* Clevedon: Multilingual Matters.

HOLLMANN, W. & A. Siewierska, 2007. A construction grammar account of possessive constructions in Lancashire dialect: Some advantages and challenges. *English Language and Linguistics* 11: 407-424.

KERSWILL, P., 1996/2007. Milton Keynes and dialect levelling in south-eastern British English. In GRADDOL, D., J. Swann & D. Leith, eds. 1996. *English: history, diversity and change.* London: Routledge, 292–300. Also in GRADDOL, D., D. Leith, J. Swann, M. Rhys & J. Gillen, eds. 2007. *Changing English.* London: Routledge. 179-188.

KERSWILL, P., 2009. Language and social class. In CULPEPER, J., F. Katamba, P. Kerswill, A. McEnery & R. Wodak, eds. *English language: description, variation and context.* Houndmills, Basingstoke: Palgrave Macmillan. 358-372.

KERSWILL, P. & J. Culpeper, 2009. Standard English and standardisation. In CULPEPER, J., F. Katamba, P. Kerswill, A. McEnery & R. Wodak, eds. *English language: description, variation and context.* Houndmills, Basingstoke: Palgrave Macmillan. 223-243.

KERSWILL, P. & A. Williams, 2000a. Creating a new town koine: children and language change in Milton Keynes. *Language in Society* 29: 65-115.

KERSWILL, P. & A. Williams, 2000b/2010. Mobility and social class in dialect levelling: evidence from new and old towns in England. In MATTHEIER, K. ed. *Dialect and migration in a changing Europe.* Frankfurt: Peter Lang. 1-13. Reprinted in MEYERHOFF, M. & E. Schleef, eds. 2010. *The Routledge Sociolinguistics Reader.* London: Routledge. 409-417.

KERSWILL, P. & A. Williams, 2005. New towns and koineisation: linguistic and social correlates. *Linguistics* 43(5): 1023-1048.

KHAN, A., 2009. Language and ethnicity. In CULPEPER, J., F. Katamba, P. Kerswill, A. McEnery & R. Wodak, eds. *English language: description, variation and context*. Houndmills, Basingstoke: Palgrave Macmillan. 243–256.

LABOV, W., 1966. *The social stratification of English in New York City*. Washington, DC: Center for Applied Linguistics.

LAWSON, R., 2011. Patterns of linguistic variation among Glaswegian adolescent males. *Journal of Sociolinguistics* 15 (2): 226-255.

MUGGLESTONE, L., 2003. *Talking proper: the rise of accent as social symbol* (2nd edition). Oxford: Oxford University Press.

SEBBA, M., 1993. *London Jamaican: language systems in interaction*. London: Longman.

SHARMA, D., 2011. Style repertoire and social change in British Asian English. *Journal of Sociolinguistics* 15: 464-492.

SHARMA, D. & L. Sankaran, 2011. Cognitive and social forces in dialect shift: gradual change in London Asian speech. *Language Variation and Change* 23: 399-428.

SNELL, J., 2010. From sociolinguistic variation to socially strategic stylisation. *Journal of Sociolinguistics* 14: 630-656.

SWANN, J. & I. Sinka, 2007. Style shifting, codeswitching. In GRADDOL, D., D. Leith, J. Swann, M. Rhys & J. Gillen, eds. *Changing English*. Abingdon: Routledge. 227-255.

TRUDGILL, P., 1974. *The social differentiation of English in Norwich*. Cambridge: Cambridge University Press.

WILLIAMS, A. & P. Kerswill, 1999. Dialect levelling: change and continuity in Milton Keynes, Reading and Hull. In FOULKES, P. & Gerard Docherty, eds. *Urban voices. Accent studies in the British Isles*. London: Arnold. 141-162.

3 LANGUAGE VARIATION 2

Patterns of Accent Variation in British English

Dr Kevin Watson

1. Introduction

It will come as no surprise to you that language varies in a wide range of complex ways. There are differences between languages (e.g., French is different from English), between different varieties of the same language (e.g., the accent of London is different from the accent of Liverpool), and there are differences within the same variety (e.g., you may talk differently to a close friend than to a prospective employer in a job interview). We have known about this sort of variation for a long time. It was noted as early as ~600BC, by the Sanskrit grammarian Panini (see Campbell 2001) and, later, Edward Sapir (1921: 157) wrote 'Everyone knows that language is variable' and added that even 'two individuals of the same generation and locality, speaking precisely the same dialect and moving in the same social circles, are never absolutely at one in their speech habits'.

What might be more of a surprise is that although we have always known that language varies, linguists have not always been interested in understanding *how* linguistic variation works. The reasons for this are rather complex, but an important contributory factor was that linguistic variation was believed to be random and unstructured. Speakers, it was thought, use one pronunciation one minute and another pronunciation the next, in such a haphazard way that we could not hope to find any patterns in their linguistic behaviour. This is clearly not a belief that is widely held by linguists today. We know now that language can vary in systematic ways according to, for example, a speaker's gender (see Cameron this volume, Chapter One) or a speaker's social class or ethnicity (see Kerswill this volume, Chapter Two). In this chapter, I explore how linguists came to start looking for patterns in highly variable language data, and I discuss some of the key patterns that have been found. My focus is on varieties of British English but, as we will see, we must begin in America, because this is where the field itself began. The discussion is focused on **accent variation** rather than **dialect variation** (that is, towards variation in pronunciation rather than grammar or vocabulary), because the field itself is somewhat skewed in this direction, especially in its early days.

2. Why is studying linguistic variation important?

As soon as we interact with someone, we make an instant judgement about them. We form an impression about their gender, their social class, their level of education, their age, and even whether they are likely to be warm and friendly or cold and distant. We make these subjective judgements about a person using a wide range of different cues, such as the way they dress or whether they smile or frown a lot, but one really important factor in the formation of our beliefs about a person is the way they talk. This is because certain features of language – certain ways of pronouncing words, certain grammatical structures, even words themselves – can be socially meaningful. This means that these features communicate not only linguistic meaning – what is being said – but also social meaning. They tell us something about the speaker. Take, for example, the pronunciation of the words *put* and *putt*. In accents of the south of England, these words do not sound the same because they have different vowels. Accents in the north of England, however, have the same vowel in each of these words, meaning they are both pronounced in exactly the same way. So, if you hear someone say the word *putt*, you will be able to make a judgement about whether they are from the north or south of England, and, more often than not, you will be correct. However, this is not the only judgement you might make. Because **Received Pronunciation** (RP), which is usually said to be the accent which has the highest status in England, has a distinction between the vowel in *put* and *putt*, then any accent which does *not* have the same distinction is likely to be viewed as being lower in status. This means that anyone with a northern English pronunciation of *putt* is likely to be judged not only as having a northern English accent (which would probably be correct) but also as being of a lower status than someone who has a southern English pronunciation of *putt*.

Of course, there is no objective reason to believe that everyone who has some regional pronunciation or feature of grammar automatically has a particular social status but, nevertheless, these views are often very widely and strongly held (see Clayton this volume, Chapter Nine). So strongly, in fact, that some people believe that they should go to elocution lessons to reduce some of the regional features of their language. On 23rd January 2012, an article in the *Daily Mail* had the headline: 'Job hunters fuel boom in elocution lessons: rising numbers want to lose regional accents to improve prospects'. In it, one person, who reportedly wants elocution lessons for her daughter, is quoted as saying: 'She has a degree and her partner is an accountant but they feel that their Essex accent holds them back from achieving successful posts and career opportunities.' This is a telling example of how our use of language is believed to have real-life consequences. By studying variation, we can learn to appreciate the fact that speakers who, for example, have the same vowel in *put* as in *putt* are not to be automatically stigmatised or immediately associated with a particular social characteristic, and we can learn to appreciate that all accents and dialects of English, and any other language, are just as comprehensive and complex as whatever the **standard** variety of that language happens to be.

3. How we got to where we are today: key thinkers in the field

For a long time, variation in language was thought to be random and unstructured. This view can be seen explicitly in an early discussion of language in New York. Commenting on an aspect of pronunciation which would later become famous in sociolinguistics – the presence or absence of the /r/ sound in words like *door* and *card* – Hubbell (1950: 48; cited by Chambers 2003: 17) wrote:

> The pronunciation of a very large number of New Yorkers exhibits a pattern... that might most accurately be described as the complete absence of any pattern. Such speakers sometimes produce /r/...and sometimes omit it, in a thoroughly haphazard pattern...it is a matter of pure chance which one comes first from his lips.

In much of the USA, speakers pronounce /r/ in words like *door* and *card*, unlike in much of the UK, where /r/ is usually omitted in words like these. In some of the USA, though, such as New York, /r/ production is variable – some speakers pronounce /r/ (perhaps only some of the time) and some speakers do not pronounce it. The view presented in the quotation above is that the choice between /r/ production and /r/ omission is random, in keeping with the view of the time about linguistic variation in general. It is in this context that the discipline which would come to be called **variationist sociolinguistics** was born. It is not an overstatement to say that this subdiscipline of linguistics was established largely by the work of William Labov (see e.g., Labov 1963, 1966, 1972), so it is important to talk about his work here, because it sets the scene for work in the UK.

It is perhaps unusual to be able to identify the time and place that an entire discipline began but, for the field that was to become variationist sociolinguistics, it is basically possible. The field started in the summer of 1961, on a small island off the coast of Massachusetts, called Martha's Vineyard. We can be so precise because this is the time that William Labov was working on his Masters dissertation, which was one of the very first empirical studies of language variation (published as Labov 1963). Before Labov's work, linguistic data had usually come from speaker intuitions, or, if speech production data was gathered, it was from just one single speaker. Labov was interested in the 'direct observation' of language in 'the context of community life from which it stems' (1963: 273). On Martha's Vineyard, Labov recorded speech data from 69 people, from both sexes, of a range of ages, who lived on different parts of the island. Labov put numerous important methodological foundations in place which are still used today.

3. Language Variation 2 – Patterns of Accent Variation in British English

To directly observe language, he designed a methodology now widely known as the **sociolinguistic interview**, which has become the most frequently used data collection technique in the field (Milroy & Gordon 2003: 61). The aim was to facilitate the collection of general conversation, but the methodology included reading aloud and other tasks, in order to collect a range of other speech styles (see also Milroy 1987: Chapter Two). Once the data was collected, there needed to be some way of working out what the patterns of variation were like. To do this, Labov introduced the notion of the **linguistic variable**. Often a variable is described as being 'two ways of saying the same thing' (see e.g., Watt 2007). So, for example, someone might say *pavement* or *sidewalk*, but be talking about the same thing (this would be called a lexical variable, since it is to do with words), or someone might say *walking* with a final [ɪŋ] on one occasion but a final [ɪn] on another (this is a phonological variable, since it is to do with sounds). Using the variable construct, it became possible to count not only where a linguistic feature occurred, but also where it could have occurred but did not. So, if a speaker pronounced words with the *-ing* variable 100 times, and pronounced 70 of the *-ing* sounds as [ɪn] and 30 as [ɪŋ], we would say that the speaker used [ɪn] 70 percent of the time. Thus, we now had a way of finding patterns in the data. On Martha's Vineyard, Labov was interested in phonological variables. He noticed that in words like *price* and *time*, some speakers sometimes – but, crucially, not all speakers always – had a particular vowel sound, which was pronounced, at its beginning, with the tongue in the centre of the mouth. Since the linguistic thinking at the time was that this variation was random, Labov was interested to know whether this really was the case, or whether speakers' use of particular vowels showed any regular patterns.

With Labov's methodological innovations, it became possible to ask the question that is now a main focus of sociolinguistics: what factors influence linguistic variation? Labov found that central vowels on Martha's Vineyard patterned in a systematic way. He found, for example, that people from rural areas were more likely to use the central vowels, and also that people with positive attitudes towards the island favoured central vowels, too. Labov put forward a number of persuasive arguments to explain these patterns. He said that vowel centralisation was a mechanism speakers from the Vineyard could use to signal their local status, to distinguish themselves from visiting tourists (see Labov 1963 for further discussion). Thus, linguistic variation appeared not to be random, and this warranted further investigation.

To do this, Labov shifted focus to a much larger community for his PhD research: New York City (NYC, see Labov 1966, 2006). He recorded speakers from the Lower East Side and analysed five phonological variables. One was the presence or absence of /r/ in words like *door* and *card*. As I mentioned above, a previous consideration of NYC /r/ had described it as the 'complete absence of any pattern' (Hubbell 1950). To test this, but before extending the

New York Study to a greater number of speakers (by the end of the project 340 individuals had been recorded), Labov wanted to test how the use of /r/ patterned across people of different social classes. He did this in a project which came to be known as the Department Store Study. Labov identified three department stores in New York which could be used as pseudo measures of social class: Saks, which sold expensive high-end items and so was deemed to be at the top of the social scale, Klein's, not far from the Lower East Side, was the least expensive and so deemed to be at the bottom of the scale, and Macy's, in between the other two, was seen as a mid-level store. To gather tokens of /r/ in these department stores, Labov (1972: 49) explains the procedure as follows:

> The interviewer approached the informant [a sales assistant in each store] in the role of a customer asking for directions to a particular department. The department was one which was located on the fourth floor. When the interviewer asked, 'Excuse me, where are the women's shoes?' the answer would normally be, 'Fourth Floor'. The interviewer then leaned forward and said 'Excuse me?'. He would usually then obtain another utterance, 'Fourth Floor', spoken in a careful style under emphatic stress.

Labov's results were startling – the sales assistants in Klein's used /r/ least often, and those in Saks used /r/ most. Assistants in Macy's had a proportion of /r/ which was in between that of assistants in Klein's and Saks. These patterns were replicated in Labov's bigger study of the Lower East Side. The Department Store Study has since been repeated, in the same stores (where possible), and the pattern Labov discovered has been replicated (see Mather forthcoming). So, it seems to be a real phenomenon, and was not just a one off. Another finding was that, across all three stores, speakers were more likely to pronounce /r/ in the *emphatic* condition, when they thought they had not been heard correctly, than when they said the word for the first time. Labov argued that as they paid more attention to their own speech, the speakers were more likely to produce the /r/ sound.

The systematic, predictable nature of this variation – both on Martha's Vineyard and in New York City – weakened the idea that linguistic variation was random and unstructured. Labov argued that instead of seeing the absence of patterns, what we in fact see is the **orderly heterogeneity** of language (Weinreich, Labov, & Herzog 1968). It is this idea – that the linguistic variation we see (the heterogeneity) is structured (or orderly) – which provided the platform on which variationist sociolinguistics could flourish. The task, then, become one of finding that structure.

Following Labov, Peter Trudgill set about investigating linguistic variation in the UK in the late 1960s (see Trudgill 1974). Prior to this, all work looking at UK varieties had been concerned with rural dialects. Since Labov had found subtly structured variation in the USA, Trudgill was interested to know if the patterns could be replicated in England. To find out, he investigated the dialect of Norwich, his native city, using a similar sampling and interview technique to Labov's in New York City. Trudgill's results, like Labov's, were very influential in shaping how researchers have examined regional and social variation in the UK and beyond. I lack space to go into detail about all of Trudgill's work here since, like Labov's, it spans many decades, and so I summarise just four key observations:

- People of a lower socioeconomic status are more likely to use non-standard linguistic variants than people of a higher socioeconomic status.

- People are more likely to use standard linguistic variants in formal settings, and non-standard linguistic variants in informal settings.

- Women are more likely to use standard linguistic variants than men, who use more non-standard variants.

- Women are more likely to over-report their use of standard linguistic variants, and men are likely to over-report their use of the non-standard variants.

All four of these observations can be seen in Trudgill's discussion of the *-ing* variable, where we see words like ***walking***, ***teaching***, ***shopping*** being pronounced with an [n] at the end rather than [ŋ]. The [n] pronunciation, resulting in ***walkin'***, ***teachin'*** and ***shoppin'***, is the non-standard form, and Trudgill found that it was used more often by working-class speakers than middle-class speakers, less often in formal styles than informal styles, and more often by men than women. He also showed that women said they used it less often than they actually did, while men said they used it more often than they actually did. Thus, we can predict when the non-standard form is most likely to occur: when spoken by working-class men speaking in an informal style. It is least likely to occur in the speech of middle- class women when speaking in a formal style. Like Labov's work in the USA, Trudgill showed that there was also orderly heterogeneity in British English.

4. More on accent patterns in the UK

The importance of work by Labov and Trudgill cannot be overestimated. This work marked the beginning of the modern sociolinguistics enterprise. It showed that there was orderly heterogeneity in language, and that language variation could be correlated with speakers' age, sex and social class, and also with the formality of the situation. Since then, very many studies have shown that linguistic variation in UK English is highly structured, along these and other lines. In this section, I provide some further examples to illustrate this, and to highlight some of the research questions that are being pursued in current work.

As well as wanting to understand the structured heterogeneity of language, Trudgill, like Labov, was also interested in how linguistic features spread from community to community. I describe two central claims here, discussed by Trudgill and others, which are (1) that language change can result from long term accommodation between speakers who come into contact with each other, and (2) that linguistic features can spread outwards from economically dominant and populous urban centres, and gradually reach localities further away.

Linguistic accommodation refers to the processes by which speakers come to sound more alike (see Trudgill 1986). This can occur as a fleeting event, during the course of a single conversation, or it can happen over a longer period. We usually refer to **short term accommodation** in the former case, and to **long term accommodation** in the latter. As an example, imagine a family of two adults and two children from London moving to the USA. When they first arrive in their new home, they would certainly still sound like Londoners – they would retain their native accent. Over time, though, we might expect them – particularly the children – to acquire some linguistic features of American English. They might initially use these features when in conversation with Americans (demonstrating short term accommodation) but, over time, they might also use them when talking to other members of their own family, or even when they came back to the UK for a holiday (demonstrating long term accommodation). The variety of English spoken by this London family, then, would have changed because of long term contact with Americans.

We can imagine a more local scenario. Imagine a suburb outside London, where many people have south eastern English accents but don't have many features of London English, but they commute daily to central London to work, and while there they talk to people with London accents. If they accommodate linguistically to these people, it's likely that they will start to use certain linguistic features not only in conversation with them, but also when they return to their suburban home. If this happens, then the potential is there for other people living in the suburb to adopt the feature without regularly travelling to London – they can adopt the feature from the suburban commuters.

This scenario is also an example of how linguistic features can spread out from place to place. One common situation is to find that a feature begins in a large, populous and economically dominant urban centre (such as London) and spreads from there to nearby smaller cities, then to smaller towns, then to smaller villages etc. This process is sometimes called **hierarchical geographical diffusion**, because we see a feature travel 'down the urban hierarchy' from urban centre to smaller town. Perhaps the best known example of a feature which has spread via this sort of geographical diffusion is *th*-fronting, where *th* sounds are pronounced as [f] in words like *three* and *both* and as [v] in words like *breathe* and *brother*. Kerswill (2003) tracks the history of this feature, suggesting that

3. Language Variation 2 – Patterns of Accent Variation in British English

Figure 1: The spread of *th*-fronting in British English, adapted from Kerswill (2003). The years represent the approximate birth year of speakers known to have *th*-fronting in each locality.

it was reasonably common in the speech of Londoners born around 1850. *Th*-fronting then reaches Derby (population 236,000) and Norwich (population 180,000) at around the same time, in people born around 1960, but appears later in Wisbech, which is geographically closer to London than Derby but has a smaller population (19,000). This fits the hierarchical diffusion model because *th*-fronting skips past closer but smaller localities, hitting larger places before smaller ones. Kerswill (2003) also tracks the spread of *th*-fronting elsewhere in the UK, using as a guide the birth year of speakers first known to use the feature. Figure 1, above, presents some of this information, adapted from Kerswill (2003: 236).

The general pattern of geographical diffusion, from south to north, should be clear from Figure 1. *Th*-fronting appears in people born in 1960 in Derby, 1970 in Middlesbrough, further north, 1980 in Newcastle, further north still, and is reported to be absent in Buckie, in north-east Scotland. Kerswill (2003) also reports that *th*-fronting is absent in other localities, such as Liverpool, but I have carried out very recent work which shows that *th*-fronting has now appeared in Liverpool in speakers born in 1994, so the feature has now reached this part of north-west England, too.

Another key issue, connected to the geographical diffusion of linguistic forms, is the **levelling** of features which are somehow 'marked' in certain accents. By 'marked', I mean a linguistic feature may be geographically restricted, appearing in a relatively small geographical location, and/or a feature may be stigmatised in a community. When levelling occurs, these marked linguistic features are replaced by other features which have a wider geographical distribution. One result of levelling is that accents begin to sound more alike, because some of the regional features which once distinguished them from other accents reduce in frequency. Two good examples of this come from Newcastle.

The first concerns the pronunciation of the /t/ sound as a [t] or a glottal stop [ʔ] in words like *city* and *water*. As well as these pronunciations, there is another, local form in Newcastle, where we see the glottal stop combined with a [t], giving [ʔt]. Milroy et al (1994) show that the regional Newcastle form (the 'marked' variant) is used less often by younger speakers, suggesting that it is being replaced by the geographically more widespread glottal stop.

The second concerns the vowel in words like *face*, *wait*, *late*, which traditionally in Newcastle sounds similar to vowels in words like *near* and *beer* in other accents. Watt and Milroy (1999) show that this regional vowel is reducing in frequency in the speech of the young, and is being replaced by a vowel which is widespread across the north of England (which sounds similar but is not quite the same as the vowel in *square* or *hair*). Here, again, the regionally marked feature is being replaced by a form which is more geographically widespread.

Why does levelling happen? It has been connected to processes of long term accommodation, introduced above. As our mobility increases, and we come into contact with more people, we have greater opportunity to converge linguistically, in some way. This means that we not only adopt features found over a large geographical area, but that our really local features, particularly those that might be stigmatised, are likely to reduce in frequency.

5. Where are we today?

Variationist sociolinguistics has a relatively short history, beginning only in the 1960s. But the field has come a long way. We now know that language variation is structured in quite complex ways, according to, for example, the age, sex and social class of the speaker, and, as more work has been carried out in different localities over the years, we have started to unravel how linguistic features can spread from place to place. However, we are far from having all the answers. In this final section, I illustrate two ways in which the field has been developing since Labov's and Trudgill's early insights.

5.1 Connecting the 'global' to the 'local'

When Labov and Trudgill carried out their pioneering studies, they divided their speech communities into various categories, according to decisions they made during the research process. We can take social class as an example. In the Department Store Study, Labov used the type of store as an indicator of social class. In his wider New York study, he used other measures, such as occupation, to place people into social class categories. Trudgill did the same sort of thing – applying a range of different socioeconomic criteria to generate a particular social class label for each speaker. However, a common criticism of this approach is that social class hierarchies based on socioeconomic indices impose categories which may not correspond to how the speakers themselves recognise their own social groups. That is, just because the analyst says that you are upper middle class or lower working class does not mean that these categories have any meaning for you. Also, there may be variation *within* social class groups (so that, for example, not all working-class people behave in the same way). The same can be said of sex – just because you are male or female does not mean you will behave in the same way as every other male or female (see Cameron this volume, Chapter One). To really understand how language works, then, some researchers argue we need to take a more local approach, and really try to understand how each specific community works. One way in which this can be achieved is by understanding a speaker's **community of practice (CoP)**. CoPs were introduced to sociolinguistics by Eckert and McConnell-Ginet (1992) and are defined as follows:

> A community of practice is an aggregate of people who come together around some enterprise. United by this common enterprise, people come to develop and share ways of doing things, ways of talking, beliefs, values – in short, practices – as a function of their joint engagement in activity. (Eckert, 2000: 65)

Here we see the three main characteristics of belonging to a CoP: (i) mutual engagement, where people come together in personal contact, (ii) a shared repertoire, of, for example, linguistic forms, such as the use of particular slang terms or features of pronunciation, and (iii) a jointly negotiated enterprise, such that people have some sort of shared goal/reason for being together.

Recent work in the UK has shown that CoPs can be used to explain speakers' language behaviour. Moore (2003) examines the language of school students in Bolton, in the north-west of England. She spent a considerable amount of time getting to know the students, and was able to learn about how their school community worked, and who belonged to particular friendship groups. She identified a number of different CoPs in the school. One was the 'Eden Village girls', who generally engaged in school activities and liked to go to each other's houses when socialising. Another group was the 'populars', who also engaged in some school activity, such as lunchtime drama and music groups, but who generally got into more trouble than the Eden Village girls, and who preferred to socialise in shopping centres or parks, often drinking, rather than go to each others' houses. Moore examined the use of *was* or *were* in sentences such as *It weren't meant to be a big party*, and found that membership of the popular group meant you were very likely to use non-standard *were* in this context, but membership of the Eden Village group meant you were very unlikely to use *were*, preferring *was*. This is a nice example of how CoP membership can predict a speaker's behaviour of a dialect feature.

In another CoP study, Clark (2009; see also Clark & Trousdale 2009) examines the language of people in a bagpipe playing band in Fife. Rather than simply assigning speakers to social class categories based on measures of socioeconomic factors, Clark asked her participants to categorise everyone else in the band, according to the groups they felt they belonged to. The pipers labelled their groups, and similarities emerged. The 'tiny wee pipers' was the label given to the youngest members of the band, and 'new folk' was used to label those people who, although slightly older than the tiny wee pipers, have spent very little time in this piping community. The 'pipe band geeks', on the other hand, had known each other for a number of years and they also all held professional positions in the band. Clark examined whether CoP membership explained speakers' use of *th*-fronting, and found that the tiny wee pipers and the new folk used this feature much more often than the pipe band geeks. Notice how this can't just be because of age differences, because there were age differences *between* the tiny wee pipers and the new folk, but they use *th*-fronting in more or less the same way.

With a CoP approach, we are able to zoom in on the local practices speakers engage in on a day to day basis, and these local practices can shed light on the complexity of linguistic behaviour.

5.2 Not just levelling, but also divergence

We saw above that increased mobility and contact between people has led to **levelling** – the reduction of regionally or socially marked forms, and their replacement with forms that are spread over a wider geographical region. However, this should not lead to the prediction that regional accents are about to disappear completely. In new work on the Liverpool accent, we have shown not only that geographically widespread forms are not particularly common (yet, at least), but also that localised forms have increased.[1]

Liverpool has a very recognisable accent, and one of its distinctive characteristics is the pronunciation of its plosive sounds, like /t/ and /k/. The /t/ sound in Liverpool, for instance, can be pronounced like [t], [ts], [s] or [h]. So the word

3. Language Variation 2 – Patterns of Accent Variation in British English

what can be pronounced with the sort of [t] we find in other localities, and in RP, but it can also be pronounced as *wos*, and *woh*. This latter pronunciation in particular is a very regionally restricted feature, and, given that we know Liverpool's accent is usually stigmatised, we might expect this feature to decline under the pressures of levelling.

To find out whether this was the case, in 2010 we recorded two groups of speakers in Liverpool – one group aged between 60-70 (called the 'Older' group below) and one group aged 16-17 (called the 'Younger' group). We were interested in how they pronounced /t/ sounds at the ends of words when followed by a pause, because this is where the pronunciation of /t/ as [h] is most likely (e.g., 'what' as *woh*). The results are presented in Figure 2.

There are several things to notice in Figure 2. First, female speakers in each age group use a higher percentage of [t] than men in the same age group – this is what we would expect, given what we know about women usually using the standard variant more often than men. Second, the glottal stop, known to be spreading across most accents of Britain via geographical diffusion, seems to have increased in the younger speakers, but only very marginally – it is only used 4 percent of the time by both the males and females. If it is increasing, it hasn't increased much yet, at least in this pre-pausal position. What *has* increased, however, is the regional pronunciation of /t/ as [h]. It is used 27 percent of the time by younger speakers, and just 3 percent of the time by

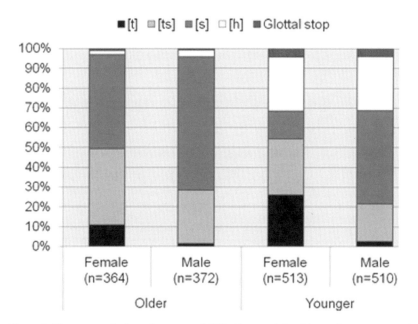

Figure 2: The pronunciation of pre-pausal /t/ in Liverpool, in older and younger speakers.

older speakers. This regionally restricted form is certainly not levelling, at least at the moment. Instead what we see is the increase of a regionally restricted form, and the divergence away from regional norms.

As we look at more varieties of English, we will probably find more examples of divergence, which need to be understood in the broader context of levelling. We can be sure, however, that whatever happens, regional accents are safe.

6. Key ideas to consider

- Language variation is not random but is structured – it shows orderly heterogeneity.
- Early work showed that standard linguistic forms were more likely to be used (a) by women, (b) by higher social classes and (c) in more formal styles.
- Recent work has shown that we need to think carefully about these 'global' categories, and also look at a more 'local' level, in order to fully understand how language variation works.
- Linguistic features spread out from populous and economically dominant and urban centres, and, when following a hierarchical diffusion pattern, reach larger cities and towns before smaller ones.
- We have lots of evidence of accent levelling in the UK, but we should be careful of assuming that all local accent features are dying out. They are not, because we also have evidence of divergence.

Endnote

[1] Work on this project was funded by Economic and Social Research Council, grant number RES-061-25-0458. I gratefully acknowledge their support.

References

CAMPBELL, L., 2001. The history of linguistics. In ARONOFF, M. & J. Rees-Miller, eds., *The handbook of linguistics*. Oxford: Blackwell. 81-104.

CHAMBERS, J. K., 2003. *Sociolinguistic theory: linguistic variation and its social significance* (2nd ed.). Oxford: Blackwell.

CLARK, L., 2009. *Variation, change and the usage-based approach*. PhD dissertation, University of Edinburgh.

CLARK, L., & Trousdale, G,. 2009. Exploring the role of token frequency in phonological change: evidence from th-fronting in east-central Scotland. *English Language and Linguistics*, 13/1: 33-55.

ECKERT, P., 2000. *Linguistic variation as social practice: the linguistic construction of identity at Belten High*. Oxford: Blackwell.

ECKERT, P., & S. McConnell-Ginet, 1992. Think practically and look locally: language and gender as community-based practice. *Annual Review of Anthropology*, 21: 461-90.

HUBBELL, Alan, F., 1950. *The pronunciation of English in New York City*. New York: Columbia University Press.

KERSWILL, P., 2003. Dialect levelling and geographical diffusion in British English. In BRITAIN, D. & J. Cheshire, eds., *Social dialectology: in honour of Peter Trudgill*. Amsterdam: Benjamins. 223-243.

LABOV, W., 1963. The social motivation of a sound change. *Word*, 19: 273-309.

LABOV, W., 1966. *The social stratification of English in New York City*. Washington: Center for Applied Linguistics.

LABOV, W., 1972. *Sociolinguistic patterns*. Philadelphia, PA: University of Pennsylvania Press.

LABOV, W., 2006. *The social stratification of English in New York City* (2nd ed.). London: Cambridge University Press.

MILROY, J., L. Milroy, & S. Hartley, 1994. Local and supra-local change in British English: the case of glottalisation. *English World-Wide*, 15: 1-33.

MILROY, L., 1987. *Language and social networks* (2nd edition). Oxford: Blackwell.

MILROY, L., & M. Gordon, 2003. *Sociolinguistics: method and interpretation*. Oxford: Blackwell.

MOORE, E., 2003. *Learning style and identity: a sociolinguistic analysis of a Bolton high school*. PhD dissertation, University of Manchester.

SAPIR, E., 1921. *Language*. New York: Harcourt, Brace, and Co.

TRUDGILL, P., 1974. *The social differentiation of English in Norwich*. London: Cambridge University Press.

TRUDGILL, P., 1986. *Dialects in contact*. Oxford: Blackwell.

WATT, D., 2007. Variation and the variable. In LLAMAS, C., P. Stockwell, & L. Mullany, eds., *The Routledge companion to sociolinguistics*. London: Routledge. 3-11.

WATT, D., & L. Milroy, 1999. Patterns of variation and change in three Tyneside vowels: is this dialect levelling? In FOULKES, P. & G. Docherty, eds., *Urban voices: accent studies in the British Isles*. London: Arnold. 25-46.

WEINREICH, U., W. Labov, I. M & Herzog, 1968. Empirical foundations for a theory of language change. In LEHMANN, W.P. & Y. Malkiel, eds., *Directions for historical linguistics*. Austin, TX & London: University of Texas Press. 95-188.

4 ENGLISH AROUND THE WORLD

Professor Jane Setter

1. Introduction

What a resilient, widely-used language English is. Spoken by an estimated two billion people around the world as a first, second or foreign language (Jenkins 2014[1]), it shows no sign of falling out of favour, even though it has been the language of conquerors, oppressors and of nations who are sometimes seen as too lazy or complacent to learn the languages of others. So what is it that drives people around the world to keep on learning and using this language? What makes it so desirable? What makes it so unique?

This chapter looks at the spread of English since the time of Elizabeth I, how it got to be in various places around the world, and what people were doing with it then and are doing with it now. It considers the features of some varieties of English around the world, how New Varieties of English can be classified, and the research that people are doing into it. We will also look at possible future scenarios for English – will it continue to grow, or will we all be speaking a different language in the future?

2. Why the topic is worth studying

Perhaps the main motivation for the global fascination with English is its chameleon-like capacity to grow and change, offering not just the opportunity for learners of English to work towards standard accents, such as Received Pronunciation (RP) and General American (GenAm), but also the chance to express oneself in an English which is very much home-grown. English does not 'belong' to native speakers anymore and, in fact, how a native speaker of English is defined is changing. If you are from the UK or the US and a monolingual speaker of English, it is necessary to step out of your shoes and walk a mile in those of an English speaker in Asia, Africa, Europe or the Middle East – to name but a few examples – to really appreciate how English works in a global setting.

And yet there is also a lot of interest in language standards and intelligibility which is also fuelling the debate on English in the world. If your English is too much influenced by other local languages, then how can it continue to be used as a **lingua franca** – i.e. to communicate between speakers who have no shared language? Are the linguistic features of a local variety innovations or just plain poor English? Should speakers all try to emulate a specific target accent or should they be eradicating features which make their English unintelligible? How do we test levels of proficiency in English if it is available in so many different forms?

3. Key thinking in this field

Research in the area of world Englishes is relatively new. Although people have been talking about learners of English for some time, it was not really until the 1980s that researchers and theorists began to propose frameworks for categorising Englishes around the world in terms of new varieties.

3.1 Kachru's circles approach

Possibly the best known framework for categorising world Englishes is Kachru's (1982/1992) **circles approach** (Figure 1). Originally proposed in 1982, the model attempts to capture the different users of English in terms of an **Inner Circle**, and **Outer Circle** and an **Expanding Circle**.

Figure 1

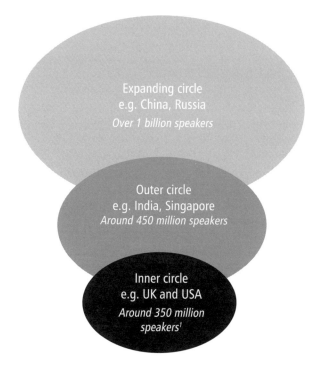

The **Inner Circle** includes speakers of British, American, Canadian, South African and Australasian Englishes. These varieties are considered to be **norm-providing** in that they are the varieties by which, historically, others are measured or with which others can be compared; speakers of them are often referred to as first language (L1) speakers or 'native speakers' of English. In terms of historical development, varieties such as American and Australian English are the result of mass migration of British and (English-speaking) Irish people to other parts of the world in order to settle and nation-build. The differences observed in the linguistic features of these varieties was initially dependent on things like when the migration took place and the contact speakers had with other languages and cultures.

The **Outer Circle** contains **norm-developing** varieties of English, typically those which resulted from the British – and more recently the Americans – initiating trade relationships with other countries around the world which developed into the provision of government and administration but not mass migration and settlement. Such countries include India, Singapore, Ghana and the Philippines. In some (but not all) cases the movement of the British or Americans into the countries in the first place was accompanied or initiated by military action; they would then stay, ostensibly in order to keep the peace. One question which could be asked is whether this has changed today.

In the case of the British Empire, it was seen as morally and intellectually necessary for the indigenous populations of the countries on the receiving end of British administration to be able to use English, and English became the main or only language of administration. In this context, we find speakers of English as a second language (L2), where an L2 is a language which is used for one or more official purpose (government, education, the law, etc.) and becomes part of a person's linguistic repertoire for that reason. These speakers are regarded as 'non-native speakers'. However, Outer Circle Englishes are not confined to L2s, as some develop into New Varieties of English with their own norms – hence norm-developing – and with native or L1 speakers. Examples of varieties which have developed to this stage are Indian and Singapore English.

The **Expanding Circle** encompasses those who are traditionally thought of as speakers of English as a foreign language (EFL), and so Expanding Circle Englishes are learner Englishes. They are described as **norm-dependent**. English itself does not have any official purpose in Expanding Circle countries; it is assumed that those who learn English in these countries are doing so in order to communicate with others who speak English – traditionally those from the Inner Circle – and are aiming towards competence in Inner-Circle native speaker norms, usually British or American English. EFL speakers comprise by far the largest group of speakers of English and, as the term 'Expanding Circle' suggests, the group is ever-increasing in size, as more and more people and nations value the importance of being able to use English for one thing or another. The motivation to do so is often instrumental rather than integrative, for example, to do business with other speakers of English rather than to integrate culturally with native speakers from the Inner Circle. Examples of countries with Expanding Circle populations include China, Brazil, Japan and Poland.

While Kachru's paradigm is useful and clear, capturing much of the complexity of the situation, it is not without its problems. One such problem is the fact that some Englishes just do not seem to fit into it very well. Let's take Hong Kong English as an example. Although Hong Kong was part of the British Empire and therefore has a linguistic history similar to, for example, India and Singapore, English in Hong Kong does not fit neatly into the Outer Circle, as some claim it is not norm-developing but a learner language and therefore norm-dependent. However, the situation is clearly different from typical Expanding Circle Englishes as English has been, and is still, used for official purposes in Hong Kong; it is one of the official languages of the law, of government and of education (particularly at university level), the other languages being Modern Standard Chinese (Mandarin/Putonghua) and Cantonese (see also Setter, Wong & Chan 2010).

Writing on this very subject, Pang (2003), points out that English in Hong Kong belongs clearly to certain domains and fields of usage and that it has remained a 'high' variety (or **acrolect**); these facts have hindered its development as a variety in its own right. This, in turn, puts its status as a full member of the Outer Circle in question. Pang suggests that the situation will not change as long as teachers of English in Hong Kong and the Hong Kong government continue to think of Hong Kong English as a learner variety, with British and American English as models. There are several languages available to Hong Kong people which perform different economic, cultural and social functions, says Pang, and English is too limited in use and remit. It is not used by indigenous Hong Kong people to speak to each other – they use Cantonese – and tends to survive 'mainly as an acrolect, not serving an integrationist function' (Pang 2003: 17).

Another criticism of Kachru's model is that the term 'Inner Circle' implies that the Englishes in this group are more important than others and 'central to the effort' (Jenkins 2014: 16). This is problematic as it seems to give Inner Circle Englishes status and influence which many believe is actually on the decline. World Englishes scholars who are interested in documenting the linguistic properties of Outer Circle Englishes, or New Varieties of English (NVEs), on their own terms prefer to do so without reference to Inner Circle Englishes, or Older Varieties of English (OVEs), other than as a point of comparison. By affording OVEs 'Inner Circle' status it implies that any other variety of English is just incorrect learner English.

3.2 Schneider's developmental paradigm

Rather than looking at types of Englishes in Kachruvian terms, Schneider (2007) proposes a developmental paradigm which he calls the **Dynamic Model of the Evolution of Postcolonial Englishes**. Schneider's classification looks at such aspects as the socio-political background, sociolinguistic conditions and linguistic effects of the various phases an NVE goes through in order to reach varietal status. The focus here is on Englishes which are typically found in Kachru's Outer Circle and, therefore, the Dynamic Model is more restricted than Kachru's paradigm in that sense. However, it allows scholars to differentiate between different Outer Circle Englishes in terms of their development towards NVE status and therefore provides a framework for more detailed description. In the case of a variety like Hong Kong English, this enables us to evaluate its development in comparison with other postcolonial Englishes rather than trying to fit it into a neat box or circle. The model has five phases:

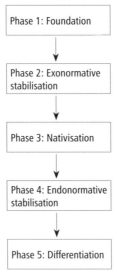

Figure 2. Diagram representing Schneider's Dynamic Model

Foundation (phase 1) can be described as the initial stage at which English is brought to a territory by a 'significant group of settlers' (Schneider 2007: 33), whether by immigration, invasion or occupation.

Exonormative stabilisation (phase 2) is the point at which English is regularly used by the settlers as the language of institutions such as government, education and the law, while still considering themselves to be in an outpost of, for example, Britain. The indigenous peoples perceive themselves to be members of a social group which is different from the settlers, but also perceive the advantage of being able to use the settlers' language in terms of socioeconomic gain, and become 'English knowing' (Schneider 2007: 39). Inter-racial marriages take place during this phase, and children of mixed race are born.

Nativisation (phase 3) involves both linguistic and cultural transformation; the intertwining of the old and the new 'is in full swing' (Schneider 2007: 40), and there is a move towards independence from the distant country of origin, politically, linguistically and culturally. Economic independence is gained, and difference in cultural background and identity is much reduced.

Endonormative stabilisation (phase 4) is not achieved until there is political independence, although Schneider (2007: 48) notes that this one criterion is sometimes not enough, and that a sense of cultural self-reliance is also required. In linguistic terms, instead of referring to 'English in X', where 'X' stands for the country, the reference is now to 'X English', where the latter indicates that the English spoken in the territory is a variety in its own right, on equal terms with other varieties.

Phase 5, **differentiation**, is seen as a turning point, a point at which there is no question of the status of the variety, and at which regional and social dialects of that variety begin to assert themselves.

If we again take Hong Kong English as an example, Schneider's paradigm has it at phase 3, although he suggests that there are still some elements of phase 2 visible, even though at the time of publication of the model in 2007 Hong Kong had not been a British colony for ten years. This is in comparison with neighbouring variety Singapore English, which Schneider suggests is well into phase 4 and so somewhat advanced in development and status in comparison with Hong Kong English.

3.3 Proficiency

Something neither of these well-known models takes into account is proficiency in English (although, to be fair, that is not what they are setting out to do). Just because a variety belongs to one of Kachru's circles or one of Schneider's phases, it should not be assumed that speakers or users of this variety are necessarily very 'good' at it. There are different aspects of a language which one can be proficient in, too: reading, writing, speaking and listening are the four skills normally looked at when language skills are tested. It is not unusual for someone to be highly fluent in a spoken language but not brilliant at reading or writing; nor is it unusual for learners of English to be very good at reading and writing but not wonderful at speaking and listening. There are many factors involved which it is not possible to go into here; suffice it to say proficiency is a complex matter. But one of the features of proficiency which has received a lot of attention recently is intelligibility in English; can and should any speaker of English be able to understand another speaker, no matter where they are from in the world?

Intelligibility is not just an issue involving speakers of Outer or Expanding Circle Englishes. For example, there was uproar in the popular press when Cheryl Cole was not welcomed on the American version of *The X Factor* because it was reported that her accent would render her too difficult for most people in America to understand.

Here's an example from my personal experience. When I was a teenager, I met one of my friend's parents for the first time at a birthday party at her house. Her father had a very broad Scottish accent and, on meeting me, said something very welcoming … which I couldn't understand at all. His actual words were: *Will you no have a chair?*, but the non-standard grammar coupled with his broad accent rendered him unintelligible to me. Her mum – probably used to dealing with situations of this kind – helped me out by asking me if I'd *like to sit down, dear?* This is actually a fond memory but it also makes the point.

Once one is used to a particular variety of English the difficulty understanding it is much diminished. I lived in Hong Kong for several years and was used to hearing local people speaking English, but businessmen flying in for a day or so who had not encountered the accent before sometimes had trouble negotiating meaning in meetings because of unfamiliar features of the Hong Kong English accent. Even now, when I'm dealing with a Hong Kong colleague I know well, I sometimes find the discourse features to be a little too forthright and have to remind myself that culture plays a part here as well as linguistics.

3.4 World Standard and the Lingua Franca Core

Linguists such as Professor David Crystal have hypothesised about the creation or evolution of something called **World Standard Spoken English (WSSE)**, a variety which would be available to all speakers of English as one of our many dialects and probably derivative of standard accents of American or British English (Crystal 2003). Whether or not it takes this form, WSSE may still come into being. He also suggests that local varieties of English around the world will adapt according to linguistic and cultural preferences and that, in fact, we will end up with dialects of English which are as intelligible to each other as my friend's father was to me, i.e. not very. Languages change: fact.

However, if English is going to continue to have an international role, people that speak it – including those in the Inner Circle – will need to be able to do so in such a way that other speakers can understand it. Setter and Jenkins (2005: 13) state that 'pronunciation is the major contributor to successful spoken communication, and how anyone learning a language can expect to be understood with poor pronunciation skills is outside of our comprehension'.

The term 'poor' here does not necessarily imply the wholesale adoption of a particular accent or dialect but, in pronunciation terms, could mean a focus on aspects of one's local variety which render it unintelligible to speakers of English from different linguistic backgrounds. One approach which attempts to deal with these features of unintelligibility is the **Lingua Franca Core**, or **LFC**, proposed by Professor Jennifer Jenkins (see Jenkins 2000).

Jenkins was interested in non-native speaker (NNS) interactions, i.e. those taking place between speakers whose first language is not English. Analysing data from learner interactions, she identified the areas in which difficulties in intelligibility arose. She also considered features of a speaker's English which arose owing to L1 background but did *not* affect intelligibility. Having concluded the analysis, Jenkins suggested a list of features as being essential for communication in English in international settings and therefore belonging to the LFC. These are summarised by her as follows (Jenkins 2002):

- All the consonants are important except for *th* sounds as in *thin* and *this*.
- Consonant clusters are important at the beginning and in the middle of words. For example, the cluster in the word *string* cannot be simplified to *sting* or *tring* and remain intelligible.
- The contrast between long and short vowels is important. For example, the length difference between the vowel sounds in *sit* and *seat* must be preserved.
- Nuclear (or tonic) stress is also essential. This is the stress on the most important word (or syllable) in a group of words. For example, there is a difference in meaning between *My son uses a computer* which is a neutral statement of fact and *My <u>son</u> uses a computer*, where there is an added meaning (such as that another person known to the speaker and listener does not use a computer).

On the other hand, many other items which are regularly taught on English pronunciation courses appear not to be essential for intelligibility in English as an International Language (EIL) interactions. These are:

- The *th* sounds (see above).
- Vowel quality, that is, the difference between vowel sounds where length is not involved. For example, a German speaker may pronounce the 'e' in the word *chess* more like an 'a' as in the word *cat*.
- Weak forms such as the words *to*, *of* and *from* whose vowels are often pronounced as 'schwa' instead of with their full quality.

- Other features of connected speech such as assimilation (where the final sound of a word alters to make it more like the first sound of the next word, so that, e.g., *red paint* becomes *reb paint*).
- Word stress.
- Pitch movement.
- Stress timing.

Jenkins' aim in specifying the LFC was not to provide 'a pronunciation model nor a restricted simplified core' (Jenkins 2000: 158), but instead to define the features of English pronunciation which will make speakers from a variety of L1 backgrounds more intelligible to one another. From that perspective, it does have obvious appeal for pronunciation teachers, although many teachers of English around the world are required to teach towards an Inner Circle model. Neither is the LFC without its critics; there is a book edited by Dziubalska-Kołaczyk and Przedlacka (2005) which contains many papers critical of the approach. The point, however, is that there should be more time spent on specific areas of difficulty which would make a difference in intelligibility in an international context, leaving other issues, which are based rather on Inner Circle speaker norms, until later in the pronunciation learning context and at the discretion of the teacher or through learner choice. Walker (2001: 8) concludes that what is in fact required is an inversion of the 'standard, negative attitude towards the learner's L1' when teaching monolingual groups.

It has become unfashionable to assert that OVEs like RP should be used as a pronunciation model in this era of global English. There are many reasons for this, not least that the imposition of any variety is akin to linguistic imperialism. In my opinion, what the target accent is should be the choice of the individual – although, in reality, in a school situation at least, this is often driven by governmental language policy. Many speakers do still strive to achieve a native speaker accent such as RP. However, for the majority of speakers, a native-like accent may not be attainable, required or desirable. The main point is that it should not matter what accent or variety a speaker has as long as intelligibility is not compromised. As Parashchuk points out, 'one of the conditions for successful intercultural communication is a certain basic degree of similarity in different varieties of English' (2000: 2). The LFC specifically targets a set of phonological features which may cause unintelligibility in international contexts and, for this reason, it is a highly sensible place for English language teachers and learners to start their work on pronunciation, assuming the goal is for everyone in the world to understand each other better in English.

Jenkins' work is under the umbrella of something known as **English as a lingua franca**, or ELF. A lingua franca is a contact language which has developed because of the need for people who do not have a common language to communicate; it has elements from many languages but no native speakers.

Thus, ELF is a 'variety' of English which has no native speakers but is used by people all over the world to communicate. This might seem odd – of course, English has native speakers – but ELF does not. Those promoting ELF are therefore saying that it belongs to nobody and everybody equally.

Where Jennifer Jenkins looks at pronunciation features, Professor Barbara Seidlhofer has worked on the lexicogrammatical features of ELF, i.e. on grammar and vocabulary. She has identified a great deal of systematicity in the lexicogrammar of ELF spoken by people from all over the world. Here are some examples of the kind of things speakers of ELF might do in terms of grammar (adapted from Seidlhofer 2004: 220):

- 'drop' the third person present tense *-s*
- 'confuse' the relative pronouns *who* and *which*
- 'omit' definite and indefinite articles where they are obligatory in English as a native language (ENL), and insert them where they do not occur in ENL
- 'fail' to use correct forms in tag questions (e.g., *isn't it?* or *no?* instead of *shouldn't they?*)
- 'insert' redundant prepositions, as in *We have to study about…*
- 'overuse' certain verbs of high semantic generality, such as *do*, *have*, *make*, *put*, *take*
- 'replace' infinitive-constructions with *that*-clauses, as in *I want that … *instead of *I want to …*
- 'overdo' explicitness (e.g., *black colour* rather than just *black*).

The inverted commas[2] around the first word in each of the points above are meant to indicate that these are considered 'incorrect' in Standard English, and efforts would be made to eradicate them in the EFL classroom (in fact, Seidlhofer says they would be regarded as 'deadly grammatical sins'!). However, if a speaker of ELF does the things above, there is no evidence that this leads to problems communicating. The sort of things that do tend to lead to miscommunication, says Seidlhofer, are the use of **idiomatic expressions** (e.g., *go the whole hog*), phrasal verbs (*get up/on/over/in …*), metaphor, and 'fixed ENL expressions such as *this drink is on the house* or *can we give you a hand*' (Seidlhofer 2004: 220). If a speaker is unfamiliar with certain vocabulary items, this is also likely to impede intelligibility.

As members of the Inner Circle – assuming you are if you are reading this – we also need to take heed and sort out aspects of our English which are not clear when communicating in international settings, assuming English is the language we'll be using. Many of us do this in code-switching contexts anyway within our own speech communities; we have a variety which we use with others we know very well and another we use with people we know less well, and these varieties will have different lexicogrammatical or pronunciation features. The variety we use with people we know less well is usually nearer to the acrolect and is sometimes referred to as a 'telephone voice'. By extension, we need a variety we can switch to when communicating with other speakers of English, and ELF and the LFC have a role here in indicating what that variety should or should not contain. If we are to be successful speakers of English in this globalised world, we need to be willing and able to accommodate.

4. Current research into world Englishes

Current research in world Englishes is taking many forms. There is interest in the role and intrusion of English in linguistic landscapes (Bolton 2012); see, for example, Lou (2012) on English in urban public signage in Washington's Chinatown and Troyer (2012) on English advertising on Thai websites, where the interesting question is why English is used in such advertising at all when it has never had a role in Thai society. Identity in English is also a hot topic, reflected in work by Lo Bianco, Orton and Gao (2009) who look specifically at the situation in China and show that beliefs and values inherent in different languages, cultures and teaching practices are often very different indeed. This can lead to an interesting conflict of identity or, alternatively, can lead the speaker to embrace a different identity when using a different language. Matsuda (2000) looks at a similar issue among Japanese speakers of English returning to Japan having lived in an English-speaking environment, and what comes through in this work is just how different a person the speaker feels he or she can be when using a language from a different culture such as English. In addition, the work into ELF continues.

5. Looking to the future

So, are we going to be using English in the future? In the *Evolving English* exhibition at the British Library (2010-2011), Professor Jenkins was very firm in her conviction that English would be going forward as the language of global communication. There are, however, a number of factors influencing a person's (or a nation's) choice of language which might confound this. Among these factors are the social, economic and political power of particular nations. For example, if China were to rise to the top of the heap, then would the scales tip in favour of Mandarin Chinese? What would happen if India, another nation on the rise, assumed the top spot? And will Britain's proposed exit from the EU have an effect on how English is used among the remaining member states?

Where Mandarin Chinese is concerned, my feeling is that the world is unlikely to adopt it as a lingua franca. The writing system, for one thing, is very complicated and needs constant study if one is to remain literate, and it is not a language which has travelled much in terms of colonisation. If India were to rise, it is likely that English would rise with it in the form of Indian English, as the language is already well established in the country and that would be an easy linguistic situation on which to capitalise. And as for English in the EU after Brexit, while some member states seem very keen to get rid of it as an official language, others claim continuing to use it will level the linguistic playing field, as it will no longer belong to any one member.

Another language spoken by a large group of people is Spanish. Currently, those using Spanish in huge numbers (i.e., speakers in South and Central America) do not have the political or economic power to influence the global lingua franca. However, one should never say never. As someone recently pointed out on a television panel show, by the time Latin was the global L2, it was no longer anybody's L1.

6. Key ideas to consider

- How do you feel when speaking to people in the UK for whom English is not their L1?

  Do you try to accommodate to them, i.e., modify how you speak to make yourself clearer?

  Have you ever assumed any of the following? Be honest!
  - They are unintelligent.
  - They're just speaking bad English.
  - They're in the UK so ought to be able to speak English like someone from the UK.

  Is it fair to assume any of these things? Why do you think so/not?

- In many countries in the world, people go to school or university where English is the medium of instruction, even though it is not the L1 of the country. How do you think this is likely to affect learning? Try to think about what it might be like to learn your subjects through the medium of French, for example.

- If you speak another language, do you feel that your identity changes when you use that language? This might be especially relevant if you're from an immigrant background with a different L1.

- What is your opinion about the likely lingua franca in 50 years' time? Will it still be English, or will we be using a different language, or more than one other language? How would you defend your position on this?

- People from Inner Circle countries are well-known for not learning other languages. Do you think we should be learning other languages, or should we give up as so many people around the world use English? What are the benefits of learning other languages?

Key abbreviations used throughout this chapter

EFL: English as a foreign language

EIL: English as an International Language

ENL: English as a Native Language

L1: English as a first language ('native speakers' of English)

L2: English as a second language (where the language which is used for one or more official purpose. These speakers are regarded as 'non-native speakers.)

GenAM: General American

LFC: Lingua Franca Core

NNS: Non-native speaker

NVEs: New Varieties of English

OVEs: Older Varieties of English

RP: Received Pronunciation

WSSE: World Standard Spoken English

Endnotes

[1] Based on figures from Crystal (2003, cited in Jenkins 2014).

[2] Jenkins points out that the publisher of the article removed the inverted commas and so she reinstates them in her book (Jenkins 2014: 90-91). The paper appeared in the *Annual Review of Applied Linguistics* and their removal begs the question of whether this was a typographical error or whether the editor meant to remove them.

References

BOLTON, K., 2012. World Englishes and linguistic landscapes. *World Englishes* 31/1: 30-33.

CRYSTAL, D., 2003. *English as a global language* (2nd edition). Cambridge: Cambridge University Press.

DZIUBALSKA-KOŁACZYK, K. & J. Przedlacka, eds., 2005. *English pronunciation models: a changing scene*. Bern: Peter Lang.

JENKINS, J., 2000. *The Pronunciation of English as an international language*. Oxford: Oxford University Press.

JENKINS, J. 2002. *Global English and the teaching of pronunciation* [online]. Available from http://www.teachingenglish.org.uk/articles/global-english-teaching-pronunciation [Accessed 21/06/2012].

JENKINS, J., 2014. *Global Englishes: a resource book for students* (3rd edition). London and New York: Routledge.

KACHRU, B.B., 1982/1992. Models for non-native Englishes. In KACHRU, B.B. ed., *The other tongue: English across cultures*, (2nd edition). Urbana, IL: University of Illinois Press.

LO BIANCO, J., J. Orton & Y. Gao, eds., 2009. *China and English. globalization and the dilemmas of identity*. Bristol: Multilingual Matters.

LOU, J. J., 2012. Chinatown in Washington DC: the bilingual landscape. *World Englishes* 31/1: 34-47.

MATSUDA, A., 2000. The use of English among Japanese returnees. *English Today* 16/4: 49-55.

PANG, T. T. T., 2003. Hong Kong English: a stillborn variety? *English Today* 19/2: 12-18.

PARASHCHUK, V. Y., 2000. International pronunciation standard of English in intercultural communication. *Proceedings of Linguapax VIII: at the threshold of the millennium: through language and culture studies to peace, harmony and co-operation.* Volume 3A. Ukraine: UNESCO and Kyiv State Linguistic University.

SCHNEIDER, E. W., 2007. *Postcolonial English: varieties around the world*. Cambridge: Cambridge University Press.

SEIDLHOFER, B., 2004. Research perspectives on teaching English as a lingua franca. *Annual Review of Applied Linguistics* 24: 209-239.

SETTER, J. & J. Jenkins, 2005. Pronunciation. *Language Teaching* 38/1: 1-17.

SETTER, J., C. S. P. Wong & B. H. S. Chan, 2010. *Hong Kong English*. Edinburgh: Edinburgh University Press.

TROYER, R.A., 2012. English in the Thai linguistic netscape. *World Englishes* 31/1: 93-112

WALKER, R., 2001. Pronunciation priorities, the lingua franca core, and monolingual groups. *Speak Out!* 18: 4-9.

5 AMERICAN ENGLISH

Professor Lynne Murphy

1. Introduction

People in the UK watch American television, listen to American music, play American video games. It's not surprising, then, to hear claims that 'American English is taking over Britain' or 'we all speak American now'.

My experience (as an American linguist in Britain) is that people from both countries tend to overestimate how much they know about the other country's English and to stereotype the language in unhelpful ways. This chapter aims to dispel some of the myths about American English (AmE) – which involves dispelling some myths about British English (BrE) too.

Before going any further, though, we need to be a bit suspicious of this terminology: *British English* and *American English*. There are, of course, many forms of English in the UK, with different accents and some different vocabulary, grammatical structures, and ways of using the language. And the same is true of English in the United States. You can probably think of types of Americans represented in popular culture who use different forms of American English – the mafia boss, the hip-hop artist, and the country singer, for example.

Given all this variation, does it make sense to talk about two national Englishes? It does sometimes, but we must be careful in how we do it. The differences exist at the national level when we talk about spelling and most vocabulary differences. *Honor* is American and *honour* is British and that's that. If you have a cut, you'd need to ask for a ***plaster*** in Britain, but a ***Band-Aid*** or an ***adhesive bandage*** in the US. This is why different dictionaries are made and sold for the British and American markets. Punctuation also tends to vary on the national level (though this can vary by publication); for example, American publications use many more commas (,) and double quotation marks (" ") than British ones. These kinds of differences are seen in formal, published English. In the spoken form, despite lots of regional variation within each country, some word pronunciations are broadly different in the US and UK. For instance, in AmE the middle syllable of ***tomato*** sounds like *may* and in BrE it sounds more like *ma*. That difference holds across most American and British English speakers, no matter which accents they have.

Accent, some aspects of grammar, and more informal vocabulary are more likely to vary within the nations, and therefore we need to be careful about how we talk about them. It doesn't make sense to talk about the *American accent* or the *British accent* because there isn't just one of either of those. But we often say things like *she has an American accent*. That can be okay, if we understand 'an American accent' to mean one American accent among many. We should be wary of broad, generalising statements if our experience of them is limited. For example, at least two British comedians have done routines that rely on the stereotype '*Americans say I could care less*'. That makes it sound like Americans don't say *I couldn't care less* – but many do, especially in writing (where it's mostly *couldn't*). So while *I could care less* is heard a lot more in American accents than in British ones, it's false to claim that Americans don't say *I couldn't care less*.

It can help to try to phrase such statements in terms of the language, rather than the speakers. It's probably never true to say '(All) Americans say X', since Americans aren't always English speakers and even among English speakers, there is variation. It's more accurate to say 'American English has X' or 'X is more common in American than in British English'.

2. Why learn about American English?

English is a world language today because the British Empire took its language into every continent. Once English is planted in a place, it can develop independently. Studying transplanted Englishes can help us to observe many historical and sociolinguistic processes in action. We can investigate issues like:

- Is a language more or less likely to change in a new place?
- How do new dialects develop?
- How are dialect differences lost?

In the 20th century, American English gained influence worldwide, particularly because of the strength of the American economy and its cultural exports, such as film, television, and music. The United States has more first-language English speakers than any other country – about five times as many as the UK. Those English speakers are doing things that change the language: making up new words and expressions, finding shortcuts for expressing meaning, following fashions of pronunciation. Some of those changes, especially now in the internet age, have spread beyond the US.

This has led to something of a panic in the British media – with commentators worrying that British English is being 'taken over' by American. The more you know about American and British Englishes and about how language change works, the better you can sift through claims about English and judge them for yourself.

3. The split between British and American English

3.1 How different are British and American Englishes?

As soon as an American starts talking, you know they're not from Britain. While there are many American accents, none of them have all the same vowel and consonant sounds as any British accents. In print, it can be harder to tell British from American. Less than 1% of our spellings differ, the grammar is mostly the same (especially in formal contexts), and I have easily written this paragraph using only words and meanings that are found in both countries – because our vocabulary is mostly the same too.

But still there are thousands upon thousands of differences at every level of language, including the following (the American is second in each pair):

- **Words:** *motorway* versus *highway*; *jumper* versus *sweater*; *abseil* versus *rappel*
- **Word forms:** *aluminium* versus *aluminum*; *maths* versus *math*.
- **Pronunciation:** *vitamin* pronounced with a 'vit' versus a 'vite'; *ballet* with the stress on the first syllable versus the second; *fertile* rhyming with *isle* versus ending with a syllabic /l/ (fert-l)
- **Morphology** (prefixes, suffixes, etc.): *dived* versus *dove*; *spoilt* versus *spoiled*; paying *tax* versus paying *taxes*
- **Word meanings:** *homely* meaning 'home-like' or 'unattractive'; *cider* as an alcoholic or non-alcoholic drink
- **Grammar:** Answering 'should I go to the gym?' with *You should do* versus *You should*
- **Spelling:** *centre* versus *center*; *travelling* versus *traveling*
- **Punctuation:** doctor as *Dr* versus *Dr.* with a full stop; Americans call punctuation dots **"periods."** British people call punctuation dots **'full stops'**. (Notice where the full stops went in those two sentences.)

It's not just which words and grammar we use, but how we use them that makes us sound 'British' or 'American'. Both Englishes use the present perfect form of verbs (*I have eaten*), but BrE uses it in places where AmE tends to use the simple past form (*I ate*). Offer a British person cake, and they'll probably say *yes, please*. An American might well say *yes, thanks*. Those kinds of differences are many, but they can be hard to measure.

How different our Englishes are thus depends on the context and topic of our communication. Here's an experiment you can do: find some American and British text on the internet, remove information about the source of the text and the location of the action, then see how far your friends or family can read before they can definitely identify the nationality of the writer. Try it with different genres of writing: local and international news, how-to instructions, fiction. A cake recipe will have many differences, but instructions for setting a secure password will have few. Topics like climate change or the World Bank are not likely to show national differences, but more local news should be easy to pinpoint, since we have different vocabulary for talk about roads and traffic, education, sports, and government.

3.2 Why so different?

The obvious reason why the US and the UK have different Englishes is our geographical separation. Language constantly changes in unpredictable ways, so when people cannot interact with each other regularly, their language is bound to go in different directions. But there must be more to it: Australia is even further away from Britain than America, but Australian English isn't more different from British English than American English is.

Why is that? One reason is time: English has been spoken in America since 1607. After Americans declared independence in 1776, immigration from Britain slowed and more immigrants from other European countries came and learned English as their second language. In comparison, English arrived in Australia in 1788, and though the distances were large, Britain and Australia kept in touch through formal ties and continued migration.

The extra years of separation were important for the development of American English, because the English of the 17th and 18th centuries was less standardized than that of the 19th or 20th centuries. Spelling, for example, was far from settled at that point (and spelling education was much more happenstance). In the late 1700s, the British were still arguing about whether *colour* should have a *u* like Norman French or whether it should follow Latin and be *color*.

Over in the US, people were arguing about it too – with a different result. Many of the spellings that we now think of as American were promoted by America's most important lexicographer (dictionary maker), Noah Webster (1758–1843). Webster argued that Americans needn't look to England for their idea of 'good English'. Creating an 'American language', he thought, would bring the new country together in its own identity. The change was not instant – not everyone was keen on linguistic independence – but today no American would think of writing *manoeuvre* and not *maneuver*.

While American spellings represented a determined effort to differ from Britain, many other linguistic differences could be considered Britain's 'fault', because it was British English that changed. Most Americans kept pronouncing the 'r' in farm while many English people stopped. American English never took on the new-fangled habit of pronouncing the 'h' in *herb*, nor has it dropped the suffix from *gotten*. Words like *sidewalk*, *period* (instead of *full stop*) and *fall* (the season) are used in the US because they came with the colonists from England. The British forgot about those words and went with other options. Americans made up plenty of new words, but then so did the British. Industrialization – and the social changes it brought on – meant that both countries had to quickly come up with lots of new words for tools, transport, banking, social care, and many other new things. And they did so separately.

That means that the common beliefs that American English is 'newer' than British English and that British English is 'purer' than American are just wrong. Sure, English started in England, but that just means that today's British Englishes live closer to the graves of the Englishes of the distant past than American Englishes do. Saying that the British English of today is 'the original English' or 'real English' is kind of like saying that your cousins who live in the same town as your grandmother are more related to her than your cousins who live in the next town over. All our Englishes are equally related to the English of Shakespeare's day; some of them just live on another continent.

4. Variation in American English

American English comes in many varieties. Some of the variation has to do with place (regional **dialects**) and some has to do with other social factors (**sociolects**), like membership in an ethnic community (**ethnolects**). In this section, we can only look at a small range of the linguistic variation present in AmE.

4.1 Regional variation

When people with similar social status but different dialects settle in the same place, the dialect of the new place tends to evolve into something similar for all the speakers. So, if Liverpudlians, Glaswegians and Bristolians ended up in the same corner of the world, their children would not speak three different dialects, but one dialect that had few of the features that separated their parents' dialects. This is called **dialect levelling**, and it's part of the reason American English dialects differ from British ones.

What's interesting about the US is that the dialects have not completely levelled. American English has more in the way of regional dialect differences than the Englishes of other former British colonies, like Canada and Australia. Part of this has to do with how America was colonized. Before there was a United States, there were thirteen English colonies on the east coast. The English people who settled in the northern colonies were mostly from different regional and social backgrounds from those who settled in the south or the middle. Protestants from Ulster (the 'Scots-Irish') tended to settle a bit further inland, toward the Appalachian mountains. Travel between these regions could take weeks (and in those days few people bothered to travel), so dialects in these regions developed on their own, with many variations at more local levels.

In the 19th century, the population exploded with immigration from many European countries. The United States expanded to the west. As new generations of immigrants learned English and people from different eastern regions mixed in the westward movement, more dialect-levelling occurred. Thus, the dialect region of the west is larger than those in the east. Map 1 shows some of the larger dialect areas. (Note that there is still variation within these.) These broad dialect areas don't cover some parts of the US, where smaller dialect areas have thrived. New England (the northeast corner) and the cities of the northeastern coast historically have rich dialect diversity, often with different dialects in different parts of a city. Few in Florida (southeast corner) sound southern because English speakers settled there later than in the rest of the east coast (it was a Spanish colony) and because of its many migrants from the north and the Caribbean. And New Orleans has been a dialect area unto itself, with dialects affected by its history of French and Spanish colonization and its status as a port at the delta of the Mississippi river, attracting migrants with many languages and dialects.

By the end of the 20th century and into the 21st, easy travel, broadcast media, and increased rates of higher education have meant that some more local dialects have lost their distinctiveness. (The same has happened in the UK.) Nevertheless, regional dialects still exist and change. Vowels in several regions are on the move, maintaining distinctions between different regions – even if they're not the same distinctions or even exactly the same regions as in historical dialects.

4.2 African-American English

African-American English (AAE; also called *African-American Vernacular English* or *Black English*) is a variety with its own pronunciations, grammar and vocabulary. Rather than a regional dialect, it is an ethnolect – a variety of English (with some local variation) spoken by many American descendants of African slaves. Many aspects of AAE are debated by linguists, but what is not debated is its status as a rule-based linguistic system, like any other English. Prejudices against AAE and its speakers are rife, however, and so it's not uncommon for non-linguists to stereotype it as 'ungrammatical' or 'lazy' English.

AAE developed through slavery and segregation. Between the 16th and 19th centuries, Europeans enslaved around 12 million African people and took them to the Americas. About 5% of those who were enslaved ended up in what would become the United States; the first Africans arrived within decades of the first English settlement in Virginia.

Slave-traders tried to move enslaved people in multilingual groups; if they couldn't talk to each other, they couldn't plot an escape or rebellion. When people from many linguistic backgrounds come together to speak a new-to-them language (and especially when their access to the language is limited by their social position), the situation is perfect for a creole language to develop, and some linguists have argued that AAE has creole roots. That is, the enslaved African people might have used a highly simplified version of English that incorporated some elements of their African languages. As this language was passed down the generations, its grammar developed and solidified. Then a process of decreolization happened, in which aspects of the variety moved closer to a standard version of English. When looking for evidence of creole origins of AAE, some linguists point to the absence of the verb *to be* as a linking verb in sentences like *She tall* or *They going home*. That is an aspect of historical AAE that seems like other English-based creoles of the Atlantic slave trade, but unlike other varieties of English.

But other linguists note the similarities between AAE and dialects of English that were brought to the American south by British immigrants – many of whom came to the US as indentured servants. The linguist Shana Poplack has shown that some aspects of AAE that contrast with other current Englishes

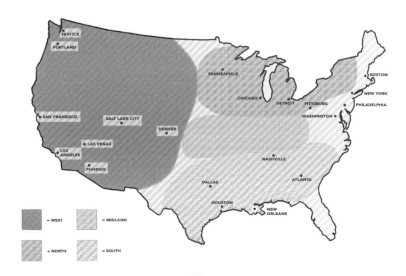

Map 1. Larger dialect regions of the United States

nevertheless have similar patterns to dialects that were spoken by English migrants to America hundreds of years ago. So, for instance, patterns of where it is appropriate to say *she sees* or *she see* in traditional AAE look a lot like the patterns of variation used by white English speakers in the early colonies and in the regional dialects they'd brought from Britain.

Slavery was always more widespread in the southern US than the north, and it stayed legal in the south until the American Civil War (1860–1865). At the start of the 20th century, over 90% of African Americans still lived in southeastern states, mostly in rural areas. Between the 1910s and the 1960s, millions left those areas in reaction to repressive laws and poor economic opportunity in the post-slavery south. By the end of this 'Great Migration' nearly half of African Americans lived outside the south, and most lived in cities. This migration brought AAE to different parts of the country, and changed the stereotypes about it; what was once a 'country' way to speak is now often associated with urban culture.

4.3 Variation upon variation

Regional variation, social variation, and ethnic variation combine in different ways to give many distinctive ways of speaking. Often variants are based in particular ethnic/immigrant backgrounds, of which the US has many. *Chicano English*, for example, describes some linguistic features that are often shared by people in Mexican-American communities. New York City dialects often employ words or grammatical patterns from Yiddish (a Germanic language historically spoken by eastern European Jews) because of the Jewish immigrant communities there. And in Southern California, particular linguistic features are associated with the mostly white subcultures of 'Valley girls' or 'surfer dudes'. Unlike in the UK (where 'talking posh' is a thing), Americans tend not to refer much to social class when talking about their speech styles, preferring instead to refer to urban/rural differences or 'educated' versus 'uneducated'. Class, of course, is interlinked with these categories.

What's important to remember is that any speaker is likely to have more than one variety of American English at their disposal. The fact that we've identified a variety called *African-American English* doesn't mean that all African Americans speak the same, or that it's the only way that African-American people speak. No matter where we're from, we can draw from a repertoire of speech styles that reflect where we come from, who we want to align ourselves with, how we want to express our identity, and how we judge the communicative needs of the context. (See Drummond in this volume, Chapter Six.)

5. Attitudes to American English in the UK

By the 1700s, British people who came into contact with American English were commenting on its differences from their own speech. Some early British travellers to the US remarked admiringly on the uniformity and conservatism of American pronunciation – the product of dialect levelling and lack of contact with the changing styles of pronunciation in London. But many back in Britain, especially the speakers of the fashionable varieties of British English, saw American English as defective in some way. If Americans made new words (like *belittle* or *congressional*), they were deemed an attack on the mother tongue. If Americans continued to use old words that had gone out of fashion in the UK (like *bill* instead of *bank note* or *brush* to refer to *fallen branches*), then they were hopelessly gauche.

In the early days, Americanisms were an affront to the tastes of British literary types. In the 20th century, they came to be seen more as a threat to British English. The US overtook Britain as an economic and world power, and the power of its language came to be felt as well. When silent films gave way to talking pictures, British newspapers printed fears that English people would soon have Hollywood accents. As the opportunities for American English to be heard increased through the television and internet ages, so have these fears and the attention that British media give to them.

These fears are stoked by misinformation, exaggeration and manipulation in the press. Take this example: in 2011 the British Library publicized their research on changing pronunciations in the UK – for example which syllable is stressed in *controversy* (CONtroversy or conTROVersy) and whether garage is garRAZH or GARridge. They concluded that British pronunciation changes have little or nothing to do with American English influence. The newer *conTROVersy* pronunciation, for example doesn't exist in American English. But *The Telegraph* ran the story with the following headline:

> The 'conTROversy' over changing pronunciations
>
> To language purists they might grate, but new ways of pronouncing words are spreading in Britain thanks to the influence of US culture.[1]

The Telegraph article goes on to quote the researcher saying that the change in the pronunciation of *controversy* has nothing to do with Americans. But by the end of a bad headline, damage has already been done. More than a third of those who click on news links don't read the article. Of those who do read, only half will make it to the end of the article[2]. Plenty of people share articles on social media using only the headline to support a point they want to make.

Now think about this BBC headline from 2017. What assumptions is it starting from? Is it trying to get a specific reaction from the reader?

> How Americanisms are killing the English language[3]

In assessing linguistic news stories, we should look for the presuppositions and metaphors used in describing English. A presupposition is a claim that must be accepted as true in order to interpret another claim that's being made. This headline expects you to accept two presuppositions: first, that the English language is being killed; they're not asking *whether* they're asking *how*. Another presupposition comes from *the*. When they write *the English language*, they expect you to make certain assumptions about how many forms of English there are (one) and who speaks it (not Americans).

Metaphors are used to frame what's happening in a particular way. In this case, if Americanisms *kill* English they must be something bad. Disease? Poison? Weapons? Assassins? It's important to notice that other possible metaphors might have Americanisms nourishing, expanding or bolstering English, rather than killing it.

Even where the media are reporting on linguistic research, they often misrepresent the careful conclusions of the researchers. For instance, one study about change in British accents (mostly caused by the strength of certain cities' accents) included one line about British communication becoming more casual, possibly because of the influence of social media platforms from the US. A *Guardian* article about the study led with the claim that ***By 2066, dialect words and regional pronunciations will be no more – consumed by a tsunami of Americanisms***[4]. There was no way to get from the report to that conclusion, but to get to the point they wanted to make, the writer gravely misrepresented the research.

You have the power to answer a lot of your own questions about American English and to check claims made in the media about language. All you need is access to the internet and a sense of which sources of information are reliable. Check a few dictionaries (more than one or you haven't really done your research – since different dictionaries offer different information). Look for presuppositions, metaphors, and poor logic, and see whether they hold up against the facts.

6. The future

Despite the worry about British English being 'Americanized', American and British English continue to do their own thing. Even with spellcheckers and autocomplete, British and American spelling are maintaining most of their differences. In fact, it's been during the internet-and-spellchecker age that British media have really started preferring the suffix *-ise* over *-ize*, apparently because of the mistaken impression that the z spelling came from America or should be left to the Americans[5]. Thus, British spelling in newspapers is looking *even more* British these days. In everyday speech, Americans and Britons continue to be easily distinguished. While the many accents in the two countries are in flux, they are not becoming more similar to one another.

The media panics about British English 'Americanizing' mostly have to do with imported vocabulary – like *cupcake* and the 'fantastic' sense of *awesome*. There are a few reasons not to panic about vocabulary movement, no matter how linguistically patriotic you are:

- Vocabulary is the part of language that is always changeable. We add new words to our vocabularies throughout our lifetimes, and most people would agree that a bigger vocabulary is helpful for communication.

- American words usually add to the language, rather than pushing British words out. Sometimes, new British uses of the formerly American words develop. For instance, the Americanism *fries* hasn't replaced the Britishism *chips*. Instead, because BrE acquired a second word that meant the same thing as one of its old words, the meanings of the two words began to specialize. In Britain, *chips* is still used for traditional fried potatoes, and *fries* used mostly used for the skinnier type that came over with American fast-food chains. This distinction does not exist in AmE, where both thin and thick fried potato sticks would be called *fries*.

- The flow of vocabulary is not unidirectional. In recent decades Americans have been adopting formerly British words that travel via the global media – words like *ginger* ('red-headed'), gutted ('emotionally devastated'), to *vet* ('to investigate candidates'), and *bespoke* ('custom-made').

- Despite some clear examples of borrowing between the dialects, the vocabulary differences are mostly holding steady. Using a very objective computer-based method of investigation, linguist Paul Baker has found 'little evidence that either variety is giving up its more distinctive words' (2017: p. 149).

In formal written language, we may see some change towards an international style, since publication is increasingly on the web, where anyone from any country can read it. Here, the US tends to lead the stylistic way, with sociolinguists noting trends in written English becoming:

- **Less formal** – for instance, you're more likely now to see contractions and personal address in textbooks like this one (for example, *you're* in this sentence).

- **Less hierarchical** – for instance, there's less use of formal titles. Above I've referred to Paul Baker just by his name, not as *Professor* Paul Baker or *Mr* Paul Baker.

- **More condensed** – in formal writing, we tend to get more meaning into fewer words than the writers of past centuries would have used. One example of this is use of the passive voice: *The book was read by the children* (7 words), rather than the active *The children read the book* (5 words). Passive usage has lessened considerably in published British English over the past 60 years, but it's lessened considerably more in American English (Leech et al. 2009; see also Baker 2017).

Those changes are particularly in published writing, though. In more local and less formal contexts, we can trust that Britons and Americans will continue to maintain separate linguistic identities for as long as national identity is important to us. Till that changes, we can expect to hear people sounding and spelling in ways that say 'I come from this place and not any other one'.

7. Key ideas and questions

1. English has changed a lot since the British colonized America – both in the UK and in the US. Geographical separation, political separation, and time have led English in the two countries in different directions.

- How much of what's different between UK and US Englishes is due to change that happened in America, and how much is due to linguistic change in Britain that happened after American colonization?

2. While we often talk about American English and British English, these labels hide a lot of linguistic variation in both countries. The United States has more regional linguistic variation than most other former British colonies, and also has a great deal of social and ethnic linguistic variation.

- How much American linguistic variation can be traced back to differences between dialects and sociolects in the British Isles? How much is due to the influence of other languages?

3. Although the idea that American English is 'taking over' Britain is often repeated, there's plenty of evidence that the two countries are continuing to differentiate themselves linguistically.

- Do attitudes to American English differ among different social groups (e.g., age, social class) in the UK?
- Why is American English the particular focus of such media stories? Are other non-linguistic factors at play?

Further reading, references, and resources

BAKER, P. 2017. *American and British English: divided by a common language?* Cambridge University Press.

This book is meant for linguistic researchers; it uses corpus linguistic and statistical tools to review differences in British and American English from the 1930s onward. It is useful for its statistics and graphs regarding how the standards of published English have changed in the two countries.

LABOV, W., S. Ash, C. Boberg. 2006. *The atlas of North American English*. Berlin: de Gruyter. http://www.atlas.mouton-content.com/

This interactive website includes maps and recordings of the various dialects of North America, with a particular emphasis on accent differences.

LEECH, G., M. Hundt, C. Mair, and N. Smith. 2009. *Change in contemporary English*. Cambridge University Press.

This book considers change in written English more generally than just US/UK differences.

MURPHY, L. 2018. *The prodigal tongue: the love–hate relationship between British and American English*. London: Oneworld.

This book is packed with facts about the history of the US–UK differences and attitudes toward them. Intended for a non-specialist audience.

MCWHORTER, J. 2016. *Talking back, talking black*. New York: Bellevue Literary Press.

McWhorter looks at the place of African-American English in the United States, including its history and structure. McWhorter is an excellent communicator about language, and can be found writing or speaking about AAE and other forms of English in many other venues on the internet as well.

POPLACK, S. 2006. How English became African-American English. In ANS VAN KEMENADE and Bettelou Los (eds.), *The handbook of the history of English*, pp. 452–476. Oxford: Blackwell.

Reviews the evidence for historical links between African-American English and the English of British settlers to the American south.

Videos: American Tongues (Center for New American Media, 1988) and Do you speak American? (WNET, 2005). Excerpts from these films can be found on YouTube and other online resources. They entertainingly document many of the varieties of English that can (or could) be heard across America.

Endnotes

[1] https://www.telegraph.co.uk/news/newstopics/howaboutthat/8305645/The-conTROversy-over-changing-pronunciations.html
[2] http://www.slate.com/articles/technology/technology/2013/06/how_people_read_online_why_you_won_t_finish_this_article.html
[3] http://www.bbc.com/culture/story/20170904-how-americanisms-are-killing-the-english-language
[4] https://www.theguardian.com/commentisfree/2016/sep/30/hsbc-dialect-dying-rab-c-nesbitt
[5] You may have noticed that while 'ise' is used throughout this book, in line with English and Media Centre's other publications, 'ize' has been used in this chapter, as it was in Professor Murphy's draft

6 URBAN YOUTH LANGUAGE

Dr Rob Drummond

1. Introduction

1.1 What is youth language?

This might sound like a question with a rather obvious answer: youth language is the language used by, well, youth. But then we need to ask ourselves which youth are we referring to? If we restrict ourselves to 'urban' youth who use some form of English for example, this still covers a very wide range of people, from 13-year-olds in Birmingham, to 16-year-olds in Detroit, to 19-year-olds in Cape Town. Even if we then restrict ourselves to a single city, there is still variation, from 15-year-old grime artists in Peckham, to 17-year-old A Level students in Notting Hill, to 18-year-old trainee chefs in Camden. And if we then add other social factors known to play a role in language variation such as gender, social class, ethnicity, sexuality, first language, and so on, the picture becomes very complex very quickly. Or maybe we should focus on the language rather than the speakers, in which case youth language is the way in which people express their 'youth' identity, regardless of who is actually using it. In this interpretation, arguably, a 35-year-old, or even a 75-year-old's language could be seen as youth language if they were using it to perform or enact 'youth' in some way.

The point is, there is no single 'youth language', even among speakers of the same language, of the same age, and who live in the same area. So what, then, do we mean by the term? In this chapter I'm taking it to mean the language used by young people aged approximately 12-20, with a focus on the contexts in which they are in some ways enacting their youth identities, for whatever reason. The fact that there is so much variation between different groups of young people is not a problem, rather it becomes a source of interest, to explore how different people from different contexts enact 'youth'.

It should be pointed out that this meaning of youth language assumes a particular approach to identity, but it is an approach I would encourage; namely, that language does not only reflect who we are, but in fact helps make us who we are. We do not simply speak in this or that way *because* of our age, our ethnicity, our gender, our sexuality, and so on, rather we *perform* our age, our ethnicity, our gender, our sexuality, and various other characteristics through the way we speak. More than this, we do not have a single fixed identity, instead we have multiple identities that are fluid and which are heavily dependent on context.

1.2. Vernacular or style?

The question as to whether we view youth language primarily as a vernacular or a style depends to a certain extent on how we view language variation more generally, and how this variation relates to identity. The word vernacular in this context refers to the Labovian (William Labov) concept of the speech we use in unguarded, casual conversation, in which we are paying the least attention to how we are speaking. Youth language as vernacular suggests that there exists an underlying, and 'natural' way of speaking consisting of language features that are specific to a particular group of (young) people. On the other hand, youth language as style suggests that young people are making conscious and often strategic stylistic choices in the language they use in order to perform or enact some kind of a youth identity (see how this relates to the understanding of identity outlined above). The most likely reality is probably somewhere in the middle – we do all have ways of speaking that are perhaps more 'natural' to us than others, but there is still a lot of room for manoeuvre in which we are able to consciously (and unconsciously) use particular language features in particular ways in order assert our 'youth' credentials. I will return to this later.

1.3 Perceptions of youth language

When we talk about youth language as a concept, we need to explore more than just the ways young people speak – we need to consider how those ways of speaking are perceived by other people. There seems to be a persistent view within (UK) society in general that young people are somehow ruining the language, that their use of slang and lack of concern for 'proper' English is leading to a permanent 'dumbing down' when it comes to linguistic standards. It is never hard to find a recent newspaper story making this argument, often blaming the decline on various other aspects of modern teenage life such as texting, or social media, or gaming, or music. But of course this has always been the case – older generations have always criticised the way younger generations use language, often blaming the decline on some new technology or cultural influence. The US linguist John McWhorter makes this point in a very entertaining way in his TED talk on text language in 2013 (McWhorter 2013). In it, he demonstrates that negative attitudes towards the ways in which young people use language, with their inability to use 'correct' grammar and punctuation in their writing, have been around for a long time. He does this by citing examples of a college professor in 1956, a school teacher in 1917, a Harvard president in 1871, a school superintendent in 1841, all complaining about their students' linguistic abilities. He finishes the examples with a 'Pedant writing in Latin, 63 A.D.', who is bemoaning the slipping standards of the language in the hands of the masses. One of the reasons to study youth language is to investigate and potentially challenge these perceptions.

1.4 Why study youth language?

In addition to seeking evidence with which to challenge negative perceptions, youth language is useful and interesting to study for two main reasons, one related to language change, and one related again to identity. We know that language changes over time; we simply have to look back at existing texts and recordings to see and hear this. And while language does, to an extent, change within an individual throughout their life, the most significant changes take place between generations: you speak differently from your grandparents and parents, and your children will speak differently from you. This means that changes are always brought about by the 'next' generation; in other words, young people. So, if we are interested in looking at the ways in which language is changing, the most useful people to investigate are the ones who are leading the change.

The other reason to study youth language is that adolescence is such a crucial and fascinating time with regard to the construction, negotiation, and performance of identity. It is a time of life when we are often working out our place in the world and who we really are; a time of life when many of us experiment with fashion, music, and behaviour in order to fit in (or not fit in) with different groups of people and in relation to different expectations of society. Canadian sociolinguist Sali Tagliamonte has written an excellent book on 'Teen Talk', and makes the point that part of what makes teenagers distinctive (and therefore interesting to study sociolinguistically), is that:

> Teenagers are in a constant state of flux. The social forces that dominate adolescent life, including increased independence, wider contacts, the imperative to separate from parents, and solidarity with peers have a corresponding impact on language. (Tagliamonte 2016:3)

Language clearly plays an important role in this process of identity construction and negotiation, and it is interesting to examine more precisely what this role is.

1.5 Why study *urban* youth language?

In many ways there is no reason why non-urban youth language should be any less interesting or less important to study than urban youth language – young people in any context are undoubtedly using language in fascinating ways. However, the urban environment generally offers more variety, with a greater number of influencing factors on both the language and the young people themselves. If we take the UK as an example – young people living in a small village in Yorkshire are unlikely to show as much linguistic (and social) diversity as young people living in inner-city London. That is not for a moment to suggest that the Yorkshire village experience (and language) is any less valid, or any less unique, but it would take a specific type of study to investigate it – one from which it would be hard to generalise outside that particular group. Urban studies, on the other hand, often look for patterns of linguistic and social behaviour which can more readily be compared with other (urban) contexts. As a result, there have been more studies, looking at a wider variety of people, in urban rather than non-urban contexts, which is why the focus of this chapter will largely be on urban youth language.

2. Previous research

In this section, I will outline some of the research that has been carried out on youth language over the last few decades. This is by no means an exhaustive list, or even a representative list, but it does provide information on some fascinating studies. In selecting the examples, I've tried to include a variety of geographical regions.

2.1 USA

One of the best-known studies into the language practices of young people is Penelope Eckert's work in a high school in Detroit (Eckert 2000). This was an ethnographic project, meaning that she spent a lot of time observing and engaging with the young people, rather than simply arranging to meet up and interview them. She made note of who hung around with who, what social practices they involved themselves in, and how they oriented themselves towards school, other people, and society in general. Eckert looked at a selection of variables (features of language that vary between speakers, groups of speakers, or contexts of speech in the way that they are produced, such as particular vowel sounds or grammatical constructions) and noticed that a lot of the variation relating to 'new' ways of using a particular feature was patterned in relation to a combination of gender, and affiliation with the two main social groups – the so-called *jocks* and *burnouts*. These two groups had been identified through the ethnographic process in advance of any linguistic analysis, and were based on 'practices that unfold in daily and mundane activity, interaction, and movement' (Eckert 2000:74). Broadly speaking, Eckert found that it was the anti-school, urban-oriented burnouts who were more likely to use the newer, incoming pronunciations, especially the burnout girls, with the pro-school, suburban-oriented jocks maintaining the linguistic norms. For example, she showed that a feature such as 'negative concord' (double negatives) was used far more frequently by burnouts than jocks, and even among the so-called 'in-betweens' it was used more by those who participated in certain urban-oriented, anti-social activities such as 'cruising' (driving through urban and suburban neighbourhoods and generally hanging out). Crucially, the young people were using particular linguistic features alongside other resources such as clothes, make-up, behaviour etc, as a way of constructing or reinforcing particular identities. They were using these resources not only as a way of enacting 'youth' but as a way of enacting particular youth identities and orientations.

Norma Mendoza-Denton undertook a similar style of project, but she focused on a specific group of young people – young Latina women who were connected to the gang scene in an area of San Francisco (Mendoza-Denton 2008). Mendoza-Denton spent a lot of time with young women affiliated to both gangs (*Norteña* and *Sureña*), both in and out of school, and again observed how linguistic features combined with make-up, clothes, hair, tattoos and other symbolic practices in order to signal social affiliation to one or other group, or else to a broader Latina-based identity. Features of particular interest in this study included the pronunciation of /ɪ/ as in 'kit' and the extent to which it became more like /iː/ as in 'keep', and the use of words like 'everything' and 'something' as discourse markers – '…I mean he was good *and everything*'. By looking at who used which features more often, combined with detailed ethnographic observations, Mendoza-Denton, like Eckert above, is able to argue that the use of such features are playing a role in the enactment of certain youth/ethnic/gang identities within that particular context.

2.2 Europe

There has been a lot of research carried out on the language of young people in various European urban contexts in recent years, much of which focuses on the linguistic and social changes brought about by increased immigration and the subsequent multilingualism and multiculturalism.

Heike Wiese works in German looking at 'Kiezdeutsch', a name which literally means '(neighbour-)hood German', and is the language of young people in multi-ethnic neighbourhoods of Berlin (see for example Wiese 2013). A particular focus of Wiese's work is the extent to which Kiezdeutsch can be seen as a dialect in its own right, alongside existing and established regional dialects. The naming of Kiezdeutsch and the description of it as a dialect has been very controversial in Germany, with Wiese herself facing a lot of personal criticism from sections of the general public and even other linguists writing in mainstream press, who see Kiezdeutsch as a sign of German being simplified, leading to a lack of language competence and subsequent educational failure among young people.

John Bellamy has looked at another youth variety of German, this time in the Nordstadt neighbourhood of Dortmund (Bellamy 2018). He finds similarities with Kiezdeutsch, but also focuses very much on the stylistic aspects of this way of speaking, gaining insights from an ethnographic study in a community/youth centre. He shows the extent to which the young people are aware of how they use language to identify with particular groups and distance themselves from others.

Interestingly, work carried out in Paris by Penelope Gardner-Chloros, Jenny Cheshire, and Maria Secova which aimed to compare the situation in Paris with that of London specifically (and other European cities more generally) obtained very different results from those in other cities. The spread of an identifiable city-specific 'multiethnolect' and the patterns of use of particular features along the lines of London (see below and Chapter Two) do not seem to be happening in the same way in Paris (Cheshire and Gardner-Chloros 2018). Future work will attempt to ascertain why this might be the case.

A particular focus of much of the work in Europe, as mentioned in relation to Kiezdeutsch above, are the ways in which these youth languages are perceived and described outside of linguistics. A key aspect of this is the choice of name given to the variety. In the Netherlands, there is 'straattaal' ('street language'), which, although often used in a negative way, was actually brought in as a replacement for the much more derogatory 'smurfentaal' ('smurf lingo') (Cornips et al 2015). Before Heike Wiese argued for the neutral term 'Kiezdeutsch', the dominant expression in public discourse in Germany was 'Kanak Sprak', where 'Kanak' is a pejorative, xenophobic word, and 'sprak' is a shortened form of 'Sprache' (language). In the UK, what linguists call Multicultural London English or Multicultural Urban British English (see below), the mainstream media often label 'Jafaican', suggesting a fake, Jamaican accent.

2.3 Rest of the world

African Urban Youth Languages have been the subject of several studies in recent years, with much of the focus being on their role as tools of solidarity, exclusion, and rebellion. Ellen Hurst (Hurst 2017) provides a useful overview of research carried out over the last twenty or so years, with descriptions of ***Sheng*** (originating from Swahili in Nairobi), ***Tsotsitaal*** (a stylistic practice that can be found in all South Africa's languages), ***Camfranglais*** (found in Cameroon), and ***Nouchi*** (popular in Cote d'Ivoire), as well as indications of others that are emerging. Hurst refers to the work of Fiona McLaughlin among others, who makes the point that

> By their very nature, youth languages are short lived and rapidly changing because they are premised on the assumption that others cannot understand them. (McLaughlin 2009: 8-9).

Indeed, this sense of exclusivity and differentiation is central to the descriptions Hurst provides, along with an underlying link between the languages, and some kind of streetwise, often criminal identity. What is also interesting is the extent to which these languages are restricted to young people. To what extent do the speakers of a particular variety continue to use it as they grow older? McLaughlin suggests that when this happens, the language may begin to be adopted by the general urban population, subsequently becoming a more established 'urban vernacular' (McLaughlin 2009: 9).

3. Current UK research

3.1 Multicultural London English (MLE)

Multicultural London English is the term given to a way of speaking, particularly among young people, that was identified in London in the early 2000s by a team of linguists led by Jenny Cheshire, Paul Kerswill, and Sue Fox (for example, Cheshire et al 2011). MLE is generally thought of as being an example of a multiethnolect – a speech repertoire (as opposed to 'variety', which suggests something more fixed) that has emerged as a result of numerous linguistic and cultural influences on the dominant mainstream language in modern, multilingual and multicultural urban centres. Cheshire and her colleagues view the repertoire as consisting of features that are selected by individuals from a 'feature pool' – a collection of words, grammar and pronunciations originating from all the different languages and dialects found in London. Particular features are selected, acquired, modified, and used by individuals both consciously and unconsciously, often depending on how they are perceived and who is already using them. One interesting aspect of this process is that features originating from identifiable languages, dialects, or ethnolects (varieties associated with particular ethnicities) often become neutralised, and available to be used by anyone, regardless of perceived heritage. (You can read more about MLE in Chapter Two.)

3.2 Multicultural Urban British English (MUBE)

But what is happening outside London? Is there a Multicultural Birmingham English? A Multicultural Glasgow English? It is very likely that there is, due to the fact that these other UK cities are also linguistically and culturally diverse and so will see similar processes taking place. As people carry out more research in a range of UK cities, descriptions of these different varieties or repertoires will undoubtedly emerge. As this happens, it is important that we look not only at the differences between cities, but also at the similarities.

Multicultural Urban British English is the name given to a possible underlying repertoire of features that is shared across UK cities, with the understanding that each location will retain some of its identifiably regional characteristics. It remains tentative at the moment as more research needs to be carried out in multiple locations, but the results of existing studies, along with anecdotal evidence of day-to-day experience, suggests it is an idea worth pursuing. Certainly, in Manchester, young people are using features that are undoubtedly associated with MLE, yet they retain other features which mark them out as being from the North-West. For example, they might use 'dem' for 'them' and even 'ting' for 'thing' (known as th-stopping, a feature of MLE), but they have the same local vowel sounds in words such as 'bath' and 'trap' (/bæθ/ /tɹæp/), and in 'strut' and 'foot' (/stɹʊt/ /fʊt/), which wouldn't be found in London.

3.2.1 Manchester

The Manchester findings come from some research undertaken by me and my colleague, Susan Dray, looking at the language of young people who had been excluded from mainstream school and who were being educated in Pupil Referral Unit learning centres in 2014-15 (see Drummond 2018). They were aged between 14 and 16, had all grown up in and around the city, but were from a variety of backgrounds. The research was carried out along the lines of Eckert's and Mendoza-Denton's studies described above, in that we both spent a year involved in the day-to-day lives of the young people and staff in two learning centres. By spending time getting to know the young people and building relationships with them, we were able to access contexts (and therefore spontaneous interactions) which would otherwise have been unavailable. Whether or not you believe there to be a 'natural' way of speaking for any individual (see the description of vernacular above), such access certainly provided the opportunity to see and hear a wide range of language styles, both in terms of inter-speaker variation (between different speakers) and intra-speaker variation (within the same speaker).

While media stories of young people 'talking themselves into unemployment' with their 'street slang' and 'ghetto grammar', often present an argument that standards are slipping, preventing them from communicating effectively, our findings ran counter to this. What became apparent early in the project was that the young people seemed more than capable of switching to a more standard variety of English when the situation required it, however they chose to speak between themselves in more casual settings. Admittedly, there may be other aspects of these young people's interpersonal skills which might be judged as less appropriate for certain formal contexts (e.g., eye-contact, posture, confidence etc.) but language itself is not necessarily an issue. In our work with the young people in the learning centres – when faced with quite a formal mock college interview scenario, all of those who took part spoke in a way that was entirely appropriate, regardless of how they spoke immediately before or afterwards with their friends. One can only assume that the people who write the newspaper articles and columns which portray the language of young people in such a negative way are basing their opinions purely on the speech they overhear on the street, rather than from any actual experience of an interview context.

3.2.2 Vernacular or style (again)?

This ability to change the way they speak depending on the context, adjusting to a more standard variety when the situation demands, strongly suggests a stylistic aspect to youth language. In other words, young people are using speech as a way of creating or performing particular identities, depending on who they are speaking to and in what social situation. When they talk to friends they are using one style of speaking; when they are in a more formal situation they are using another. However, despite it being a natural part of communication, this process can be viewed negatively, sometimes characterised as people 'putting on' a particular speech style and being somehow 'fake'.

But how accurate is this? To what extent is this kind of style-shifting between different ways of speaking the same as putting on a 'fake' speech style? Whether any way of speaking is viewed as being 'put on' rather depends on the extent to which you subscribe to the view that we all have a 'natural' way of speaking. If we accept this idea, then one could argue that young people will each have a natural, unguarded way of speaking (the vernacular discussed earlier), and then they put on a relevant youth language variety in order to enact a particular youth identity. Or it could be the other way around, and the youth language could be their unguarded vernacular, and the more standard variety is used in order to enact a more mainstream identity. But whichever style is seen as being more natural, both are performing a particular function and 'doing' something in relation to identity. In which case, it is probably useful to view all speech styles used by an individual as equally important stylistic and identity resources rather than as something either 'natural' or 'fake'. This is especially true when we bear in mind that we are usually only talking about relatively minor differences between styles (such as specific pronunciations, words/phrases, or grammatical structures) rather than a completely different dialect.

Some research into youth language has tended to focus on how it represents a fundamental change in the vernacular, or the underlying and natural speech of the young people (for example much of the work on MLE), and other research has tended to focus on it being used as a stylistic resource (see, for example Quist 2008). However, most people would probably agree that there is value in both approaches, and that urban youth language represents both a change in underlying grammar, lexis, and phonology, as well as a tool for young people to use alongside other resources as a way of constructing and performing identities.

To put it another way, we know that language changes over time and between generations, and young people will almost invariably be leading that change (see Tagliamonte 2016 for a good description of the idea of 'incrementation' – the process by which each generation builds on the language of the previous generation by using more of the new and incoming features). In urban centres across the UK and Europe especially, the changes taking place are influenced in no small part by the variety of languages, ethnicities and cultures that exist in these diverse contexts. In this sense, the underlying vernacular of young people is changing in this multilingual/multicultural direction. However, in addition to this, young people are using some of the available linguistic features both unconsciously and consciously (and therefore to an extent strategically) in order to construct and perform particular identities. Whether you happen to view the underlying change as more important, or the use of language as a stylistic resource as more important is in many ways simply a reflection of personal research interest and focus. People who focus on each one are often asking different questions in the pursuit of different answers. Research which explores the developments in underlying vernacular addresses questions about why and how language is changing in this way; whereas research which explores the use of language as a stylistic resource addresses questions about how particular features came to mean what they do when being used in identity performance. In other words, why should the use of a certain pronunciation, word, or syntactic structure be perceived as a marker of 'youth' identity? How do linguistic features acquire their social meaning? One way they do this is through music.

3.2.3 Music

Music has always played an important role in the lives of many young people, often serving as a shared experience through which to strengthen social groups and boundaries. Musical tastes and allegiances go hand in hand with issues around fashion, attitude and behaviour, and are therefore central to issues of identity. If you ask any group of young people about the different broad social groups that exist among people their own age, many of these groups will have a specific type of music (and fashion and set of behaviours) associated with them. For some, the music will be *the* defining characteristic that brings members of the group together and separates them from others.

One particular type of music that is of interest here is the broad genre of rap and hip-hop, and, specifically in the UK context, grime. Grime is a style of music that grew out of early 2000s East London, and one which, while sharing similarities with US hip-hop, actually has its roots in UK garage, bashment, jungle and dancehall[1]. Grime is gritty, urban, and strongly associated with issues around hardship, disenfranchisement, and 'street' culture. As a genre, it exudes an attitude and identity of streetwise, gang-related toughness. (Whether it is always perceived in this way is of course, as with any intended identity performance, debatable depending on the context).

Linguistically, grime and MLE are strongly connected. MLE is in many ways the default language of grime, with many artists (e.g., Dizzee Rascal, Stormzy, Wiley, Plan B) serving as ideal illustrations of what MLE actually is. And it is this connection that is so important – it allows the process of association between language features and social meaning to take place. The process is illustrated in figure 1 and goes something like this: language feature (A) is used as a way of signifying allegiance to a particular social group, who use a particular variety/repertoire of language (MLE) (B), and who engage in a particular type of music (grime) (C). Engagement with grime then triggers an association with a particular tough/street culture (D), resulting in a situation where the language feature itself starts to become associated with that street/

tough culture (E). In other words, the language feature acquires its social meaning through its association with grime.

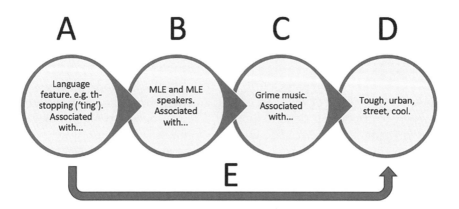

Figure 1. The process by which a language feature acquires social meaning.

I describe an example of this process in action in Drummond (2018). The context was a recording of a conversation between a group of four boys and one adult youth worker during an art class. The boys were discussing somebody they all knew (let's call him Marcus) who was soon to be released from prison, and each of them was recalling when they had last seen him. As the conversation progresses, each of the boys tries to show how well they know Marcus, and although they aren't trying to outdo each other, they are certainly making sure the others are aware of their association with him, and by extension, his way of life. And as they do this, it becomes noticeable that they start to use [t] for 'th' more often, having earlier been using the more frequent [f].

My interpretation of this is that in trying to align themselves with Marcus, and with his tough and even criminal way of life, the boys start to use a particular feature of speech (th-stopping) which somehow helps to enact a certain identity. This interpretation only works if there is some mechanism which links th-stopping to that identity, which is shown in the process illustrated above.

Of course, we have to be careful when we ascribe social meaning to linguistic features. We cannot simply claim a link and use isolated examples just because they suit the story we are trying to tell. Rather, we need to gather the evidence that supports this interpretation. In this context, the evidence was provided through the ongoing observations of the day-to-day practices and language use of the boys, and noticing when and in what contexts particular features were used.

4. Lexis and slang

One final area which is always of interest in relation to youth language is the way in which words and phrases come in and out of popular use, often subtly changing their meaning in the process (see Julie Coleman's book *The life of slang* for an excellent and detailed overview).

Below are a selection of words and phrases that were in popular use among the young people we observed in Manchester in 2014-15. Even when I went back a year later, some of the phrases had already dropped out of use, so this should be seen as a snapshot of what was current among a particular group of people at a particular point in time. I share the examples here in part to encourage you, as future researchers, to go out and capture what is in use among your own networks, as that way we can start to build a more complete picture of the changes as they happen.

Allow It (Verb) /əˈlaʊ ɪt/ Leave it, let it go, don't worry about it.

Just allow it man, it's not your business.

Bait (Adjective) /beɪt/ Being obvious or acting suspiciously when the situation demands a bit more secrecy or subtlety.

I didn't want to look bait so I went the other way.

Dead (Adjective) /dɛd/ Boring, rubbish. 'Semi-dead' can be used to describe something as 'not that bad'.

This lesson's dead.

Long (Adjective) /lɒŋ/ Something that requires effort, is boring, or will take ages. It refers to more than just time, the effort aspect being central. Can also refer to people

This is long (usually lo:::::ng)

You're long, you = you're taking ages.

Macca (Adjective) /ˈmækə/ Rubbish or shit. It can also mean 'dead' (see above) or 'boring'. It's often used in the phrase chatting macca, that is, talking rubbish.

He was chattin' macca about the Taliban and all that.

Peak (Adjective) /piːk/ Shame, bad luck, embarrassing, gutted. When something bad happens to someone, it can be described as 'peak'

Ha ha! That's peak, that.

Time (Noun) /taɪm/ Although still carrying the standard meaning, it's the grammatical structure that's of interest. Used in phrases such as I haven't seen you for time, or He hasn't been here in time, it essentially means the same as the informal 'ages', to refer to a seemingly long period.

I haven't seen you for time.

5. Future work

Due to the nature of adolescence as a life stage, and the fact that language is always changing, research into youth language will always be interesting and enlightening from both linguistic and social perspectives. Research into *urban* youth language will be of increasing importance as we use sociolinguistics as a way of making sense of the rapidly changing make-up of our cities. However, it is very important to also keep an eye on what is happening in non-urban spaces; when particular urban-based language features start being used elsewhere, it can start to tell us about how they become available to be used as stylistic resources. Whatever the focus, urban or non-urban, it is vital that we try to build up as complete a picture as possible by researching in as many locations as we can. This way we can compare youth language between countries and between cities. In the UK we need to ensure that it isn't just London (or Manchester) that gets the focus – we need to document what is happening in Leeds, in Liverpool, in Swansea, in Glasgow, in Belfast. Is there a similar style of speech emerging in UK cities? And if so, how is it spreading, and how are local identities being maintained (are they being maintained?)? Is music important, or is there something else helping to drive the changes and provide stylistic and identity-related meaning?

The great thing is – these are questions that any kind of research can help to answer, however small-scale the project. Wherever you live, you will have access to young people, which means you will have access to youth language. So start listening!

Endnotes

[1] At the time of writing (summer 2018) there is a lot of talk about drill music taking the place of grime in London, but even if this is the case, there are enough similarities between the two for them to be seen together in this context.

References

BELLAMY, J. 2018. 'Ein Remix-Deutsch'. Marginalisation, linguistic practices and identity construction amongst young people in Dortmund. tbc

CHESHIRE, J., P. Kerswill, S. Fox, and E. Torgersen. 2011. Contact, the feature pool and the speech community: the emergence of Multicultural London English. *Journal of Sociolinguistics 15*, 2: 151–196.

CHESHIRE, J., and P. Gardner-Chloros. 2018. 'Introduction: multicultural youth vernaculars in Paris and urban France'. *Journal of French Language Studies Special Issue: Multicultural Youth Vernaculars in Paris and Urban France 28* (2018), 161-164

COLEMAN, J. 2012. *The life of slang*. Oxford University Press.

CORNIPS, L., J. Jaspers & V. De Rooij. 2015. The politics of labelling youth vernaculars in the Netherlands and Belgium. In NORTIER, J. and B. A. Svendsen (eds) *Language, youth and identity in the 21st century*. 45-70. Cambridge University Press.

DRUMMOND, R. 2018. *Researching urban youth language and identity*. Palgrave Macmillan.

ECKERT, P. 2000. *Linguistic variation as social practice: The linguistic construction of identity in Belten High*. Oxford: Blackwell.

HURST, E. 2016. African (Urban) Youth Languages. *Oxford Research Encyclopedia*. OUP.

MCLAUGHLIN, F. (ed.) 2009. *The languages of urban Africa*. London: Continuum.

MCWHORTER, J. 2013. "Txtng Is Killing Language. JK!!!" TED Talk. February. http://www.ted.com/talks/john_mcwhorter_txtng_is_killing_language_jk?language=en.

MENDOZA-DENTON, N. 2008. *Homegirls: language and cultural practice among Latina youth gangs*. Malden and Oxford: Blackwell.

TAGLIAMONTE, S. 2016. *Teen talk: The language of adolescents*. Cambridge: CUP.

WIESE, H. 2013. From feature pool to pond: The ecology of new urban vernaculars. In *Working papers in Urban Language and Literacies* 104.

7 SPOKEN ENGLISH

Dr Sue Fox

1. Introduction

Why study spoken English when we have access to so many written resources? Doesn't the written version tell us everything we need to know about the structure and use of English? The answer is 'no' because although they are, of course, both forms of the same language there are also many important differences between the two and these differences are due to the fact that we use speech and writing in very different communicative situations. Speech is 'time-bound, dynamic, transient' (Crystal 2003: 291); it takes place in the here and now as part of an interaction in which both speaker and listener(s) are usually present. It is important for interpersonal relationships, completing daily transactions and for general social integration. It is usually (though not always) unplanned, spontaneous and brings immediate feedback from the addressee. Writing, on the other hand, is 'space-bound, static, permanent' (Crystal 2003: 291); it is usually planned, can be revised and edited to change the sequential order and it can be read and re-read by the recipient many times over (see Crystal 2003 for a more detailed account of the differences between speech and writing).

There is a tendency to think of the written variety as *the* language and as the standard against which spoken language is measured; any speech that doesn't come close to the written standard then comes to be seen as somehow 'incorrect' because written English is the standard form that society tends to value the most. However, it is important to remember that speaking is the primary form of communication and that anyone born with a normal ability to learn will acquire speech and listening skills long before they acquire the ability to read and write (if they ever do and many people around the world do not). As Crystal (2003: 236) notes, 'The origins of the written language lie in the spoken language, not the other way round.' It is clear that the vast majority of English use is speech, thus emphasising the importance of spoken language as the main channel within which human interaction takes place.

So what is interesting about spoken language? There are many linguistic features that are characteristic of speech that we do not find in writing. Unique to speech, there are prosodic features of intonation and rhythm – we can convey meaning by altering the pitch, loudness and speed of our talk or we can use silence in the form of a pause. We can also make use of body language in the form of facial expressions and gestures to help us convey and understand meaning. None of these things can easily be represented in writing. The fact that we have to think about what we are producing while we are actually talking means that the construction will probably be looser than written language, with more repetition and rephrasing and the opportunity to reformulate when clarification is needed. False starts, overlapping speech and interruptions are also common in spoken language. There are no clear sentence boundaries in speech, rather utterances that may consist of combined clauses, sometimes lengthy and complex and which may be left unfinished, perhaps due to the situational context or to the shared knowledge of the speakers.

Having highlighted some of the differences between speech and writing, it should be pointed out there is sometimes some crossover between the two mediums. For example, speech is not always spontaneous; rhetorical speeches, lectures or sermons are often prepared in advance and will therefore be coherently structured with no false starts, repetitions or other features of more spontaneous talk. We may not always be able to make use of body language or gesture, such as when we are talking on the telephone, or there may not be another participant in the interaction, as in the case of talking into a telephone answering machine. It should also be acknowledged that there are also many current forms of writing which are rather closer to speech forms than to formal writing; written electronic communication quite often displays interaction features such as reformulations and clarifications as well as **discourse-pragmatic features** (which are discussed in the following sections). We must therefore bear in mind that features of spoken language are tendencies rather than hard and fast rules. We must also consider that spoken language is a vast topic area and that most people engage in many different types of speech in their everyday lives, for example telephone conversations (both private and business), shop and other transactional encounters, negotiations, debates, interviews and many other types of speech depending on our occupation and the contacts we have with other people. It is difficult to know what proportion of our time is taken up with each type of speech but there seems no doubt that for most people the most frequent type of speech is casual conversation. In the rest of this chapter, then, we will explore further some general features of spoken language that occur mainly in casual conversation.

2. Backchannels

Interaction is a two-way process, involving both the speaker and listener(s), who jointly produce the conversation. The listener plays an important and complex part in this process and does not simply have a passive role; in order to keep the conversation running smoothly, the listener must signal active listening to the speaker, otherwise there is the risk of a breakdown in communication. These signals support the speaker's turn and usually communicate that the listener is engaged and acknowledging the talk but that they are not attempting to take over the speaking turn. They tell the speaker that her message has been received, understood or that it has produced either agreement or some other reaction (surprise, for example) from the listener. The way that listeners do this is to provide feedback to the speaker by using what are called **backchannels** (or sometimes **minimal responses** or **listener responses**). In most cases, these backchannels overlap with the speaker's turn and are usually skilfully placed at the end of the clause to which the listener is responding. Backchannel communication occurs in all languages and cultures. In English, typical backchannels are small words or items such as *yeah*, *no*, *oh*, *right*, *mm*, *mhm* and *uh-huh* but there are many other possibilities, depending on what the listener wishes to signal to the speaker. The following are some of the main functions that have been attributed to backchannels (the list is by no means exhaustive).

2.1 Backchannels functioning as 'continuers'

This is probably the most common form of backchannel, the type that keeps the conversation flowing and maintains the turn with the current speaker (S). Here is an example[1], with backchannels from the listener (L) shown in square brackets:

> S: that was our pastime there go to the theatres up west [L: *mhm*]. and er . have a meal up there I love the lights [L: *yeah*] I love the lights mind you its all different now ah I never even see it anymore . I don't even bother to go anymore but I go more Essex way now where the family is . er . so yes I do go to the theatre occasionally . which I love [L: *mhm*]. and when I go away its usually a show on there they have shows I mean you get your entertainment of a night so but er the main thing indoors is if I haven't got that now mine packed up so I haven't got one anymore but I have the talking books you know [L: *oh yeah*] from the library

In the above example, the backchannels all function as continuers because they encourage the speaker to continue her turn; they do not express any particular attitude or stance towards the content of what is being said.

2.2 Backchannels which seek to align with the speaker

Sometimes backchannels are used to signal a shared opinion or agreement with the speaker. The range of backchannel items used to signal allegiance is wide but might include words such as *sure*, *indeed*, *absolutely* or may even be short phrases such *you're right there*, *I agree* and *that's true*.

> S: very agricultural region [L: *yeah*] and of course the other way . was farmland as well [L: *that's right*] where the White Hart Lane estate [L: *yeah that's right*] that was all farmland wasn't it

The above example occurred during a sociolinguistic interview and speaker (S) is explaining to the interviewer how the area in which she lives has changed since she was a child. The listener (L), her friend, is not attempting to take over the turn but provides backchannels to show her engagement in the conversation, her alignment to the speaker and to confirm her agreement with what the speaker is saying. We can see from this example that backchannels are also an important way of collaborating to produce a story.

We can also include in this category backchannels that demonstrate empathy with the speaker. These might be expressions such as *oh no*, *oh dear*, *that's awful*, *that's terrible*, *poor you* and *you poor thing*, among many others.

2.3 Backchannels which function as 'newsmarkers'

These are used to show that what is being said is newsworthy in some way. They could include expressions such as *wow*, *really*, *blimey*, *oh my god* and *goodness me*.

> S: and you've got to jump across a ledge [L: *yeah*] . then go round a big tree post [L: *yeah*] walk across a wooden bridge with no handles [L: **<u>oh my god</u>** <*laughs*>] yeah . and then you've got to go across a wire [L: *yeah*] .. then a catwalk .[L: **<u>my god yeah</u>**] . and then there's a rope where you gotta lean back and that if you fall well [L: **<u>my god</u>**] you're just hanging there like

Note that the three backchannels highlighted in bold and underlined come after the three most dangerous (i.e. newsworthy) activities described by this speaker in relation to his experience of completing an outdoor assault course.

2.4 Backchannels that have an assessment function

These forms of backchannels are used to show engaged listening but they also evaluate the talk of the speaker and can include expressions such as *good idea*, *that's nice*, *oh*, *lovely* and *that's a shame*. We can see how these work in the following example:

> S: I went up there and I stayed up there for five years [L: *excellent*] with lord (name) he's a nice old gentleman him quite a few judges I had up there but my official whatsname was official referee . place I still got me briefcase .. .. [B: *oh very smart*] there are . official referee . that's what it's that's not the official referee stuff in that's all the clubs books [L: *aah*] cos I have to keep you know I still have to er keep check of all the money I spend you know cos I . I was sponsored by different people letting the hall out and all that so I had to keep a record of everything I spent and where I whatsname we just had our christmas dinner at Southend [L: *nice*] last week everything quite a nice day . the weather was good and dry so [L: *that's good*] alright well it was raining when we left but when we got down there weather changed it went . dried out

Of course, we must remember that backchannels can also be non-verbal but that they still signal engaged listening to the speaker. Non-verbal backchannels include nodding or shaking of the head, eye contact, raising eyebrows, frowning, smiling or other facial expressions. You can often see these techniques being used by news reporters and TV interviewers who are trained to 'minimise their vocals' because it avoids hearing the interviewer's voice during the speaker's response. To sum up, backchannels perform important functions in the discourse and they highlight the fact that the listener's participation is crucial to successful interaction.

3. Clause combining

In writing, clauses tend to be linked with a variety of conjunctions such as *and*, *but*, *because*, *or*, *so* and pairs such as *neither/nor* and *either/or*, and sentences may also contain many subordinate clauses introduced by conjunctions such as *when*, *since*, *until*, *however* and *therefore*. There are, however, only so many clauses that a sentence can contain before it becomes unwieldy and difficult to read and at this point it is usual to end the sentence and start a new one. However, as mentioned previously, there are no clear sentence boundaries in spontaneous speech and because speakers do not have time to plan how clauses are to be linked in the variety of ways that they might use in writing, clauses in spoken language tend to be combined with the most commonly used conjunction *and*, which often expresses a very general meaning of addition. Utterances can consist of many clauses combined in this way and could go on indefinitely. The following example is from an 8-year-old girl describing to the interviewer (interviewer's responses shown in square brackets) how she and her sister make spiced chicken:

> S: me and my sister do chips and chi. erm do do the
>
> chicken [Int: *yeah*] yeah .
>
> we always put like different type of stuff .
>
> when we just peel this erm stuff away
>
> **and** then we wash it .
>
> **and** rinse it away
>
> **and** put it away .
>
> **and** then we took some like ingredients and stuff .
>
> **and** then we put some pepper inside [Int: *wow*]
>
> we put some curry

we put some er ghee

put some salt [Int: *nice and spicy*] yeah and stuff like that

and then when we just put it inside the oven for some minute

and then it was erm . done . erm my bro ..

and it was nice [Int: *mm*]

cos of the curry

but my dad . but my dad wasn't there .

erm cos erm . my dad is allergic to curry

This young speaker's turn consisted of many more combined clauses (you can see the full transcript and listen to the audio file at http://sllf.qmul.ac.uk/englishlanguageteaching) but the above excerpt highlights the extensive use of the conjunction *and*. Of course, this might be a feature that we would expect of children as they develop their language skills but the next example demonstrates that this linking device is also common among adult speakers. In this extract, the female speaker is over 70 years old and is describing her husband's younger days during World War II.

S: and erm they grew up with all this farmland around them

and I mean they used to be over the fields

and of course you get him talking about during the war

and there was the anti-aircraft battery up on . (name of road)

up the top there

well the farm the fields just led straight there

and they were out working or helping o. in the fields one summer

and erm a German plane got shot down

and they didn't half get a telling off

cos they all went running over <*laugh*>

and they said the pilot could have come out shooting

Other conjunctions are also used in spoken language but less so since they have more specific meanings. The speaker in the first example uses *but* which expresses contrast. Other conjunctions commonly used (though again less frequently than *and*) are *so* or *so that*, used to suggest that what follows is a result of what has just been said and *or*, which introduces an alternative. In the above two examples we see the use of *because* (commonly shortened to *cos* in connected speech) which links the main clause to a subordinating clause (a clause which expands an element of the main clause and cannot stand alone) and, in the first example, provides a reason why the chicken tasted nice and, in the second example, provides a reason why her husband and his siblings got a 'telling off'.

4. Conversational historical present

The **conversational historical present** (**CHP**) refers to the use of the present tense when talking about past events. In conversation, people tend to do this when they are narrating a story, when the use of the present tense makes the story more vivid and gives the sense that it is happening right now. It's particularly common to use it when quoting one's own words or the words of others (see **quotative expressions** below). It is important to note that no story is ever told entirely in the conversational historical present but rather that it alternates with past tense forms, as in the following example:

> S: I went to (name of) station yeh
>
> I put money in the mach. in the machine
>
> I put in . ten pound note in the machine
>
> and then they **say** there's no change
>
> so I **cannot** buy the ticket
>
> so I **take out** that money
>
> and **go** outside to a new. newsagent to give me change
>
> but they wouldn't
>
> so I had to come inside
>
> stand in there for a little while
>
> **go** inside
>
> **come** outside
>
> I was just going up and down yeh .
>
> then I got it changed

The speaker in this extract had been arrested for acting suspiciously at a train station and was explaining the circumstances and his behaviour leading up to the arrest. Notice the point when he switches to the CHP (in bold), which seems to foreground the information that is important in this story.

The historical present is also used in other genres of spoken language such as radio and TV news headlines, for example *Archaeologists **find** treasure buried for more than 5,000 years*. Sports commentators frequently use it when describing past sporting events, for example when looking at video clips as in *here he **passes** the ball down the line, it**'s** picked up by Beckham who **shoots** for goal….ooo and it **comes off** the bar*.

5. Deixis

Spoken language often contains **deictic expressions** that refer directly to the immediate situation. This is because the participants usually have visual contact with each other and the listener can therefore 'see' what the speaker is referring to and the context makes the meaning clear. In interaction, the pronouns *I* and *you* are very common because it is obvious that they refer to the speaker and listener present. Similarly, *here* and *now* are frequently used, again because it is obvious that they refer to the time and place in which the interaction is occurring. *This, that, these* and *those* are used to refer to things that can be seen in the immediate context or to refer to things that have just been mentioned. In writing, these expressions would be ambiguous and therefore tend to be avoided. The following extract has many examples of deictic expressions – perhaps you can guess the context in which this interaction is taking place.

S: 1		now, **this** is a very special machine.
	2	I'm going to clip it onto **you** like **this**…like **that** . ok? .
	3	and then I'm going to give **you this** .
	4	shall I clip **this** onto **you** . somewhere .
	5	onto your trousers? .
	6	ok . now that makes **you** a film star . a television star .
	7	do **you** like **it**? .
	8	and can **you** see **this**? .
	9	every time **you** speak .
	10	**you** see when I speak, **these** lines are going up and down.
	11	if **you** speak **you**'ll see your lines going up and down as well.

12	try it ....
13	can you see it?.
14	every time **you** do that
15	**you**'re making **that line** go up and down .
16	when **I** speak **that line** goes up and down

The above extract comes at the start of a sociolinguistic interview where the interviewer is introducing her 5-year-old participant to the recording equipment. The *special machine* in line 1 is a wireless radio microphone transmitter and the *this* in line 3 refers to the clip-on lapel microphone. In line 8 the *this* refers to the recording machine itself and *these lines* in line 10 refer to the sound frequency display during recording. None of these things are made explicit during the interaction because the context makes the meaning clear to the participants.

6. Discourse-pragmatic markers

Discourse-pragmatic markers are important features of spoken language. While they make very little contribution to the literal meaning of what is being said they perform many different important functions in interaction. For example they can:

- mark the beginning or end of a turn – *right*, *ok*, *I mean*, *so*, *anyway*, *then*, *like*
- mark the start of reported speech – *I said*, *he goes*, *she's like*
- mark information that is new to the conversation or mark the start of a new topic – *so*, *I mean*, *right*, *actually*, *like*
- show how the speaker feels about what they are about to say or what they have already said – *I think*, *of course*, *really*, *so*, *kinda*, *sort of*, *to be honest*
- check that the listener is following – *don't you?*, *aren't they?*, *isn't it?*, *innit?*
- create solidarity with the listener – *you know*, *do you get me?*, *do you know what I mean?*, *and stuff like that*, *and all that*.

As can be seen from the above examples, many discourse markers are not restricted to just one function and in fact can be multi-functional (indeed, they can also have other grammatical functions such as verbs (*like*), conjunctions (*so*) and adverbs (*actually*)).

Because discourse markers do not primarily carry information or add to the content of an utterance, they are sometimes subject to stigmatisation and are often regarded as being meaningless or even thought of as careless speech. However, all speakers use them as indispensable tools in the structuring of what they say and how they want what they say to be interpreted by their interlocutors. They are therefore essential for successful signposting in conversation. In the following sections, we'll look at some language features, all of which might be considered to be discourse-pragmatic markers.

6.1 General extenders

General extenders are expressions such as *and stuff, and stuff like that, or something, or whatever, and all that* and *and things*. They are pervasive when we are talking in informal contexts and have important functions in spoken language. They are called general extenders because they often indicate that the previous word is part of a set, so they extend the meaning of that word without having to name all the members of the set. For example, the *and stuff* in *teenage magazine, just problems and quizzes **and stuff*** refers to a set of features that someone is likely to find in a teenage magazine.

However, referring to a set is not necessarily their most important function. Sometimes, speakers do not want to give exact or precise information, or they may genuinely be unsure about the information they are giving, so these expressions come in handy to express vagueness. For example, in *the kids had it like a big knot and two black stripes or three black stripes **or whatever*** the speaker is indicating that the precise number isn't relevant to the story and in *I can't remember .. uh yeah do you know er . (name of park) **or something** it's called* the speaker seems unsure of the exact name of the park. Perhaps even more importantly, general extenders function as a way of creating solidarity between speakers. When a person uses a general extender it suggests to the person they are speaking to that they have shared knowledge or shared opinions, so there is no need to be explicit.

6.2 Hedges

When people talk they will often avoid making direct statements, preferring instead to tone down their comments or soften the force of what they say by using expressions such as *kinda/kind of, sort of* and *a bit* (e.g., *he's **kinda** thuggish; she's **a bit** stupid*). These **hedging devices** are also used if someone is not sure of what they are saying (e.g., *it's **about** seven thirty; he's **around** 45 years old*), and the use of modal verbs is common if a speaker wishes to be intentionally vague (e.g., *I **might** come along later; sorry, we **may** be out tomorrow*). Lots of adverbs such as *probably, perhaps, slightly, maybe, generally* and *basically* also lessen the force of what is said.

6.3 Intensifiers

We all use adjectives or adverbs to describe things (e.g., *pretty* in *that's a **pretty** dress*; *clever* in *she is **clever***) but sometimes we want to boost the strength of our adjectives and adverbs with **intensifiers** such as *very*, *really* or *so* (e.g., *that's a **really** pretty dress*; *she is **so** clever*). There is nothing new about this; we can find examples of intensifiers being used in the works of Shakespeare and Chaucer for example:

> The better angel is a man **right** fair (W. Shakespeare. Sonnet 144, c. 1596)

> He was a **well** good wight, a carpenter (Chaucer, 'Prologue', *The Canterbury Tales*, c. 1390)

What is interesting about intensifiers in spoken language, though, is that different intensifiers tend to fall in and out of fashion over time so it is an area of grammar where there is constant change and renewal. It seems that young people do not like using the same intensifiers as those of older generations! Barnfield and Buchstaller (2010) looked at the changing use of intensifiers over four generations of speakers over the last 60 years in Tyneside. They found many examples of *very* and *really*, particularly among the older speakers, but in the 1990s there was an explosion in the use of *dead* (e.g., *she's **dead** gorgeous*) and it became the most popular intensifier to be used among people aged 18-40. However, by 2007 its popularity had lost ground and it was by then the *least* frequent intensifier used by young people, perhaps an example of a linguistic 'fad' (you can read a summary of the Barnfield and Buchstaller article at http://linguistics-research-digest.blogspot.co.uk/2011/11/reallyverydeadso-interesting-how-to.html).

The use of *very* and *really* is well established across all generations in the UK but innovations in the use of intensifiers tend to vary from one region to another. For example, Pearce (2010) notes that in the north-east of England *geet/git* can function as an intensifier (though it also has other functions as a discourse marker and a quotative expression – for a summary of the Pearce article go to http://linguistics-research-digest.blogspot.co.uk/2011/11/im-geet-excited.html) as in *your songs on here are **geet** good*. In London, *bare* (e.g., *I'm **bare** hungry*) and *well* (e.g., *I woke up **well** early*) are popular forms used by young people, although *bare* mainly functions as a quantifier to mean 'a lot of' (e.g., *I just caused **bare** trouble; it makes **bare** noise*).

6.4 Question tags

Question tags are mini-questions that we often put at the end of an utterance in spoken English, particularly in informal contexts of interaction. They generally consist of an auxiliary/modal verb and a subject, in that order – *does* *he?, won't she?, wouldn't I?, can't you?*. When the statement is positive, the tag is usually negative and vice versa (e.g., *there was a lot of traffic, **wasn't there?**; it isn't very busy, **is it?**)*.

Question tags have several functions in discourse including:

- looking for confirmation from your listener – *it's been in the local papers I think, **hasn't it?***
- inviting the listener to agree with you – *he's really nice, **isn't he?***
- asking somebody to do something for you in a polite way (usually with a negative statement and positive tag) – *you couldn't close the door, **could you?***

There are many non-standard and regional varieties of question tags, including *ain't it/he/she/they?* (fairly widespread but perhaps particularly associated with London English), *in't it?* (north-east England) and *din't I?* (Greater Manchester area) but perhaps the question tag that has attracted the most attention in recent years has been the innovative tag, *innit*. The tag *innit* has been around for some time as a derived form of *isn't it?* (e.g., *it's raining outside, **innit**?*) but in recent years it has been increasing not only in frequency but also in its use as an **invariant tag** i.e. it doesn't match the verb and subject of the preceding clause (e.g., *I asked my mum **innit** but she never told me*). There have also been innovative functional uses attributed to *innit* in London (Pichler & Torgersen 2009) including its use after a noun phrase to signal a topic shift (e.g., *I mean **the sister**, innit, she's about five times bigger than you*), after an if-clause to foreground new information (e.g., ***if you got beef**, innit*) and utterance-initially before the statement over which it has scope, to draw attention (e.g., *there is (.) innit, **there's a scary one in the club***). Pichler and Torgersen's study also shows that the innovative uses of *innit* are most frequently used among London speakers from minority ethnic groups. The use of *innit* has generally received negative criticism because it does not conform to the standard rules for question tags but perhaps this criticism can be viewed as resistance to language change generally. As demonstrated above, *innit* is not randomly used at any place in the discourse but, like other discourse-pragmatic features, fulfils important functions in interaction for its users.

6.5 Quotative expressions

The quotative verb system refers to the range of expressions used to introduce direct speech in spoken language. This is something that all speakers do almost every day of their lives when they want to tell somebody something that another person has said. Direct speech is even used by speakers when they want to repeat something that they themselves have said (or even thought) earlier. Direct reported speech (*she said 'aaah, there's a spider in my bed'*) is more lively and interesting than indirect reported speech (***she shouted that*** *there was a spider in her bed*) because by quoting someone, even if they are not the exact words that were used, the speaker almost acts out what they are reporting. Note that quotative expressions are not just used to introduce direct speech but also reported thought (*I was thinking 'move away!'*), non-lexicalised sound (*I was like 'ugh'*) and gesture (*I went <shrugs shoulders>*).

Traditional grammar usage books tend to state that quoted speech is introduced using the verb *say* (*Sue said 'I feel ill'*) but research has shown that speakers use a range of quotative expressions, as shown in the following examples:

Say

    (i) *I <u>said</u> 'if you wanna find out'*
       I <u>said</u> 'you better phone the Salvation Army'

    (ii) *I <u>says</u> 'I'm sorry I can't tell you that'*

    (iii) *I <u>was saying</u> 'god it was only a bag of crisps'*

Think

    (i) *I'm just <u>thinking</u> 'when did I get this?'*

    (ii) *you come from like this age now and you're <u>thinking</u> 'oh my mum and dad are gonna say no'*

    (iii) *and I just <u>thought</u> 'oh my god I'm gonna die'*

Go

    (i) *he <u>goes</u> 'no man I'll let you off this time'*

    (ii) *I <u>go</u> 'yeh mum I am still'*

    (iii) *she <u>was going</u> 'what you looking at?'*

    (iv) *yea and I <u>went</u> 'oh look who it is'*

Zero form (speech or thought introduced without the use of a quotative expression)

    (i) *he said 'I hear you had a bit of trouble last night'*
       (<u>zero</u>) 'yeah . police picked me up'

Tell

    (i) *so they just <u>tell</u> me 'whagwan why did you do?'*

    (ii) *I <u>told</u> my olders 'I don't like this boy'*

Be like

(i) *I met her on the bus and we **was like** 'oh I'm going (college)' and she **was like** 'so am I' I **was like** 'I'm doing hairdressing' and she **was like** 'so am I'*

(ii) *I**'m like** 'I. I didn't do nothing innit . flippin ask your son yeh'*

(iii) *it's been a couple of times where I've **been like** 'uuurr can't smoke no more'*

There are also forms which are more regionally localised:

Here's me (used in Northern Irish speech)

(i) *Here **was I**: 'Then I must be hard of hearing or something – you rapped the door and I didn't hear you'*

(ii) *Here**'s me**: 'Have youse took leave of your senses?'*

(examples taken from Milroy & Milroy 1977)

Geet/Git (used in north-eastern England speech)

(i) *I **was geet** 'ahh'*

(ii) *Stacey **was git** 'where's me burger then'*

(both examples taken from Pearce 2011)

This is + Subject (used in London speech)

(i) *this **is them** 'what area are you from . what part?'*

(ii) *this **is me** 'I'm from (name of place)'*

(iii) *this **is my dad** 'hmm so you want to go mixed school yeh and mess about with girls'*

Research has shown that older speakers of English tend to use *say* or *go* to introduce direct speech, or there may be no introduction at all (the *zero* quotative, page 109, above) if it is clear whose speech is being reported. Younger speakers also use these quotatives but they are much more likely to use *be like*, which has been increasing in use since it was first reported in the 1980s. In London there is the even newer quotative expression *this is + subject* (as shown above), demonstrating that the quotative verb system is another area of language where there is change and renewal.

7. Key points to consider and further reading

- Spoken language is the primary form of communication and the main channel through which human interaction takes place.

- The origins of written language lie in spoken language, not the other way round – the vast majority of English use is speech.

- Many features of spoken language may not add to the factual content of an utterance but they are indispensable for their important interactional functions in spoken discourse.

- An accessible book which provides lots of examples of spoken language with commentaries is Carter and McCarthy (1997).

Endnotes

[1] All extracts unless otherwise stated are taken from two studies of London English: *Linguistic innovators: the English of adolescents in London* http://www.lancs.ac.uk/fss/projects/linguistics/innovators/ and *Multicultural London English: the emergence, acquisition and diffusion of a new variety* http://www.lancs.ac.uk/fss/projects/linguistics/multicultural/index.htm.

References

BARNFIELD, K. & I. Buchstaller, 2010. Intensifiers in Tyneside: longitudinal developments and new trends. *English World-Wide* 31 (3): 252-287.

CARTER, R. & M. McCarthy, 1997. *Exploring spoken English*. Cambridge: Cambridge University Press.

CRYSTAL, D., 2003. *The Cambridge encyclopedia of the English Language*. Cambridge: Cambridge University Press.

MILROY, J. & L. Milroy, 1977. Speech and context in an urban setting. *Belfast working papers in language and linguistics*. Vol. 2.

PEARCE, M., 2011. 'It isn't geet good, like, but it's canny': a new(ish) dialect feature in North East England. *English Today* 27/3: 3-9.

PICHLER, H. & E. Torgersen, 2009. It's (not) diffusing, innit? The origins of innit in British English. Paper presented at NWAV 38, October.

8 LANGUAGE CHANGE

Dr Graeme Trousdale

1. Why does English change?

This chapter provides an overview of one of the most intriguing aspects of human language – the fact that it changes. In some respects the fact that it changes is trivial. If you invent a new product (like a *PlayStation* or an *iPad*), you often need a new name for it, and so you create a new word, and that is a kind of language change (because there has been an addition to the English lexicon). You don't always have to invent a new word: you can take an existing word and either give it a new form and/or meaning (since the fifteenth century, *mobile* has been used as an adjective meaning 'capable of movement'; it is now also used as a noun to refer to a kind of phone), or even build on an old meaning of a word that fell into disuse (an iPad is one of a range of *tablets* – historically, a tablet was a slab on which something was written). We might ask 'why those particular forms?', but the motivation for creating a new word, or a new meaning for an existing form, is rather simpler: there is a need for a new means of referring to a new entity when it comes into being.

But this is just a tiny area of language change. Even if we restrict ourselves to discussing new words and new meanings, it is clear that there is not always an objective need for a new term. Speakers of English are not short of ways to describe someone as 'physically attractive' – there are plenty of forms like *hot*, *sexy*, *stunning*, *gorgeous*, and so on, which do that job – but that did not prevent a new meaning of *fit* becoming a conventional way of referring to someone as 'attractive' (as well as 'athletic'). Furthermore, when we think of language change, we typically think of new things coming into being, rather than old things disappearing. But we might well wonder why we no longer refer to people who are spiritually blessed as being *silly*, or people who are cunning as being *pretty*, though these were conventional meanings at earlier stages in the history of English.

And what about changes elsewhere in the language? If certain features of English pronunciation had not changed over time, we would *fneeze* and not *sneeze*, and no-one would ever pronounce *elf* and *health* in the same way, as some currently do. If certain features of English syntax had not changed over time, we'd have a word order more like contemporary German, and have clauses in which the verb is at the end (something like *I married a woman who*

I at work met). And, of course, we often think about 'English' has having a beginning, when in fact it was simply the continuation of a range of Germanic dialects brought over to the British Isles by a series of invaders from continental Europe from around the fifth century CE onwards (and transported to other parts of the globe by subsequent series of invaders ever since), a point I return to at the end of this chapter.

Language is in a constant state of variation, with new features appearing at the fringes, and sometimes gaining currency, often at the expense of other features. And English, as a language with a well-documented history and a significant contemporary global spread, provides us with a wealth of data to consider both how language changes (the mechanisms involved) and why it might change (the motivations for change). In this chapter, I will outline some of the reasons linguists have proposed for both mechanisms and motivations.

2. Who cares about language change?

Some non-linguists care about language change a lot. They write to the newspapers or post blog entries lamenting, for example, that young people (and it is usually young people, because most cases of language change are naturally associated with new acquirers of language) don't know the difference between *disinterested* and *uninterested*, or that they don't pronounce the 't' in *better*, or the 'g' in *running*. In England, people complain that people pronounce *drawing* as something like *droaring*, saying they shouldn't because 'there's no 'r' in the spelling' – but they never seem to complain that people *don't* pronounce the 'r' in *bar* when there *is* an 'r' in the spelling.

This final point is relevant particularly because it highlights the arbitrariness inherent in linguistic systems. It cannot be 'better' linguistically to pronounce the intervocalic consonant in *butter* with an alveolar stop [t]than it is to pronounce it with a glottal stop [ʔ], because such a claim would be tantamount to suggesting that one sound is better than another. And it is clear that speakers don't object to glottal stops per se, or to other instances of the same general linguistic process (known as lenition, or the weakened articulation of a consonant sound) which happens in other languages – after all, it would be strange to argue that the Latin word *vita* 'life' was any better than the Spanish word *vida* (where the intervocalic consonant has also undergone lenition).

Another misguided view on language change is that the older way of doing things is always better. Again, this value judgement is hard to substantiate. In the earlier history of English, speakers used to make use of a four way distinction in the pronoun system when referring to a singular addressee, as shown in Table 1.

	Singular	Plural
Subject	ðu	ge
Non-subject	ðe	eow

Table 1. Some forms of the second-person pronoun in Old English

This persists in some non-standard varieties of English as *thou, thee, ye* and *you*, but this is rare. How can it be 'better' to merge all of these helpful grammatical distinctions in one form *you*? And if it is better, why are some speakers of English using more recent plural forms like *yous* (which is very widespread) and *y'all* or *yeeze lot* (which are more geographically restricted)? A similar misunderstanding holds for the use of multiple negation. Expressions like *I ain't never done nothing wrong* in contemporary English are often considered to be illogical on the grounds that two negatives make a positive (so saying *I did not eat no sweets* suggests that I did in fact eat some, because the speaker negates the assertion 'I ate no sweets'). But this fails entirely to understand how the system of negation works in dialects which have preserved this historical pattern. In describing the parson in the 'General Prologue' to *The Canterbury Tales*, Chaucer (a literary figure admired by many speakers of Standard English for the beauty of his language and his poetic craft) wrote *A bettre preest I trowe that nowhere noon is* (literally, 'a better priest I believe that nowhere no one is'). He certainly did not mean that there were lots of better priests elsewhere, which is what you would have to claim if you followed the 'logic' of those who condemn multiple negation. In fact, Chaucer – just like those people today who say *I ain't never done nothing wrong* – used multiple negative markers for emphasis. *I ain't never done nothing wrong* emphatically negates the assertion 'I did something wrong'; *a bettre preest I trowe that nowher noon is* emphatically negates the assertion 'someone somewhere is a better priest'. By attempting to enforce a kind of language change (e.g., by attempting to proscribe multiple negation), self-appointed guardians of English often show themselves to be misguided about the nature of English and its history, and about the regular, systematic nature of linguistic variation.

3. An overview of some work on language change

Research on language change has usually been concerned with both the mechanisms of change (how does a change take place?) and the causes of language change (why does a change take place?), though interest in the latter is more recent than the former. We will address both mechanisms and causes in this section; and we will also consider both internal and external factors. By 'internal' factors, I mean factors that are concerned exclusively with the language system, and the properties of the individual and aspects of the human body which are directly associated with the production and perception of language (that is, the brain and the vocal tract in the human head and neck). By 'external' factors, I mean factors concerned with human interaction that indirectly lead to linguistic innovations and their conventionalisation and spread (e.g., speakers of English coming into contact with speakers of the native American language Narragansett during the early colonial period in America, and borrowing an abbreviated form of the word *asquutasquash*, i.e. 'squash', as a term for a particular kind of vegetable).

3.1 Mechanisms of change

I will talk about three main mechanisms of language change: **borrowing**, **analogy** and **reanalysis**, and illustrate these mechanisms with examples from a range of varieties of English.

Borrowing is a well-attested mechanism of change in the history of English, most closely associated with the expansion of the vocabulary. Ever since speakers of Germanic dialects arrived in the British Isles (usually dated to the mid-fifth century CE), there is evidence of a sharing of lexical items across speakers in a community. From Celtic borrowings (such as *brock* for 'badger') in Old English (OE), to borrowings like *sushi* from Japanese in more recent times, the wordstock of English has regularly been updated by adopting, and often adapting, lexical items from other languages (compare English and French pronunciations of the word *restaurant*). But borrowing is not restricted to lexis, though lexical borrowing is far more common than phonological borrowing is. Sometimes we do borrow words that contain sounds that up to that point were not part of the English phonological system. For instance, words which contain the /ɔɪ/ phoneme (e.g., in *coy*) are not attested in OE, but first appear in Middle English (ME), subsequent to significant contact with speakers of French. In the same period, in the north of England, contact with speakers of Old Norse led to borrowings into the grammar, many of which have persisted into the present (e.g., the *-s* ending on third-person present tense verbs, like *speaks*, or the *th-* pronominal forms like *they*, *their* and *them*). Notice that such grammatical borrowings are rare and limited to fairly extensive contact (e.g., in bilingual communities) between speakers of different languages.

Analogy is another mechanism of change, where speakers use their sense of proportion to regularise what appear to be anomalies in the system. For instance, most past tense forms of verbs in English are marked by an inflectional ending (e.g., *play – played*), but some are marked by a change in the vowel of the verb stem (e.g., *run – ran*). Over time, verbs that historically belong to the latter set have shifted into the former set, as a result of analogical thinking (if the past tense of *play* is *played*, then the past tense of *X* must be *Xed*). Thus Milton was able to write *So clomb this first grand thief into God's fold* in *Paradise Lost* in the mid-seventeenth century, but we would write (and say) *climbed*. *Clomb* was the older past tense, and speakers of English in the past produced the more regular *climbed* as a result of analogy. The likelihood of a form being regularised seems to correlate with frequency – high frequency verbs (like *run* or *speak*) are likely to retain their irregular forms, while low frequency words are more likely to regularise. We can see this in a small set of verbs ending in *-ive* /aɪv/. Infrequent forms like *thrive* have regularised (very few speakers, if any, have *throve* as the past tense), while frequent forms like *drive* have not. There are also some cases which show variation between and across English-speaking communities. For instance, some speakers have adopted a regularised form, while others have not (Americans typically say *dove*, British speakers say *dived*, as the past tense of *dive*); and many people are not sure whether the past tense of *strive* is *strove* or *strived*, so there is likely to be significant variation in the community). Notice again how futile a prescriptive argument is here: it makes no sense to say that the 'correct' form of the past tense of *dive* is *dived*, otherwise Americans are always wrong. Instead of thinking in terms of correctness, it is more appropriate to think about conventions, and how those conventions may change, and may be variable in different communities.

Finally, **reanalysis** is another significant mechanism of change, affecting all levels of the language. A lexical item like OE *garlēac* 'spear leek' (so called because the leaves of the plant resembled spears, and the OE word for 'spear' was *gar*) comes to be reanalysed as a single word (rather than a compound word), *garlic*. An expression like *as far as* is reanalysed from a way of talking about relative distance (as in the expression *if you live in Darlington, Edinburgh is as far as London is*) to a way of delimiting the topic of the discourse (as in the expression *as far as your essay's concerned, you did a very good job*). This works also in phonology. In OE, speakers did not use the opposition between voiced and voiceless fricatives[1] in order to make meaningful distinctions between words. In other words, there were no words in OE where the difference between [f] and [v] (as in Modern English *half* vs. *halve*), or [s] and [z] (as in *sip* vs. *zip*) was the only difference between words. That doesn't mean that OE speakers never used the sounds [v] or [z] – we can hypothesise that they did, in words like *ofer* 'over' and *wisan* 'wise', but that these pronunciations were conditioned by the linguistic environment in which the words appeared – so [v] and [z] only appeared in positions that were in between other voiced sounds. This explains the Modern English (ModE) alternation between *wolf* and *wolves*, for example: in OE, the singular form written *wulf* ended with a [f], but the plural form was *wulfas* [wulvas] – the spelling changed to reflect the fact that this is a voiced sound. Crucially, these voiced sounds like [v] and [z] never appeared at the beginning of words. But in the ME period, with borrowings from French, we get words like *fine* and *vine*, where the only difference between the two words is the opposition between the voiceless [f] and voiced [v] sounds – this means that the difference was reanalysed as a phonological (systemic) rather than a phonetic one. This distinction is particularly interesting, as it shows that lexical borrowing can have phonological effects – in other words, one kind of change can have repercussions elsewhere in the language.

3.2 Causes of change

There are a number of ways to think about different causes of change. In this section, we will look at some of the internal factors, as well as the external motivations for change to occur.

Internal factors sometimes make reference to properties of a speaker's mental capacity for language, or to aspects of human physiology relevant to language. For instance, semantic change is said to be motivated by a speaker's desire to be expressive, which can often lead to exaggeration or hyperbole. Thus an instruction for a driver to proceed *dead slow* cannot be interpreted literally (because deadness implies no movement at all): it has to be figurative, so it means 'so slow that no-one can distinguish between whether the mover is dead or alive', and this clearly involves exaggeration. However, once this gets conventionalised, the hyperbole weakens, and so *dead* comes to work as a degree modifier, meaning something like 'very', as in *he was dead clever*. The fact that *He's dead quick* means 'He's very fast' in contemporary varieties of British English is a wonderful example of how languages change – OE *dēad* meant 'dead', while OE *cwic* meant 'alive' – so an OE speaker would be completely baffled by the idea that someone could be both 'dead' and 'quick' at the same time. (A comparable example is *pretty ugly* 'reasonably ugly', which only sounds odd to a speaker of contemporary English when he or she actually stops to think about it.)

External factors in change often relate to the social context in which language is used. For instance, we saw in 3.1 that borrowing from another language is one way in which a language can change, and borrowing is often the product of contact between speakers of more than one language. In the early Modern English period, there was increased contact between speakers of English and speakers of other languages as new settlement patterns, increased trade and increased military operations further afield meant that speakers of English travelled far beyond the British Isles. Evidence from the *Chronological English Dictionary* suggests that in the early seventeenth century, words were being borrowed not just from traditional sources like Latin and French, but also from native languages of Peru, and from Arabic, for example (Nevalainen 2006: 51).

The social context of language use has also been shown to be very important for an understanding of contemporary, ongoing language change. **Variationist sociolinguistics** (a field of study which involves the systematic collection of linguistic data from a range of speakers in a given community; see Watson this volume, Chapter Three) has provided us with a great deal of information about how patterns of synchronic variation may reflect ongoing change. Typically, research in this domain looks at the linguistic behaviour of older and younger speakers, to see if a particular variant is found predominantly in the speech of younger members of the community (in which case, that variant may be an innovation), or in the speech of older members of the community (in which case, that variant may be a relic). However, the relationship between linguistic variation and time is more complex than this. For instance, it is possible for a speaker to use a higher proportion of a given variant at the earlier and later stages of his life, and a higher proportion of a different variant in middle age, a phenomenon known as **age-grading** (see further Meyerhoff 2006: 145). This pattern repeats generation after generation, so there is no change over time.

However, there are clearly cases where one variant is ousted in favour of another. As suggested by spellings like *for* and *fort*, it used to be the case that speakers of English pronounced the 'r' (I'll use the phonetic symbol [ɹ] to represent this sound from now on) not just in pre-vocalic positions like in *roof* and *proof*, i.e. in the onset of syllables, but in positions after the vowel too, i.e. in the coda of syllables. While this is still a feature of some English accents (e.g., in Scotland and in parts of north America), few speakers of English in England pronounce the [ɹ] in coda positions. What kinds of external factors might bring about a linguistic change like this?

First, a number of speaker variables need to be taken into consideration. For instance, research into ongoing change has found that it is often the case that speakers who use the highest proportion of an innovative variant in a community tend to be located in the interior of a social class hierarchy; they also typically have a number of contacts outside their immediate neighbourhood; and they are often women (Labov 2001). Second, addressee variables are also relevant. For instance, speakers may use a higher proportion of innovative forms when addressing others with whom they are on an intimate basis, rather than with a stranger. Third, the nature of the speech act may also have a role to play in the propagation of an innovation in a community. For instance, speakers may tend to use more conservative language if they are speaking in a formal situation (such as giving a presentation in a classroom or at a business meeting, or speaking in court). Social and discourse factors can therefore have an important role in the propagation of change.

4. Rethinking language change

Like any intellectual discipline, research on language change is constantly evolving, as new ways of thinking about change emerge. Equally important are changes as to how research is carried out, i.e. what new methods have been developed. We will consider both of these issues in this section.

One important new direction in the study of language change has been in the area of dialect and language contact. Contact can lead to new varieties emerging: in the case of dialect contact, new local dialects, and in the case of language contact, **pidgin** and **creole** languages. Traditional work in dialectology often attempted to minimise the effects of contact by selecting particular kinds of speakers as the informants for the various research projects. Traditional dialectologists were also interested in language change, but they were especially interested in the outcomes of changes that had taken place some time ago, and so they were looking to find speakers who were relatively isolated socially and geographically, who had not come into contact with speakers from different dialect areas, because it was believed that such speakers were 'true' dialect speakers, and would preserve some of the reflexes of older changes. When the shift of emphasis to research on urban dialects took place (beginning about fifty years ago), it became clear that the effects of contact could not be ignored. More recently, the effects of dialect contact – particularly, the notion of **dialect levelling** – have come to the fore in sociolinguistic research. The dialects of new communities (e.g., in new towns like Milton Keynes) have been investigated to establish precisely the shape of varieties that have emerged when speakers of different dialects come together. For instance, researchers were interested to find out whether the local dialect of the area would prevail, or whether a different variety would emerge. Research in Milton Keynes itself (see, for example, Kerswill 2002) suggested that speakers born in such new communities did not adopt the local variety, preferring instead a more general south-eastern accent that was not clearly localisable. This forms part of more general research into dialect levelling, 'a process whereby differences between regional varieties are reduced, features which make varieties distinctive disappear, and new features emerge and are adopted by speakers over a wide geographical area' (Williams & Kerswill 1999: 149). Similarly, in the case of language contact, the issue of pidgin and creole languages has raised important questions about the nature of change, and the role played by internal and external forces and constraints on change. For instance, if a creole variety develops from a pidgin (which typically has a very reduced and simple grammatical system), how do the children who are the speakers of a new creole get the extra bits of grammar that are absent from the simplified pidgin that provides their linguistic input? What does this tell us about the nature of the human mind, and about the place of language in human cognition?

As for methods, one very important development has been the availability of computerised corpora of texts that can allow researchers to search for examples of particular words, or particular kinds of grammatical patterns and how they have evolved over time. Much work in philology involves the examination of individual manuscripts (and in some cases, edited versions of those texts). More recently, linguists have taken these older texts and created searchable corpora, which makes it much easier to find examples and track changes in frequency of various forms. Imagine, for instance, you want to investigate some of the ways in which the frequency of various **quotative constructions** has changed over time in English, from the early Modern English period to the present day. (Quotative constructions are grammatical patterns used to introduce direct speech or thought, as in ***he said***, *'Don't come in!'* or ***I was like***, *'Don't come in!'* – see this volume, Chapter Seven.) One way of doing this is to look at a random selection of texts, and read them all, to find how many instances of ***quoth***, ***said***, and ***be like*** (for instance) there are in each text from each period. But this is far more time consuming than searching a corpus for relevant examples, and many more texts can be investigated more rapidly.

These are just two ways in which principles and methods associated with language change have developed. There are many other topics (such as the relationship between linguistic and biological evolution, and computer simulations of such evolutionary developments) which are revolutionising how we think about variation in language over time. Finally, we should also consider how we understand narratives of change in particular languages. The narrative of the history of English is often the narrative of the evolution of the standard variety. But perhaps a more realistic view is to consider the history of English as a history of varieties. Evidence from the earliest records of English points to a number of varieties of Germanic being spoken by the invading tribes from the continent. And contemporary varieties of English across the globe highlight the persistence of variation in the course of time. It may be instructive to think of contemporary English not as a unified language, but as a family of related varieties, some of which are closer to one another, some of which are more distant (just as was the case with Germanic).

5. Key ideas to consider and further reading

- Language change is a normal product of speaker interaction.
- Change has its roots in patterns of **synchronic variation**.
- Variation in words (their form and meaning) is often a good way to begin thinking about language change. Have you noticed different speakers in your community using new words, or using new meanings associated with old word forms?
- Linguists distinguish the mechanisms of change (how a linguistic change takes place) from the causes of change (why a change takes place).
- Mechanisms of change involve borrowing from another language, analogy to an existing pattern elsewhere in the language, or reanalysis of an existing structure into a structure new to the language.
- Contemporary English is no better or worse than the English of Shakespeare. And contemporary English is no better or worse than the English of the twenty-fifth century will be.
- A good, accessible book on language change is *Why Do Languages Change?* (Trask 2010).

Endnotes

[1] If you are not sure about the difference between voiceless and voiced sounds, try saying the first sound you make in the word *file*, then saying the first sound you make in the word *vile*. Then put your fingers in your ears as you alternate between the two consonants – you should hear the difference!

References

KERSWILL, P., 2002. Koineization and accommodation. In CHAMBERS, J.K., Peter Trudgill and Natalie Schilling-Estes, eds., *The handbook of language variation and change*. Oxford: Blackwell. 669-702.

LABOV, W., 2001. *Principles of linguistic change, volume 2: social factors*. Oxford: Blackwell.

MEYERHOFF, M., 2006. *Introducing sociolinguistics*. London: Routledge.

NEVALAINEN, T., 2006. *An introduction to Early Modern English*. Edinburgh: Edinburgh University Press.

TRASK, R. L., 2010. *Why do languages change?* Cambridge: Cambridge University Press.

WILLIAMS, A. & P. Kerswill, 1999. Dialect levelling: change and continuity in Milton Keynes, Reading and Hull. In P. FOULKES & Docherty, G. eds., *Urban voices: accent studies in the British Isles*. London: Arnold. 141-62.

9 Attitudes to Language Change

Dan Clayton

1. Why study attitudes to language change?

While the history, processes and patterns of how the English language has changed are interesting and important to study in their own right, how different people *respond* to language change offers us a glimpse of something more than just the language itself. It gives us an insight into its users and their beliefs, attitudes and personalities. At the risk of sounding pretentious, it gives us a chance to learn more about human nature and what it is to be a living, breathing, speaking, writing, texting, emailing, tweeting human being.

The feelings people have about language change can range from the celebratory to the protective, and from the welcoming to the cautious. Language change is a particularly contentious area, not least because we will all see the language that we used as young people change as we grow older. And while we might see change as an inevitable, even positive, process, seeing and hearing the language that we grew up with change before our very eyes is bound to make us feel *something*. When we extrapolate that individual feeling across thousands of years and billions of people, we can see that it's a big deal.

That we often feel strongly about language shouldn't come as much of a surprise to a student of English Language; after all, from looking in this collection at social and regional variation (Kerswill, Chapter Two and Watson, Chapter Three), technology (Goddard, Chapter Ten), urban youth language (Drummond, Chapter Six), gender (Cameron, Chapter One), you'll have seen that language and identity are tightly bound up with each other.

Another thing that makes attitudes to language change such an important topic to study is that while the pace of language change might be speeding up – with factors such as technology, movement of peoples and social change all having an influence – the concerns remain perennial. For example, there is frequent concern expressed in the UK media about American words that have been adopted by British English speakers, but in the sixteenth century a very similar concern over 'inkhorn' terms – words imported from Latin, Greek and French – was prevalent. Equally, some commentators today are concerned about the rise of social media and their supposedly negative impact on young people's literacy, yet when the printing press first became popular as a technology in the fifteenth century, it too raised concerns, this time over whether its machine-produced fonts could convey human emotion as well as the written word. Language changes but the concerns remain the same.

In this chapter we will look at some of the historical complaints about language change and the various reasons for them, before moving on to look at specific areas of language that have aroused fierce debates, among them slang, new words, political correctness, changing technologies and non-standard usages. Along the way, we will try to look at the bigger picture – the overarching patterns that characterise many of these debates about language – and then look to the present day and beyond.

Idiot speak?

- The language is going to pieces before our eyes, especially under the influence of the debased dialect of the Cockney, which is spreading from our schools and training colleges all over the country. (S.K. Ratcliffe 1909)

- If you allow standards to slip to the stage where good English is no better than bad English, where people turn up filthy ... at school ... all those things tend to cause people to have no standards at all, and once you lose standards then there's no imperative to stay out of crime. (Norman Tebbit 1985)

- This is nothing but idiot speak. If you hear your children using it, it means they are brainless morons. Next stop = tattoos, binge drinking & ASBOs. (*The Sun* message board 2010)

- You can hear this Jafaican crap on buses, in benefit centres and McDonald's across London – anywhere but where money is earned. As if these kids didn't have little enough chance in life as it is, speaking a patois derived from some of the most pointless countries in the world is hardly going to help. (*London Evening Standard* message board 2011)

- The whites have become black. A particular sort of violent destructive, nihilistic gangster culture has become the fashion and black and white boys and girls operate in this language together. This language which is wholly false, which is this Jamaican patois that has been intruded in England and that is why so many of us have this sense of literally of a foreign country. (David Starkey 2011)

It ought to be clear from just this selection of quotations from the media that the language use of others excites strong reactions in many people. George

Bernard Shaw (1916) once said that 'It is impossible for an Englishman to open his mouth without making some other Englishman hate or despise him', and while Shaw probably had accents in mind when he wrote this, it holds true for so many different aspects of language.

Some might object to contractions such as ***shouldn't*** and ***won't*** in formal writing, and how they can easily lead to more apparently egregious usages such as ***must of*** (in place of ***must have*** or ***must've***) or ***your*** (in place of ***you're***), while others are more concerned with grammar and the use of multiple negation (*I never did nothing*), past participle forms used instead of past tenses (*I done it twice*), adjectives instead of adverbs (*I'm good* instead of *I'm well*) or subject and verb concord (*we was* and *I weren't*), or the most recent bugbears: quotatives like (*I was like 'ZOMG?!', and she was like 'Whatever'*) and the invariant tag question ***innit***.

On the surface, it's the lexis (the words themselves), the semantics (the word meanings), the grammar (the structure of the words, phrases and clauses) and the phonology (sounds) that cause concern, but as Henry Hitchings puts it in *The Language Wars* (2011):

> Arguments about English have always been coloured by feelings about tradition, the distribution of power, freedom, the law and identity.

He adds (in an interview for *emagazine* in 2011) that:

> these debates quickly become heated because they involve people's attitudes to – among other things – class, race, money and politics.

So, when David Starkey talks about a 'wholly fabricated Jamaican patois' his argument is not so much with the language (which isn't in fact anything like Jamaican patois) but with the users of it (white kids 'talking black' or just black people in general, if we take his dubious arguments about gangsta culture at face value). Likewise, negative comments about the pernicious influence of new technologies upon young people's literacy are often more to do with concerns about the leisure habits of young people (and the fact that they are just, well, *young*), than the language they use, while concerns about slang terms creeping into the language from Jamaican patois or American popular culture are probably more to do with nationalism and fears about cultural identity than the words ***battyriders*** or ***gotten*** in their own right.

2. Raising the standard

Clearly, the English language has changed over time. New words appear, old words disappear, and some grammatical patterns change gradually over time. Graeme Trousdale looks at the mechanisms and motivations for much of this in more detail in Chapter Eight. As well as these quite natural changes, there

9. Attitudes to Language Change

have been conscious attempts to shape the language we use and one of the key movements in the development of English has been **standardisation**. This is the process of developing an agreed, nationally recognised form of the language that can be understood by all speakers of whatever background, which is then passed on from generation to generation. Lesley and James Milroy (1991) describe standardisation as 'the consequence of a need for uniformity that is felt by influential parts of society at a given time' and by Nevalainen and Tieken-Boon van Ostade (2006: 273-4) as 'a change from above, that was both consciously implemented and consciously adopted'.

While standardisation's golden age probably coincided with the later Middle English period and was spurred on by the growth of printing technology from the end of the fifteenth century, earlier attempts had been made to provide a standard for English, initially (and ironically, perhaps) through the use of Latin – the language of the Christian church that had been brought to England in the sixth century, during the Anglo-Saxon period – but later by the adoption of West Saxon as the prestige form. As Henry Hitchings points out in his excellent overview of arguments about 'proper' English, *The Language Wars* (2011), many of the arguments about a standard form of English were as much about establishing English as a national language in opposition to Latin and French as they were about establishing a set of rules and regulations for English itself. In many ways, creating a language that could be called 'English' was one of the key aims of those involved in standardisation, and that combination of English as both a national identity and a language remains interwoven into the fabric of arguments about language change that still rage today.

Leith, Graddol and Jackson (2007: 83-84) identify four processes involved in standardisation: **selection**, **elaboration**, **codification** and **implementation**.

In the case of English, the **selection** of the East Midlands dialect as the form upon which the standard should be based was linked to the area's wealth, proximity to governmental, religious and educational establishments and its geographical location.

Elaboration involves 'ensuring that the new language can be used for a wide range of functions' (Leith at al. 2007) and the increasing use of English as the language of government, science and education fulfilled these criteria.

Codification took the form of establishing rules of spelling, drawing up definitions of word meanings and agreeing norms of grammar usage. This last one has remained something of a sticking point ever since, because some of the earliest **grammarians** (the writers of early 'grammars' of English) often turned to Latin for grammar rules, meaning that the realities of English grammar were often not addressed head-on.

Implementation was then required to set and maintain the new standard. Works in Standard English needed to be made widely available and then used in all spheres of life. A sense of prestige and value had to be built up around the use (and therefore users) of Standard English, often through the dismissal of non-standard forms as inferior, uneducated or dubious, and again arguments around these judgements – about the status of regional dialects, the place of new words in English, the extent to which we should allow language to change (and indeed whether we have any control over it at all) – are at the heart of language debates today. To implement the standard, the language would need to be policed, and this laid the ground for the grammarians of the eighteenth century to ply their trade.

In the early 1700s, inspired by the apparent successes of the French in regulating their language, Jonathan Swift put forward a proposal for an English Academy which would '...find many words that deserve to be utterly thrown out of our language, many more to be corrected, and perhaps not a few long since antiquated, which ought to be restored on account of their energy and sound' (quoted in Baugh & Cable: 265). Such an academy would rule on how English should be and 'fix' a standard for all time.

Swift's proposal did not succeed, but as Baugh and Cable explain (op cit) 'What could not be imposed by authoritative edict might still win adoption through reason and persuasion', so those who believed that English needed regulation and rules took their arguments to the educated classes in books about grammar. By the end of the eighteenth century, not only did English have its most famous dictionary (Samuel Johnson's *Dictionary* of 1755) but Joseph Priestley, Robert Lowth, John Ash and Lindley Murray had all published books about how to use (and not to use) English grammar and had set out their definitions of what constituted 'correct' English.

As Hitchings (2011) explains, history has not treated many of these grammarians very kindly, often painting them as prissy pedants, hung up on half-baked Latin rules shoehorned into English grammar. In reality, they were a mixed bunch, some (particularly Lowth and Priestley) with a much more nuanced understanding of how English was actually used in speech and writing. However, one thing they had in common was a belief that there was generally a right way to speak and write English, and any other ways were inferior or just plain wrong. Such prescriptive views are returned to later in this chapter when we look at debates about rules and usage.

3. Lowering the standard

Of course, the development of a standard form of English meant that there was now something tangible to kick against, so for those who wished to express their opposition to convention or the norms of polite society, non-standard forms (which had always existed in one form or another, particularly

9. Attitudes to Language Change

in spoken language and regional varieties) now had a standard to which they wouldn't adhere. Regional variation, using non-standard forms of lexis and grammar, could now – arguably – be seen to express a sense of rebellion and non-conformism as well as regional identity. And as Standard English gained polite, perhaps stuffy, respectability – what might be termed by sociolinguists **overt prestige** – non-standard varieties linked to region, class, criminality and rebellion came to be seen as attractive and energetic to those who didn't wish to conform, were excluded from the mainstream in some way or who wanted to signal some kind of outsider status. **Slang** was (and is) one such means of doing just that.

Jonathon Green (2000), the renowned slang lexicographer, defines slang in many ways in his works but one particularly pertinent definition is that slang is a 'counter-language': a language that runs against the norm. And as soon as you have a standard, you'll have a counter-standard. Slang and slang-users tend to be looked down upon in society but also have a degree of kudos outside the mainstream. While slang often makes creative use of language resources – changing word meanings, altering grammatical functions and combining existing words or parts of them – it's generally treated as being outside the standard, even as a threat to the language, or the morals of society itself. But even this is changing to some degree.

Julie Coleman in *The Life of Slang* (2012: 71) comments that:

> The term slang was originally condemnatory, and it sometimes still is, but through the course of the twentieth century...it came to be used in a more celebratory sense. Slang was once considered a sign of poor breeding or poor taste, but now it indicates that the speaker is fun-loving, youthful and in touch with the latest trends.

Some attitudes towards language have clearly shifted as time has gone on, with a growing tendency towards informal, down-to-earth language: a process that the linguist Geoffrey Leech refers to as **colloquialisation** where 'written language progressively adopt(s) norms of spoken language' (2006). So, as usage among the population becomes less formal, slang terms which were once well outside the mainstream now creep into wider use among older age groups and higher social classes. But none of this is happening without a fight, often in the form of strongly-worded editorials in national newspapers, pronouncements from MPs or angry online comments about kids who say *innit* and *whatever*, often written without appropriate capital letters, spelling or even basic grammar, as in the case of 'mick' from Scunthorpe who was moved to write the following on *The Sun's* website in 2008:

> keep talking like that and see were it get's you, muppets no wonder some kids are as thick as to short planks.

Exactly.

4. Techno-fear

Technological advances have also caused consternation to language commentators who worry that the proliferation of new technologies will adversely affect the language we use and veer away from the standard. Writing in the *Daily Mail* in 2007, the Radio 4 broadcaster (and author of a number of books about declining standards of language), John Humphrys, claimed that:

> ... the texters, the SMS (Short Message Service) vandals (who) are doing to our language what Genghis Khan did to his neighbours eight hundred years ago. They are destroying it: pillaging our punctuation; savaging our sentences; raping our vocabulary. And they must be stopped.

But it's not just the most recent advances such as email and text messaging that have worried some commentators; writing itself was initially viewed with a degree of distrust. Dennis Baron reports in *A Better Pencil* (2009: 3) how in Plato's *Phaedrus*, Socrates warns that:

> This invention will produce forgetfulness in the minds of those who learn to use it, because they will not practice their memory. Their trust in writing, produced by external characters which are no part of themselves, will discourage the use of their own memory within them.

Baron goes on to explain that each and every 'word technology' from the pencil, through to the printing press, the telegraph, the typewriter and the computer has created a form of moral panic about the damage that would be done to language. Humphrys' hyperbole about the dangers of texting is clearly part of a wider culture of complaint that runs through the history of English. We are probably quite familiar with recent media reports of how texting and social media are damaging people's (usually young people's) literacy, but it is perhaps surprising to see that at one stage the printing press was viewed as equally dangerous. But like so many other complaints about language, while the battlefields might change, the core fears often remain the same.

If the mainstream media in the UK is to be believed, texting is felt by many to promote laziness in spelling and grammar, over-reliance on abbreviation and even shortened attention spans. A key concern is that the more young people text, the more likely they are to use textisms (abbreviations, deviant spellings etc.) in their school assignments or in the workplace. The UK had its moral panic about texting in the early 2000s, but the USA is (for once) a relatively late adopter of this technology and its media has recently been full of scare stories about poor spelling, declining standards and texting-while-driving accidents. But does the evidence against texting stack up? Inspired to look at the links between texting and literacy in young people, researchers from Coventry University carried out a number of studies between 2008 and 2011.

In one report on the team's research for the British Academy, Dr Clare Wood said, 'We were surprised to learn that not only was the association strong, but that textism use was actually driving the development of phonological awareness and reading skill in children. Texting also appears to be a valuable form of contact with written English for many children, which enables them to practise reading and spelling on a daily basis'.

While the researchers can't actually lay claim to a causal link between texting and higher literacy skills, the research goes some way towards deflating some of the more exaggerated claims about the damage texting can do to literacy. So, why isn't the general public persuaded and why are so many language commentators unconvinced? As we've already seen, there's a long tradition of complaint when it comes to standards in English, a tradition that the writer Robert Lane Greene (2011: 48) refers to as **declinism**, a belief that the language is in a state of perpetual and irreversible decline: 'Not only is declinism not new, as hundreds of years of examples show. It is not particular to the Anglophone world, either. Not only have English and American schoolmarms worried about 'kids these days' for centuries, similar concerns have nagged speakers of languages around the world throughout recorded history'.

Greene goes on to discuss fears about declining standards in a piece for *The New York Times* (2011), pointing out that in 1870 20% of the US population was classed as illiterate (unable to read and write in any language), while in 1979 that figure was 0.6%:

> A century ago, a nation of 310 million engaged with the written word on a daily basis was unthinkable. Now its uneven results are taken as proof by some that language skills are in decline. That is far from obvious. We may just be seeing more of language's real-world diversity – dialect, nonstandard grammar and all – in written form, whereas 150 years ago those same people would never write. That's something to celebrate, not to complain about.

If we look at the research into texting and Greene's points about literacy together, we can see that declinist arguments don't really hold water. Perhaps something else is at work, however. In the early days of Standard English, very few people were educated enough to read or write, but those who *were* tended to be very well educated. Nowadays, many more people can read and write; many more people do read and write (text, email, blog...). Perhaps what the declinists object to is the democratisation of language, its movement from the preserve of an elite to the wider populace.

5. Prescription and description

As discussed earlier in this chapter, the development and maintenance of Standard English required a degree of policing. If a form of language – a spelling, a way of constructing a sentence, a word's meaning – veers away from the standard, it will be judged, and the opposing positions that can be taken on such usage can be divided broadly into **prescriptivism** and **descriptivism**.

Jean Aitchison (1991: 14) distinguishes between these two positions by describing the aims of prescriptivism as laying down 'artificial rules in order to impose some arbitrary standard of 'correctness'', and descriptivism as a means of describing 'what people actually say'. She goes on to make a distinction between the two uses of the word 'rules', arguing that for descriptivists 'rules are not arbitrary laws imposed by an external authority, but a codification of subconscious principles or conventions followed by the speakers of a language'.

Here we can see that prescriptive views are very much part of the purist tradition of 'fixing' the language, settling on an agreed standard and then maintaining it, while descriptivism is perhaps a more recent perspective, influenced by the growth of Linguistics in the twentieth century and its focus on the realities of language as it is used in all its varieties. As Hitchings (2011) makes clear, it would be too simplistic to cast all of the eighteenth century grammarians as arch-prescriptivists, but for many of them the written word in elegant, refined Standard English was their benchmark of 'correctness' and spoken forms, particularly those non-standard forms of the regions and lower classes, fell way short. For modern linguists, there is much more of an understanding that spoken language is the primary medium through which most of us communicate and that to compare it unfavourably with formal written English is a pointless task.

So, while modern linguistics now offers us a chance to look at which forms of language are used, who uses them, why this might be and what they might mean – the underpinning of most A Level English Language and undergraduate programmes in English Language – there still remains a prescriptive tradition of complaint. Aitchison characterised this tradition with three models in her Reith Lectures of 1996 as 'the damp spoon', 'the crumbling castle' and 'the infectious disease'.

Each model reflects a prescriptive complaint about language change. 'The damp spoon' model quotes the 'queasy distaste' felt by journalist Mary Stott 'at seeing a damp spoon dipped in the sugar bowl or butter spread with the bread-knife', and relates to breaches of manners or etiquette in language matters. (While Aitchison's analogy is apposite, the very nature of social customs is such that for many young people, the whole idea these days of using a sugar bowl, or even a bread knife, might seem alien when we all know that sugar comes in paper sachets and bread comes pre-sliced.)

'The crumbling castle' model relates to a common complaint that the English language is crumbling away from a once glorious state of perfection, where changes have eroded and debased it. But as Aitchison argues, 'This view

9. Attitudes to Language Change

itself crumbles when examined carefully. It implies that the castle of English was gradually and lovingly assembled until it reached a point of maximum splendour at some unspecified time in the past. Yet no year can be found when language achieved some peak of perfection, like a vintage wine. The 'beautiful building' notion presupposes that rigid systems, once assembled, are better than changing ones. This is untrue. In the animal world, flexibility is a great advantage, and animals that adhere to fixed systems often lose out' (Reith Lectures 1996).

'The infectious disease' model paints change as something that is contagious: we catch change from others and ought to fight it as we fight diseases. But again, as Aitchison herself points out, while we do pick up changes from other people, we often want to pick up new language features from others and do it consciously, unlike diseases.

Many of the prescriptive arguments about language are rooted in a form of conservatism (usually with a small 'c', but often with a big 'C' too) in which grammar achieves a significance far beyond language. Deborah Cameron (1995: 111-112), discussing arguments about English teaching and grammar instruction states that:

> Grammar was made to symbolise various things for its conservative proponents: a commitment to traditional values as a basis for social order, to 'standards' and 'discipline' in the classroom, to moral certainties rather than moral relativism and to cultural homogeneity rather than pluralism. Grammar was able to signify all these things because of its strong metaphorical association with order, tradition, authority, hierarchy and rules.

Here, once more, the arguments that appear on the surface to be about language use are really about other things. Language – in this case, grammar – becomes a proxy battlefield for conservative forces that want to halt social change. So, if prescriptivism is essentially conservative, does that mean that descriptivism is essentially radical and progressive?

Probably not. For a start, such a depiction of prescriptivism is probably a touch unfair. Many prescriptivists care deeply about language and that surely has to be a good thing. Even those who put together the first grammars and dictionaries acknowledged that English had changed and would continue to do so. So, to caricature them all as finger-wagging fuddy-duddies might be a low blow. It is also the case that not all of those who disapprove of certain kinds of language change are necessarily conservative in outlook. There's a strand of what might be called 'benign prescriptivism' that runs through an organisation like the Plain English Campaign whose raison d'etre is to ensure that companies and government bodies use clear, jargon-free language in their communication. Likewise, there are those on the left of the political spectrum, as well as the right, who object to the Political Correctness movement's attempts to reform language and remove potentially offensive and discriminatory words, not because they support discrimination but because they object to any form of language control from above.

Perhaps then, caricaturing descriptivists as let-it-all-hang-out, anything goes, hippies is just as bad. For a start, most linguists don't necessarily pass any judgement on language change. They acknowledge that it happens, describe its characteristics and usage, then move on. Doing this doesn't necessarily mean that they approve or disapprove of the features they are describing. Jean Aitchison (1991: 210) points out that language change is 'natural, inevitable and continuous', but that doesn't make it either good or bad. Some changes 'disrupt the language system'; others 'repair it'. It's difficult to judge whether a change might be viewed as an improvement or a step backwards.

Aitchison (1991: 221) concludes by saying that 'there is no evidence that language is either progressing or decaying. Disruption and therapy seem to balance one another in a perpetual stalemate'. It's a similar view to that of David Crystal (1997: 5) who in *The Cambridge Encyclopedia of Language* stated that:

> If metaphors must be used to talk about language change, one of the best is that of a system holding itself in a state of equilibrium, while changes take place within it; another is that of the tide, which always and inevitably changes, but never progresses, while it ebbs and flows.

In a sense, those who wish to innovate with the language and those who wish to preserve it are locked in a similar relationship, one that resembles a tug of war. One side pulls language in one direction, before the other drags it back. So, at a given point in time, the descriptivists may have the upper hand in the public debate about language change. For example, there might be a generally accepting approach to new words that are used to label new discoveries because they are perceived as meeting a clearly identified need. At another point in time, the prescriptivists might pull harder and drag the debate back to their terms, perhaps arguing that the proliferation of new words is causing confusion and fragmentation.

Part of the very dynamic of language change is the tension between different attitudes towards it. In essence, not only are attitudes to language change important to our study of the subject of English Language because of what they tell us about being communicative humans, but they are important too because they exert a control over the path of language change itself. As we've already seen, whatever new forms of language emerge in the years to come – languages spawned by new technologies, varieties of English from different parts of the world, or new forms of slang – the debate will continue and the sides will probably remain the same, locked in an everlasting tug of war.

6. Key ideas to consider and further reading

6.1 Key ideas

- Arguments about language are often about issues connected to identity, rather than the language itself.
- Gripes about language usage are not just a recent phenomenon and often address the same usages century after century.
- Technology, in all its forms, has always affected language use and caused concern to prescriptivists.
- Prescriptivism and descriptivism offer two different mindsets for viewing language change.
- Literacy rates have steadily increased over the centuries, but concerns remain for some that standards are falling.
- While standardisation creates a version of the language that provides mutual intelligibility and a model to be acquired through education, it also offers something to kick against for users of non-standard forms.

6.2 Further reading

Books which offer a good overview of arguments about language use are: Jean Aitchison's *The Language Web* (1997). Anderson and Trudgill's *Bad Language* (1990), Crystal's *The Fight for English* (2006), Hitchings' *The Language Wars* (2011), Greene's *You are What You Speak* (2011) and my own *Attitudes to Language* (2018).

References

AITCHISON, J., 1996. *Language change: progress or decay*. Cambridge: Cambridge University Press.

BARON, D., 2009. *A better pencil*. Oxford: Oxford University Press.

BAUGH, A. & T. CABLE, 1978. *A history of the English Language* (3rd edition). London: Routledge

CAMERON, D., 1995. *Verbal hygiene*. London and New York: Routledge.

COLEMAN, J., 2012. *The life of slang*. Oxford: Oxford University Press.

CRYSTAL, D., 1997. *The Cambridge encyclopedia of language*. Cambridge: Cambridge University Press.

GREEN, J. 2000. *Cassell's dictionary of slang*. London: Orion.

GREENE, R.L., 2011. *You are what you speak*. New York: Delacorte Press.

HITCHINGS, H., 2011. *The language wars*. London: John Murray.

LEECH, G. 2006. http://www.lancs.ac.uk/fass/doc_library/linguistics/leechg/mai_and_leech_2006.pdf (accessed 12.08.12).

LEITH, D., D. Graddol & L. Jackson. 2007. *Changing English*. London and New York: Routledge.

MILROY, L. & J. Milroy, 1991. *Authority in language*. London and New York: Routledge.

NEVALAINEN, T. & I. Tieken-Boon van Ostade, 2006. In HOGG, R. & D. Denison, David eds. *A history of the English language*. Cambridge: Cambridge University Press. http://www.britac.ac.uk/news/news.cfm/newsid/14 (accessed 12.08.12).

10 LANGUAGE & TECHNOLOGY

Professor Angela Goddard

1. Introduction

The topic of language and technology is not about technology. That is, it's not about being a 'techie'. You don't have to know how aspects of technology work, such as knowing how computers function or how phones process text messages. Of course, that kind of knowledge is useful, particularly if you are thinking about a career in the communications industry. But the study of language and technology is really about language.

What does help to build a good foundation for this area is an interest in how people communicate, and how new forms of communication shape their language choices. For example, how does it change the way we write when we know we can only use a limited number of words, or when we have to send a message in a real hurry? It helps to have some experience yourself of modern communication systems – but these are now so embedded in our everyday lives that it would be odd if you didn't.

This topic is not just about how we communicate. It's also about our attitudes towards communication, and the public issues that surround its use. Almost every day there is a news item about how new forms of communication are affecting our lives. Sometimes these are hopeful, happy stories – for example, long-lost relatives who rediscover each other via the internet. On other occasions the stories are full of fear and hurt, such as cyberbullying and online fraud. Often, you can find the same technology written up both positively and negatively, depending on the political standpoint of the writer. One example of this is the way mobile phones were implicated both in the public disorder in UK cities in the summer of 2011 (where phones were seen as a bad thing) and in the struggles for change in the Middle East in the 'Arab Spring' in that same year (where phones were seen as a good thing).

You might feel that sending your friend a text message or updating your status on a social media site is a bit different from global politics. But what links them together is language use. When you use language, you are representing yourself in a certain way, creating a story about yourself; and the same process of storytelling is involved when journalists or advertisers or writers of novels present accounts involving new types of communication. Studying this area therefore encompasses personal, social and political perspectives, so you have lots of choice about where to focus.

2. Why the topic is worth studying

This is a fascinating topic because it's all about our everyday behaviour and therefore is easy to relate to. It's an important topic because it helps us to stand back and take a critical view of language, so that we are better able to see how language can be manipulated. On a more pragmatic level, the topic affects all the other dimensions of language that are required study for English Language A Level and beyond, into undergraduate study.

Children are familiar with new forms of communication at a very young age, so it's impossible to study language acquisition without taking account of new communication technologies. Adults are also experiencing a type of language acquisition, because we are all constantly learning how to use new tools and platforms. In an interesting reversal, there are now many situations where younger members of communities are helping older participants to acquire new communication skills.

New technologies also have a significant role in language change, and this has been true through the ages. Technological advances regularly produce brand new artefacts that need a name, and sometimes this results in a wholly new word. An example of this is the *telephone*, which was created from Greek roots meaning 'distant' (*tele*) and 'sound' (*phone*). At other times, existing words are applied to new contexts, in a metaphorical extension: for example, the terms posting and mailing as used in digital contexts were 'borrowed' from the idea of the traditional postal service. These are small examples of much larger discourses that surround all our new technological experiences and activities. Changes in discourse provoke strong attitudes, triggering many language debates in the press and elsewhere where descriptive and prescriptive approaches clash.

There is no such thing as a single type of communication that cuts across all new communication contexts, so the area exemplifies different varieties of language use. New tools are bought and sold, resulting in a strong strand of persuasive language that can be studied for aspects of representation. New forms of communication are often seen as having characteristics of both speech and writing, so ideas about mode are prevalent in any data analysis.

Variety is also evident in how people express themselves online, with both individuals and groups creating their identities by their language choices. The distance in time and space that's often part of digital communication can be a factor in miscommunication, but can also generate creative play and humour as participants find ways to reach out to each other.

Finally, studying language and technology quickly brings us to some quite philosophical questions about language, questions which have pre-occupied thinkers for centuries, long before new technologies came on the scene. For example, is language the same as behaviour? When we say something, is it the same as doing something, or is it simply an abstract representation? So is the internet 'just words' or a world where language use has the same real consequences as in 'real life'? There are no easy answers to these questions but the area offers many genuine opportunities for language investigations and productions.

3. A historical overview of the key thinking in this field

The previous section focused particularly on new technologies, such as **computer-mediated communication** (CMC). But the phrase 'new technologies' itself needs more scrutiny.

The term *technology* is derived from Greek roots meaning 'the study of art, craft, or skill'. In other words, the tech bit of technology has quite a broad scope and doesn't just refer to electronic communication or, indeed, to communication at all. Any application of a tool of some kind, from the earliest cave flints of pre-history, can be considered a technology. However, researchers in the field of language and technology will have a particular interest in the technologies that are connected with communication, and that enable new sorts of communication to take place.

There is, of course, no technology that remains 'new' for all time, as what we consider new now will soon become familiar, and a new 'new technology' will take its place. The history of different communication technologies, and how they were understood when first introduced, is an interesting subject in its own right. For example, early users of the first telephones in the late nineteenth century were offered advice on how to make a phone call – both how to hold the receiver, and what to say (Goddard & Geesin 2011: 3).

Technologies can look very different from each other across the centuries – quills and parchment seem a world away from keyboards and screens – but the issues and debates they generate can be surprisingly similar. For example, the great 'new technology' for the philosopher Aristotle, in the Greece of fifth century B.C., was writing itself. He saw this new technology as a dangerous invention which would interfere with human thinking and memory – something that has recently been suggested of computers.

It isn't possible here to go through the history of every new communication technology, but it is worth thinking about some former inventions that radically changed the way people communicated. When William Caxton set up the first printing press in England in 1476, it meant that writing could be duplicated and broadcast to multiple audiences for the first time. After Alexander Graham Bell's first phone call in Ontario in 1876, and Marconi's first radio transmission from Cornwall to Newfoundland in 1901, the human voice stopped being something you could only hear if you were within earshot. The idea of broadcasting communication across time and space was at the heart of these older technologies and this same crossing of physical barriers is also one of the key features of our modern digital communication systems. Changing the parameters of time and space in communication contexts has a powerful shaping effect on the nature of language use and therefore is a major focus for language research.

The internet was originally a network called 'Arpanet', named after the US military's Advanced Research Projects Agency, which developed it in the late 1960s. But it wasn't until the 1990s that internet service providers offered private households the ability to access online networks. Since that time, however, the speed of technological change has been phenomenal, with commentators now looking back at the history of earlier stages of web development and charting significant points of change within what is really quite a short timespan.

A significant step-change in the experience of being online was termed 'Web 2.0' by the web designer Darcy DiNucci in 1999. She was referring to the change from the web as a medium where people could only read webpages provided for them ('Web 1.0'), to one where anyone can compose pages as well as read them. Personal authorship was made possible by many factors coming together, including the development of broadband communication with faster and bigger download possibilities, new templates requiring little skill for the construction of webpages, cheap or free software, and the merging of technologies so that material could be both multimedia and mobile.

All this meant that we became – and still are – constant producers of communication as well as consumers. Sometimes you see a blended term – *prosumers* – used, to signal this new role. This term, coined by Alvin Toffler (1980: 37), was intended to suggest that new communication technologies were likely to generate a new kind of society where information is bought and sold much as other kinds of 'produce' had been traded in former times. In this process, we produce the same things that we consume.

To understand the concept of the prosumer, think about what you do on social media sites, such as Facebook, Twitter, WhatsApp, or Instagram. And of course this is by no means simply a UK phenomenon. The use of social media is both widespread and international with well over 2 billion active Facebook users, 1.5 billion on WhatsApp, 1 billion on Instagram and 330 million on Twitter, along with platforms such as WeChat and QQ, based in China having 1 billion and 800 million users respectively (source: Statista.com 2018). You are producers of communication and also you 'consume' others' products. These products are information about yourselves – what you've been doing, your views and reactions, your personal data. The language you choose creates an online persona, rather as an author creates a narrator to tell a story in a novel. You are also a reader of others' online presentations of themselves and, as you read, you interpret their language use in particular ways. See Goddard (2003) for a comparison between the language strategies used in online 'chat' and those used in literary texts. Platforms such as Facebook are also commercial companies, and they make money by selling your data to advertisers and other groups who want information about the habits and interests of social groups. In 2016, Cambridge Analytica, a UK 'data mining' company, used the personal data of 87 million Facebook users in order to analyse personality types and target them with specific messages to help Donald Trump win the US Presidency. So the 'likes' and 'dislikes' you express on Facebook are much more than a simple piece of communication shared between friends.

At a personal level, language choices online were – and still are – seen as constructing an identity for the user. Identities are not fixed: in 2006 Chandler talked of our identities being constantly 'under construction' as we choose, subconsciously or otherwise, how to present ourselves online. Chandler was researching at the point where ordinary individuals were just starting to create their own personal homepages, and he devised a checklist-style framework for analysing individuals' online output. He called this research tool a 'Bricoleur's Webkit', the word 'bricoleur', from the sociologist Claude Levi-Strauss, referring to a kind of creative tinkering. The idea of the webkit was to offer some simple starting points for analysing the way people endlessly 'tinker' with their online identities – for example, focussing on what types of material have been included by the author, what has been left out, what is being alluded to indirectly, and so on.

Early webpages created by private individuals marked a shift from advertising created by commercial companies to promote their products towards advertising created by individuals to promote themselves. Nowadays, some individuals still have their own websites, where they collect together information about themselves for particular reasons: for example, novelists and academic researchers. However, more of us distribute information about ourselves across a number of domains, both professional and personal. The idea of Chandler's webkit is still relevant, but to output across a range of sites rather than to any total assemblage in one space alone.

So far, the focus has been on the idea of writing as an act of identity-creation, considering how that might have changed. But the nature of readership – specifically, who we think might be 'reading' us – has also changed. While commercial companies are constantly looking for ways to segment their market so that they can target specific groups, individual users of the internet have faced a much broader potential audience of unknown others who might be reading and interpreting them. In that respect, online communication between individuals can be seen as less like the certainty of face-to-face situations, and more like the ambiguous contexts of published writing, where meaning is negotiated somewhere between the writer's use of language and the reader's interpretation of it.

As the internet has developed, researchers' ideas about the nature of language use within it have also changed. Early commentaries on internet communication tended to have a rather utopian view of language and human behaviour, thinking that because we couldn't see who we were communicating with, this might remove some of the social stereotyping associated with language differences – for example, regional and foreign accents, speech impairments, and so on – and that, as a result, we would be much nicer to each other. Haraway (1990) talked of the idea of a 'cyborg' body, having a kind of free-floating consciousness that allowed people to move beyond physical markers of difference such as gender, race and disability. However, it soon became clear that, rather than feeling liberated by leaving all our identity markers behind, an absence of information could increase people's efforts to mark their identities. For example, Hall's research on gender suggested that computer-mediated communication leads not to 'cyborgs' but to 'goddesses and ogres':

> Rather than neutralising gender, the electronic medium encourages its intensification. In the absence of the physical, network users exaggerate societal notions of femininity and masculinity in an attempt to gender themselves (Hall 1996: 167).

More recently, we have the phenomenon of 'trolling', where anonymous individuals deliberately disrupt online communities by creating malicious identities (see Hardaker 2013; Tagg, Seargeant & Brown 2017).

Hall's early research was focused on situations where complete strangers were communicating with each other; and this is clearly still possible, as Hardaker's research shows; see also Seargeant and Tagg (2014). But Susan Herring (2001; 2004) noted at quite an early stage that our internet interactions were becoming much more embedded in our everyday lives, and involving people that we already knew. Soon, the idea of a cyberspace 'out there' and a real world 'in here' evolved into our current situation, where we are not simply 'online' or 'offline' but where aspects of electronic communication are threaded through our lives. To test this idea, try writing a 'day in the life' for yourself, focusing on your communication during a typical day, noting particularly where and how communication technologies feature in your routines.

If Web 1.0 was all about users as the receivers of pre-made information, and Web 2.0 has been all about human interactivity, Web 3.0, sometimes called 'The Internet of Things', is all about machine communication – that is, machines communicating both with humans and with each other.

The area of Artificial Intelligence (AI) has a long history of research and development. An important question asked by Alan Turing, the founder of modern computing, in a research paper in 1950, was 'Can machines think?' This question provoked many tests, which came to be known as variants of 'the Turing Test', during which human subjects tried to assess whether they were communicating with another human or a machine; and of course it was language use that formed the evidence for their judgement. For example, in 1966 Joseph Weizenbaum created a 'bot' called Eliza, which simulated a psychotherapist's language; while in 1972, Kenneth Colby created 'Parry', a bot based on the language of a paranoid schizophrenic patient. In neither of these cases were the human participants particularly successful in detecting the AI nature of their interlocutors. However, the fact that these machines could use the structures of human language and perform its routines did not mean that they had understanding. In recent times, there have been more sophisticated robots such as Sophia, which has a human-like appearance, uses voice recognition and has 50 facial expressions and a visual capacity via eye-based cameras.

If the advent of bots such as Sophia seem to be in the sci-fi realm, think about the automated systems that you may have already encountered. For example, you may have spoken to automated voice software on the phone, or used 'smart speakers' such as Siri or Alexa or Echo to send voice-to-text messages, give instructions, or get information. If you used a chat facility on a sales website, how much of the language that came your way was ready-made? And how many applications are interacting with each other behind the scenes in your everyday life, or generating automatic messages for human consumption? For example, how do you know whether the newsfeeds you read are real? Twitter has admitted deleting more than 50,000 posts generated automatically by Russian 'bots' targeting American voters (Swaine 2018). There are similar concerns about 'fake news' having influenced the UK's 2016 referendum on EU membership.

For language researchers, these ideas are all very relevant but they are not the end of the story. There are also important questions about the nature of electronic language itself, particularly in the light of linguists' traditional categories and theories.

Early researchers discussed computer-mediated communication as if it were one type of language, and tended to give it a single label: for example, Crystal (2001) termed it 'netspeak'. As time has passed, it has become clear that we should be thinking not about a single genre of communication, but about a range of types, and work continues on how these different types should be described.

Language researchers continue to be particularly interested in ideas of **mode** – that is, in the relationship between our traditional notions of spoken and written language, and the new communication tools we use. CMC was quickly labelled as a 'hybrid' form of communication, where elements of spoken and written features combine. For example, real-time writing such as instant messaging was thought to resemble writing because it is composed at a keyboard using written symbols, but also thought to resemble speech in being synchronous (i.e. occurring in real time). However, our traditional concepts of speech and writing are themselves not particularly clear. For example, speech doesn't always occur in real time: think of a formal speech which has been recorded and broadcast. At the same time, writing can be a joint, informal, face-to-face activity: think about working with a friend to get some wording right on a birthday card. See Goddard (2004) for more discussion of our ideas about speech and writing.

One approach to analysing the characteristics of different types of electronic text – or 'outputs', as Crystal (2011) terms them – is to consider their **affordances** (what the communication tool allows users to do) and their **limitations** (drawbacks, or aspects that limit what it's possible to do). This approach was used by Sellen and Harper (2002) in looking at the functions of paper and of electronic communication, in an office setting.

A further, more detailed approach is Herring's (2007) use of 'facets', or dimensions of variation between different CMC genres. Her framework splits analysis into aspects of the tool being used (for example, whether it's synchronous or asynchronous) and aspects of the social context (for example, whether you are chatting with friends or planning a work project with colleagues). Herring's classifications mirror the earlier work of Erving Goffman, who was writing about communication and language long before the development of the internet. Goffman's (1981) view of communication was that it could be split into 'system constraints' (the nature of any technology used) and 'ritual constraints' (the conventions of the language community in question). The idea that lies behind the work of both these scholars is that the available technology does shape our language use, but so does the communication context – who we are communicating with, why we are communicating, and so on. The technology alone doesn't determine how we use language: you can email a friend with a message full of abbreviations, errors, in-jokes, **emojis** and general playfulness, but the same communication tool can also convey your CV in a formal job application. You would be a poor communicator if you used the same language in both these contexts. In that sense, there is no single 'language of email', or of any other communication tool.

Having said that, researchers have recognised that there are certain features of language use that occur in more than one digital context. This transfer of language practices from one environment to another is hardly surprising, if you think about the way different tools have converged in a single apparatus: for example, most mobile phones have texting and email functions, as well as web applications. In addition, built-in cameras allow phone owners to attach images and video to messages and sites, producing multimodal communication that is not simply a 'hybrid' of speech and writing but an intertwining of several modes at once.

While social scientists were researching new communication environments some time ago, it took a while for linguists to start doing the same. The language of texting (or 'txting', as it has sometimes been spelt, in order to differentiate messaging outputs from 'texts' in general) was particularly overlooked for a while. One of the first serious treatments of this new language practice was by Thurlow (2003), who offered what he called some 'sociolinguistic maxims' that might lie behind certain language choices. His maxims included the need for speed and brevity, but also the need for the writer to communicate some of the non-verbal and prosodic aspects that are missing in written texts – such as facial expression, and vocal contours such as volume and intonation. Later, Shortis (2007) discussed the creativity of text spelling, which he likens to some older forms of language play; Goddard (2011a) explored how 'cries' such as laughter and other expressive noises are conveyed both in real-time and asynchronous writing; while Crystal (2009) tackled the way texting has been represented in the media.

The various ideas above about brevity, speed, and the linguistic creativity of writers to simulate vocal effects can be a useful starting point for thinking about why authors in many different electronic genres, such as emails, blogs, Twitter and other social media sites use particular language strategies. For a more detailed account of Thurlow's maxims, see Goddard (2009). Thurlow et al (2004) offers further analyses of CMC.

More recently, linguists have started to look in detail at the roles played by emoticons and emojis in conveying implicit meanings – especially sarcasm and irony – in CMC messages that would otherwise be lacking in any equivalents of vocal effects or facial expression (see Evans 2017). Schnoebelen (2012) reviews the 28 most common emoticons and explores their subtle variations of use.

4. Possible limitations of some of these approaches

Language and technology is a big area and it's tempting therefore to ask 'big' questions, such as how all the communication tools we are using today will change aspects of the language we use. Unfortunately, we have no way of knowing the answer to such a question, which would require a god-like perspective on global communications. Within this large area, therefore, there is a need to think small, as with other aspects of language research, and arrive at do-able investigations with a modest scope and as sharp a focus as possible on a limited range of things.

While bearing in mind the warning above, there are problems with aspects of the research tradition as it has developed so far in that it has had a very Western focus. Sometimes there's an assumption that the whole world has networked computers, which is far from the case; at other times, there's an assumption that the rest of the world will simply 'catch up' with Western societies and go through the same stages of technical development in exactly the same way. This is a bit like expecting every country to have had a version of the UK's Industrial Revolution. The reality is that different technologies have developed in different ways across the world, and even within Western societies a lot of variation is apparent. For example, some areas of the USA don't have broadband because of the vast distances between settlements. In some parts of Africa, mobile telephony is much more common than computer use, and this could be seen as a more advanced stage of development than the fixed terminals that many Western users are still connected to. In short, there needs to be more research in different cultures around the world, in order to give us a better picture of how different technologies are used in specific contexts.

A further problem in some studies results from the difficulty of capturing the original communication process. If we liken real-time writing to the speech context, we are aware that spoken language in its original form is different from a transcript of it. In the same way, a chatlog of an interaction is different from the original experience of it, where a participant's line may have ended up in a different place on the screen from where they intended it to go. Also, interactive writing – ie online 'chat' – unfolds in real time, so users experience each new piece of writing as a new occurrence; when we read a transcript or chatlog, we can see the end of the text. Researchers therefore have to think about how to get back to the original communication and not regard the recording as the thing itself. The idea of real-time writing as a physical, material experience is discussed in Goddard (2011b).

Although there are always research concerns about the objectivity of any analysis, it doesn't help when analysing CMC to have no experience of it. Good studies often arise from an understanding of a particular online community, rather than ignorance of it. However, being part of a community then involves particular responsibilities for ethical behaviour on the part of researchers. In general terms, any site that involves password protection is considered a private space and permission needs to be obtained for use of data.

5. What people are researching now

While we need more information about how new technologies are used in different parts of the world, we also need more information about how intercultural communication works online. The ability to communicate with people in different parts of the world is an exciting and fascinating aspect of our new communication tools. International communication in the early years of the internet tended to consist of playful explorations, but it is now serious business: many workplaces are global corporations employing an international workforce, with expectations that employees communicate with each other successfully from remote locations. So what language strategies do successful online communicators employ?

New technologies have also transformed teaching and learning, with educational establishments of all kinds having their own virtual learning environments. However, we still have much to learn about how new technologies work in educational contexts, and particularly how to assess the communication skills we are trying to develop. New sources of information are now available to learners, involving new ways of reading. Older ideas of paper-based literacy are being challenged and notions of individual creativity re-examined. Young learners are of particular interest because they are growing up with new technologies from the outset: see, for example, the toy mobile phones pictured in Goddard and Geesin (2011).

And we still have no real answers to the more philosophical questions about language use, particularly to what extent we can be held to account for 'just words'. Over the years, especially since the proliferation of terrorist attacks, using language has increasingly been seen as an act in its own right, with laws around hate speech and language that radicalises and incites violence. The big platforms such as Facebook and Twitter are regularly criticised for not taking down offensive posts. But to what extent do these providers 'own' the language that occurs on their sites? And whose definition of offence should prevail? There are no easy answers to such questions.

6. Looking to the future

The first wave of computer use in the UK in the 1980s involved humans learning a new language in order to send commands to their machines. As time passed, the situation reversed: manufacturers recognised that in order to sell computers to a mass audience, people had to feel that computers 'spoke their language'. The Web 3.0 project involves a search for a common language for use between computers themselves. The vision set out by Tim Berners-Lee, the inventor of the web, was of a world where a web of data is processed by machines, database linking with database, freeing humans from routine tasks. Whether his idea of 'the Semantic Web' is possible – machines communicating with understanding – remains to be seen. But what is certain is that we will see increased connectivity in our lives, and increasingly sophisticated tools for communication on all our many devices.

7. Key ideas to consider

- How many different communication technologies have you had to learn so far? How did you learn the new conventions associated with each one?
- What differences do you observe about the different social groups you participate in, and how they use new communication tools? For example, are there age or gender differences in the language you see?

- Do you know people who appear very different online compared with their face-to-face identity? How are they different?
- Start a collection of stories you see in the press and elsewhere, about new technologies. Can you classify the themes that recur? How do you explain some of the public attitudes to language and technology?
- How aware are people that their communication on social media sites is owned by the site and acts as a 'product' which is sold to advertisers?
- How important are new technologies to our need for play and pleasure?
- Try to find out about new technologies in other countries and cultures. For example, Ito (2006) offers an account of mobile phone use in Japan.

References

CHANDLER, D., 2006. Identities under construction. In J. Maybin, ed., *The Art of English*. Maidenhead: Open University Press.

CRYSTAL, D., 2009. *Txtng: the gr8 db8*. Oxford: OUP.

CRYSTAL, D., 2001. *Language and the internet*. Cambridge: Cambridge University Press.

CRYSTAL, D., 2011. *Internet linguistics: a student guide*. London: Routledge.

EVANS, V., 2017. *The Emoji Code: How Smiley Faces, Love Hearts and Thumbs Up are Changing the Way We Communicate*. London: Michael O'Mara Books.

GODDARD, A. 2003. 'Is there anybody out there?': creative language play and literariness in internet relay chat (IRC). In SCHORR, A., B. Campbell and M. Schenk, eds., *Communication research and media science in Europe*. Berlin: Mouton De Gruyter. 325-343.

GODDARD, A. 2004. 'The way to write a phone call': multimodality in novices' use and perceptions of interactive written discourse. In SCOLLON R. & P. Levine, eds., *Discourse and technology: multimodal discourse analysis*. Washington, USA: Georgetown University Press. 34-46.

GODDARD, A. 2009. Language and new technologies. In MALMKJAER, K., ed. *The linguistics encyclopedia*. London: Routledge.

GODDARD, A. 2011a. 'Type you soon!' A stylistic approach to language use in a virtual learning environment. *Language and Literature*, 20/3: 184-200.

GODDARD, A. 2011b. . look im over here Creativity, materiality and representation in new communication technologies. In CARTER, R., R. Pope, & J. Swann, eds., *Creativity in language and literature: the state of the art*. Houndmills, Basingstoke: Palgrave Macmillan.

10. Language and Technology

GODDARD, A. & B. Geesin, 2011. *Language and technology*. London: Routledge.

GOFFMAN, E., 1981. *Forms of talk*. Oxford: Blackwell.

HALL, K., 1996. *Cyberfeminism*. In S. Herring, ed. 147-170.

HARAWAY, D., 1990. A manifesto for cyborgs: science, technology and socialist feminism in the 1980s. In HANSEN, K.V. & I. J. Philipson, eds., *Women, class, and the feminist imagination*. Philadelphia: Temple University Press. 580-617.

HARDAKER, C., 2013. ' 'Uh…..not to be nitpicky,,,,,but…the past tense of drag is dragged, not drug.': An overview of trolling strategies'. *Journal of Language Aggression and Conflict 1*(1): 57-85.

HERRING, S., ed., 1996. *Computer-mediated communication: linguistic, social and cross-cultural perspectives*. Amsterdam: John Benjamins.

HERRING, S., 2004. *Slouching toward the ordinary: current trends in computer-mediated communication*. New Media and Society 6/1, 26-36.

HERRING, S.C., 2007. A faceted classification scheme for computer-mediated discourse. Language@Internet, 4, article 1. Available from http://www.languageatinternet.org/articles/2007/761/ [accessed 10.2.12].

ITO, M., 2006. *Personal, portable, pedestrian: mobile phones in Japanese life*. Cambridge, Mass.: MIT Press.

SCHNOEBELEN, T., 2012. 'Do You Smile with Your Nose? Stylistic Variation in Twitter Emoticons,' University of Pennsylvania *Working Papers in Linguistics*: Vol. 18 : Iss. 2 , Article 14. Available at: https://repository.upenn.edu/pwpl/vol18/iss2/14

SEARGEANT, P., and Tagg, C., 2014. *The Language of Social Media: Identity and Community on the Internet*. Basingstoke, UK: Palgrave Macmillan.

SELLEN, A.J. & R.H.R. Harper, 2002. *The myth of the paperless office*. Cambridge, Mass.: MIT Press.

SHORTIS, T., 2007. Gr8 txtpectations: the creativity of text spelling. English Drama Media. *NATE*: June edition. 21-26.

SWAINE, J., 2018. 'Twitter admits far more Russian bots posted on election that it had disclosed', *The Guardian*. 20 January. Available at: https://www.theguardian.com/technology/2018/jan/19/twitter-admits-far-more-russian-bots-posted-on-election-than-it-had-disclosed

TAGG, C., SEARGEANT, P., and BROWN, A., 2017. *Taking Offence on Social Media: Conviviality and Communication on Facebook*. London: Palgrave Macmillan.

THURLOW, C., 2003. Generation txt? DAOL 1 (1). Available at: http://www.shu.ac.uk [accessed 10.2.12].

THURLOW, C., L., Lengel, L., and Tomic. A, 2004. *Computer Mediated Communication: social interaction and the internet*. Sage.

TOFFLER, A., 1980. *The third wave*. New York: Bantam Books.

11 CHILD LANGUAGE ACQUISITION

Dr Paul Ibbotson

1. Introduction

Flatworms (*Pseudoceros bifurcus*) take part in 'penis fencing' battles to determine who becomes the female of the species. The loser does – the life of the female flatworm is much harder work. Ants (*Protomognathus americanus*) steal eggs from neighbouring species of ants, take them home and raise them as slaves, making them do the foraging, cleaning and babysitting. Female mites (*Histiostoma murchiei*) make their own husbands by laying eggs that don't need fertilising. When they hatch the female has sex with her four-day-old offspring, after which the son/husband promptly dies. The resulting female babies are fathered by their dead brothers. If you were cataloguing remarkable animal behaviour on Earth you would have to add to this list the human capacity for acquiring and using language. The human entry in such an encyclopedia might say '*Homo sapiens* likes to live in groups, uses sound to get thoughts and feelings from one brain to another, learns to do this by three years of age'. When you look at it like this, **child language acquisition** is another extraordinary aspect of the natural world that begs an explanation.

Researchers want to know how language acquisition works not just because many people find language inherently interesting, but because it bears on some fundamental questions of human nature: learning and innateness, the relationship between language and thought, and human uniqueness. At its heart, the process involves children learning the relationship between sound (**phonology**), sentence structure (**syntax**) and meaning (**semantics**). In trying to understand how humans acquire language, with all its subtlety, power and complexity, researchers break the bigger question into smaller sub-questions.

First, how do children find the words in what they hear? Figure 1 (overleaf) shows an image of someone saying *would you like a jelly baby?* Notice that sometimes the gaps in the sound line up with the edge of a word but often they don't. When someone speaks, there is an illusion that each word is separately articulated with a_convenient_space_between_each_word. The effect soon disappears when you don't know what the words mean, like when you listen

11. Child Language Acquisition

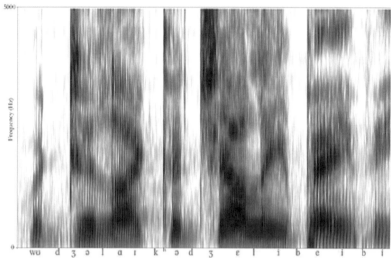

Figure 1
Time is left to right. The dark areas represent sound frequencies. Phonetic transcription of speech (across the horizontal axis) shows how the words map onto the speech.

to someone speaking a foreign language, making it sound like one continuous unintelligible stream of speech. The child faces a similar problem in trying to work out where the words are – except they have to do it without the aid of any foreign phrasebooks or formal instruction. Not only do different speakers have different ways of saying the *same* words, the *same* speaker has different ways of saying the same words – and this depends on lots of different factors including what other words it appears with, what they are trying to emphasise or whether they have a cold or not. Somehow the child has to work out what all the relevant building blocks are and start to put together their vocabulary. And then, when they want to say something they have to somehow translate what they have heard into speech – a phenomenally complex task that involves choreographing the tongue, lips, soft palette and vocal folds. Impressively, at 5 months-old infants can tell the difference between a video of someone speaking their native language and the same person speaking a foreign language ... even when there is no sound!

Second, how do children work out what are the acceptable combinations of words? For example, on a Monday a child hears her mother say sentence (1a) and then (1b). On Tuesday she then hears sentence (1c) and the child decides to say (1d). The child may have reasoned that the structure of (1a) and (1c) are quite close – they overlap in many of the way the words are organised into a sentence. On that basis, she thought, if you can say (1b) after (1a) then I should be able to say (1d) after (1c).

(1a) The baby seems to be asleep.

(1b) The baby seems asleep.

(1c) The baby seems to be sleeping.

(1d) The baby seems sleeping.

Somehow the child has to learn which generalisations are possible and which aren't. Going beyond simple imitation of the input is a crucial feature of language and all theories of language have to explain how we do this. This is why researchers are so interested in errors such as *She giggled me*, and *I go-ed to the shops*, because it shows children are generalising from what they have heard to say something new. These errors (called **overgeneralisations**) give researchers a glimpse into the learning mechanism that children might be using to acquire their language.

Thirdly, how do they work out what words mean? When a mother says to a child a word they have never heard before, the child might think: 'what do they want me to pay attention to?' If they are in a park, and the mother says a new word, she could be referring to the name of a dog (Colin), dogs in general (dogs), part of a dog (a leg), the action the dog is doing (running), the way the dog is running (quickly), the colour of the dog (red), the type of dog (red-setter), what she thinks of dogs in general, a question about dogs or nothing to do with dogs at all. Somehow the child has to learn what people intend to communicate when they say something.

In one way or another these are all problems of finding patterns; so we can think about language learning as the skill of learning to find the right patterns and then using these patterns to communicate.

These are the types of questions that researchers in the field of child language are trying to answer. Exactly how children learn language is not fully understood – it's quite a complicated process! The work of a scientist is often likened to that of a detective; piecing together evidence to reconstruct a plausible version of events. Sometimes the question seems so complicated that the task seems hopeless. At least we have an abundance of clues to work with – language is all around us. Due to the sustained effort by scientists all around the world over the past fifty years, we now have a good idea about how many of the basic principles work. In this chapter we will look at some of the key thinkers and developments that have driven this progress.

2. A brief history

> In certain basic respects we do not really learn language; rather, grammar grows in the mind. (Chomsky 1980: 134).

The study of language acquisition over the past fifty years has been massively influenced by the work of linguist and political philosopher Noam Chomsky. Consider the following set of sentences.

(2a) She painted the green house.

(2b) She painted the house green.

(2c) She knew the green house.

(2d) She knew the house green.

As in the previous example (1a-d), on the basis of (2a-c) a child might think it is possible to say (2d). This pattern is probably something you haven't really thought about before, yet you have hundreds of thousands of these intuitions about what makes a well-formed sentence in your language – you have a grammar. Chomsky's point was that the patterns of our grammar (like the ones above) are essentially too difficult and abstract to learn with a simple set of learning mechanisms, such as associating a stimulus with a reward. So here is the problem. If we end up knowing more about language (our set of intuitions) than it was possible to learn with these simple mechanisms, then we need somehow to explain how we reach adult-like language. Chomsky said that a set of innate linguistic principles helps the child by guiding them towards their adult language. He called this **Universal Grammar** as everyone is born with it, as part of their DNA, and it defines all possible human languages, past, present and future.

Now, if Universal Grammar is going to do anything, it needs something in it – some set of principles that will guide the child towards their native language. It is no good building in what will only work for an English-speaking child as Universal Grammar doesn't know if it is going to be born into a culture of English-speakers or Japanese-speakers! And this is the first problem. The principles need to be specific enough to help the child learn their particular language yet general enough to capture the variation across the 6000 languages that currently exist. The second main problem is that these principles need to be described in quite a general, abstract way – again if they are to capture the different way in which all languages work. This means that a child needs a way of linking their general grammatical principles to the day-to-day utterances they hear and say, like *doggie gone* and *more juice*. Despite over fifty years of trying, linguists haven't been able to define *the content* of Universal Grammar in a way that satisfactorily solves both problems. There are other problems with the idea of UG, for example how it could, in principle, evolve to be a human adaptation and also whether the theory itself is falsifiable – a scientific theory should have some way of showing how it *could* be false. But as much as weaknesses in the theory and a lack of progress undermined Chomsky's ideas, it was not until a serious alternative was developed that the consensus started to shift on what language is and how it might be acquired.

3. Cognitive-functionalism

> Putting together novel expressions is something that speakers do, not grammars. It is a problem-solving activity that demands a constructive effort and occurs when linguistic convention is put to use in specific circumstances. (Langacker 1987: 65)

About twenty years after Chomsky made his first proposals, a growing band of linguists and developmental psychologists dissatisfied with his approach began to move in a different direction. They wanted to understand language in terms of how the mind works – how it categorises things and makes analogies, how it directs attention, how it remembers and how it forgets, how it reasons about actions, objects and people. Remember, Chomsky saw grammars as so abstract, so complex, and the principles that govern them so subtle and highly specific to their purpose that they effectively couldn't be learned without the aid of Universal Grammar. At this time there wasn't a convincing theory of learning that would fully answer Chomsky's criticism, but despite this, the Cognitive-Functionalists thought their view of language had several advantages.

First, remarkable claims require remarkable evidence and a theory which says 6000 different languages are built out of the same innate linguistic building blocks is a remarkable claim about human nature. It requires dedicated mental machinery (Universal Grammar) evolved for the purpose of learning language. As we have seen, it is debatable whether the evidence is as remarkable as the theory. Instead, what if language was a by-product of a broader adaptation, say for finding patterns, reading other people's intentions and for cultural life in general? To illustrate the cultural diversity of language: if all the languages in the world were equally distributed over the inhabitable parts of the world you would have to walk less than 50 miles on average to meet a new language. The odd cultural variation in handshake in chimpanzees is impressive but it doesn't really compete with over 6000 ways of saying *hello*! (Foley & Lahr 2011). So the first advantage is that many of the things that make language work – pattern finding, reading peoples' intentions, cultural imitation – can be understood independently of linguistic theory. And in science there is generally a preference for the simplest explanation if two theories can equally well describe the data (although people argue over whether they do equally explain the data and what 'simple' means).

Second, in **Cognitive Functionalism** the fundamental linguistic unit to be learnt is the **construction** – a pairing of form and function. That means a symbol which links some kind of pattern – a word, an idiom, a sound, a syntactic pattern – with a particular meaning. That includes patterns which are regular (e.g., ***John kissed Mary***), irregular (e.g., ***Him be doctor!***), abstract (e.g., ***Subject Verb Object***) and concrete (e.g., ***I wanna***). Everybody agrees that the child has to learn all the idiosyncrasies of their language: the sounds of the language and structures that don't conform to the regular patterns like idioms such as *the more the merrier*. If children can learn these particulars of their language, maybe they can learn their grammar too. A Cognitive-Functionalist approach may be more 'child-friendly' in another way. If grammar is no longer separate from the rest of cognition (as it was in Chomsky's theory), we no longer have the same problem of linking an abstract, meaningless grammar to the external world. We can also recruit general psychological processes, like **categorisation** and **analogy**, for language learning. More than this, we predict that there will be a close relationship between cognitive development and linguistic development. There is a growing body of evidence that the nature and properties of at least certain patterns in language are learnable on the basis of general categorisation strategies (Goldberg 2006). Moreover, we now know that the kinds of motivations to learn and learning mechanisms that children bring to the task of language acquisition are much more sophisticated than the kind of learning that Chomsky was criticising.

3.1 The process of learning

The Cognitive-Functionalist picture of what language is and how it works laid the theoretical foundations for a more **Usage**-based view of language acquisition. 'Usage' because (1) linguistic knowledge in the mind builds up as a function of the child's linguistic experience and (2) language structure emerges from language use – this goes for language change as well as language acquisition. One of the consequences of this is that researchers are interested in the relationship between what children actually hear and their language development (see section below). One of the most influential figures in this approach has been the psychologist Michael Tomasello (Tomasello 2003). Decades of research by his lab and others has shown that young children begin by learning very local patterns, for example *Where's the X?, I wanna X, More X, It's a X, I'm X-ing it, Put X here, Mommy's X-ing it, Let's X it, Throw X, X gone, I X-ed it, Sit on the X, Open X, X here, There's a X, X broken*. The 'X' here is the variable element, a slot that can be filled by different items, such as *Where's the toy/book/dog?* Once a child has heard variation like this in their language, they build up more abstract constructions by analogising across exemplars – this means finding similarity in the way things work or the way things sound (Gentner & Markman 1995). The idea is that these reliable patterns (called **slot-and-frames**) give the child a foothold into learning more complex syntax. For example, when the child is trying to comprehend two sentences like *the goat ate the woman* and *a woman tickled a goat*, they do not begin by aligning elements on the basis of the literal similarity between the two goats, but match the goat and the woman because they are both construed as playing similar roles in the event, such as actor or undergoer. There is much evidence that people, including young children, focus on these kinds of relations in making analogies across linguistic constructions, the most important being the meaning of the words involved, especially the verbs, and the spatial, temporal, and causal relations they encode. Of course, making analogy is not unique to language (Figure 2, below).

X is like Y in way Z
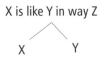

The two sentences are alike as they involve someone doing something to someone else.

The goat tickled the woman.   The man bit the dog.

An atom is like a solar system in the way that they both involve something orbiting something central.

Figure 2
Analogy works across different domains (e.g., perception, language) and different scales (e.g., atom, solar system, word, sentence)

Analogy also functions at the level of words and sounds. When a learner says *I goed to shops* it is by analogy to a set of verbs which mark past tense in English with *-ed*. Likewise, *I brung it* is produced by analogy to 'phonological neighbours' which show similar sound alternations, such as *sing-sung* → *bring-brung*.

Having discussed ways in which the child is a powerful analogy-maker we now need a way of controlling generalisations so they don't make analogies indiscriminately. Returning to an earlier example, on the basis of (1a) and (2a) a child might correctly generalise (3a), but overgeneralise to (4a) (examples from Goldberg 2006).

(1a) She painted the green house.

(2a) She painted the house green.

(3a) She knew the green house.

(4a) She knew the house green.

However, if we paraphrase the meaning of each sentence…

(1b) She painted a house that happened to be green.

(2b) She caused the house to become green by painting.

(3b) She knew a house that happened to be green.

(4b) She caused the house to become green by knowing.

we see some generalisations might never enter the mind of a child because quite simply they don't make sense. However, this still leaves a lot of generalisations that do make sense but are nevertheless rarely made. For example, it is not that *the magician disappeared the rabbit* is incomprehensible, we just don't say it – but why not? Just how to deal with these cases within the Cognitive-Functionalist approach is an area of ongoing research (see Box 1).

Box 1 Constraining generalisations

Usage-based approaches to language acquisition have developed three main proposals that would help children rule out some overgeneralisations.

1. Entrenchment – the more often a child hears a verb in a particular syntactic context the less likely they are to use it in a new context they haven't heard it in. Example: *John slept* entrenches the verb into the intransitive construction, making it less likely to be generalised to *John slept Mary*.

2. Pre-emption – if a child hears a verb in a construction that serves the same communicative function as a possible generalisation, then the child infers that the generalisation is not available. Example: Where a child could have expected to hear *John goed to the shops*, based on analogies with other past tense formation in English, *went* pre-empts its use in this position.

3. Indirect negative evidence – the intuitive reasoning is 'I would have encountered this construction if it existed, I haven't, therefore this construction does not exist'. Example: If a child repeatedly hears the verb *made* used in the syntactic context of *The magician made the rabbit disappear*, in situations involving direct causation, the child may infer that *The magician disappeared the rabbit* is not acceptable.

3.2 What children hear and what they say

The availability of online transcripts of child language and **child directed speech** (**CDS**) has greatly improved our understanding of the relationship between language acquisition and the language children hear. For example, Cameron-Faulkner, Lieven and Tomasello (2003) estimated that on the basis of their sample of English child directed speech children hear something in the order of 7,000 utterances per day including 2000 questions! More important than the raw quantity of items perhaps is the way these items are distributed. A small number of lexical (word) based frames account for a large amount of the data. For example 69 percent of all utterances beginning with the word *What's…* followed a pattern.

The idea is that these islands of reliability allow the child a foothold into the language on their way to generalising more abstract categories.

There is evidence that there are close links between the way adults use particular words, morphemes, and phrases in CDS and the way children learn them. For example, the way children use particular syntactic categories of verbs is strongly related to the way their mothers used those particular verbs (Theakston et al. 2001). The acquisition order of *wh-* questions (*What, Where, When, Why, How*) is predicted from the frequency with which particular *wh-*words and verbs occur in children's input (Rowland & Pine 2000; Rowland, Pine, Lieven & Theakston 2003). Children's proportional use of me-for-I errors (e.g., when the child says *me do it*) correlates with their caregivers' proportional use of *me* in certain contexts (e.g., *let me do it*, Kirjavainen, Theakston & Lieven 2009). The pattern of negator emergence (*no* → *not* → *'nt*) follows the frequency of negators in the input; that is negators used frequently in the input are the first to emerge in the child's speech (Cameron-Faulkner, Lieven & Theakston 2007).

One obvious criticism of these types of studies is that they are usually based on one or two hours of recording every few weeks, massively under-sampling crucial early stages of child development. One extreme solution to this has been adopted by Deb Roy of MIT Media Lab. He has placed cameras and microphones all around his house and recorded his son's development, gathering approximately 10 hours of audio and video on a daily basis from birth to age three. The resulting corpus, which already contains over 100,000 hours of multi-track recordings, constitutes the most comprehensive record of a child's development made to date. While only based on one child, this data provides many new opportunities to understand the fine-grained dynamics of language development.

3.3 Statistical learning

It is important to note that when Usage-based theorists talk of learning they mean something different from what the Behaviourists had in mind – a branch of psychology that looked at learning in the context of trial and error, rewards for successes and stimulus-response. The modern conceptualisation is something much more sophisticated and diverse than that. For example, by attending to transitional probabilities (the chance that one thing will be followed by another) children are able to find 'words in a sea of sounds' and treat these newly acquired words as part of their lexical inventory (Saffran 2001). Eight-month-old infants are sensitive to the statistical tendency that transitional probabilities are generally higher within words than across words (Saffran, Aslin & Newport 1996). Children are also able to discover syntactic regularities between categories of words as well as the statistical regularities in sound patterns (Marcus et al. 1999). By twelve-months-old, infants can use their newly discovered word boundaries to discover regularities in the syntactic distributions of a novel word-string grammar (Saffran & Wilson 2003). And by fifteen months old, infants are able to combine multiple cues in order to learn word-level grammatical patterns (Gerken, Wilson & Lewis 2005).

The following sentences, created by the developmental psychologist Brian MacWhinney shows that if the child knows something of the distributional properties of items in their language (English in this example), they are able to guess what kind of item *pum* might be from the syntactic context – the relationship to the other words it appears with. This is a probabilistic process – the initial guess offers the best hypothesis given the evidence (child directed speech), which might be revised as more evidence comes in.

(1) Here is a pum (count noun).

(2) Here is Pum (proper noun).

(3) I am pumming (intransitive verb).

(4) I pummed the duck (transitive (causative) verb).

(5) I need some pum (mass noun).

(6) This is the pum one (adjective).

4. Social-cognitive development

Suppose you see a woman take keys out of her pocket while approaching the front door of a house. Not only do you perceive the physics of the scene – the solidity, acceleration and trajectory of the objects – you naturally think of mental motivations for her actions – 'she wants to open the door', 'she's trying to get in her house', 'she believes the key will open the door'. If she knows you are watching the scene she will have beliefs about what you believe of her 'you think I'm trying to get in the house', and so on. So, fundamental to interpreting human behaviour is our capacity to think about other people's actions in terms of their underlying goals, intentions and beliefs. As well as the ability to read behaviour in this way, we seem to possess an intrinsic, and perhaps species-specific, motivation to share psychological states (and know that we share these states) with other people. There are even those who argue that it is this kind of thinking that leads to a kind of consciousness, which happens when the model of the world is so detailed and flexible that it includes a model of itself.

What's all this got to do with language? The central idea here is that language is a code that rests on a deeper code about how people work. We understand the mundane utterance *Can you pass the salt?* as a transparent request rather than, say, as an enquiry about condiment passing abilities, because we can work out what is relevant from the perspective of the speaker. One way to work out what's relevant for them is to have a model in your head of their beliefs, desires and attitudes. Research in infants suggests that language begins to take off shortly after infants show signs of this mind reading ability (e.g., Carpenter et al. 1998). Once this deeper code is understood the next code can be learnt – what sounds does this particular language use to direct people's attention?

Learning language, then, is seen as part of a broader adaptation to cultural learning. In the old view of language, the paper-and-pen analysis of grammatical patterns led linguists to conclude that there was a problem for the child; there was not enough data in the language to get where you needed to be as an adult speaker (part of why Chomsky suggested Universal Grammar in the first place). Researchers are starting to realise that this isn't the same problem children are faced with as social agents grounded in a communicative context.

The last fifty years of research has begun to uncover the rich social and cognitive learning skills that children bring to the language acquisition process. Firstly, a child learns that language is an attention-directing skill; a communicator wants the recipient to attend to something: an action, an object, some aspect of the scene, the speaker's attitude toward a scene, or a proposition (remember the dog in the park example?). Second, the communicator is also likely to have a social motive for doing so: they want me to do something, to feel something, to know something, or to share something that they think I will find useful or interesting, and this assumption of helpfulness guides my search for communicative relevance (Sperber & Wilson 1986, 1995; Tomasello 2008). By comparison, our closest evolutionary relatives, the chimpanzees, are rarely motivated to share information for the sake of sharing information – their communicative motives seem to be more driven by food, sex and group hierarchy (although you might be able to make the same argument about some of the people you know!). Finally, in ongoing discourse these communicative acts are modified by what the speaker-recipient know together, the common ground and joint attention that they have established over the course of their communicative history. For example, the first time we mention somebody new in the conversation we might refer to them as *John the fisherman* then the next time *John* and the next time *him*. To get the message across we need to respect what the other person knows, so at the start of the conversation we spend more time and effort making sure we set the scene so that the new information to come later makes sense against this background. This is just another part of the way language works, and another aspect that children need to learn.

Possessing a powerful set of social-cognitive and social-motivational tools is logically prior – both in the development of the species and the development of the individual – to recipients treating utterances as language and not just a string of sounds (e.g., Tomasello 2008). Many of the claims about the processes involved in language acquisition – statistical learning, analogy – are likely to be true of other species (and computers too). However, once our view of language, and more generally of communication, is one of a social act, it is possible to say why cognitive processes and even species-general processes might be necessary but not sufficient for language acquisition.

> **Box 2 What was the context of Chomsky's big ideas?**
>
> Chomsky's big ideas neatly fitted with the intellectual spirit of times. In 1950, Claude Shannon programmed an electronic mouse with a set of rules to find its way through a maze towards a target. He gave it a memory so it could learn from experience and a set of simple rules that were general enough to solve a variety of different mazes. By the standards of today, not a particularly ground-breaking achievement, but at the time Behaviourists thought psychology should concentrate on the respectable business of measuring stimuli and responses. Shannon's mouse showed how one could sensibly talk about how stimuli are processed and stored to produce responses; he preferred to talk about *information*, the currency of what was to become Cognitive Science. The target-finding maze-navigating behaviour of the mouse looked intelligent – it used knowledge of the way the world worked to obtain goals in face of obstacles. Maybe the things that are important to us – reasoning, language, music – could also be described with the abstract mathematical approach that had worked for Shannon and his mouse. It was very much in this spirit that Chomsky set out to describe UG.
>
> But if Shannon designed the program for his mouse where did UG come from? Chomsky's answer to this fitted with the second trend. Evolutionary biology was showing how much behaviour could be explained by genetics rather than culture. Chomsky's conclusion was that the human linguistic capacity rests on dedicated mental structures, many specific details of which (i.e. UG) evolved to become an innate biological endowment of the species. At this point a satisfying and non-trivial description of language acquisition seemed tantalisingly within reach; all linguists had to do was define the content of Universal Grammar that allows a child to learn language. This more or less defined what the followers of Chomsky and his followers did for the next fifty years.

5. Criticism of the cognitive-functional approach

One of the main challenges is to specify in greater detail the learning mechanisms that underpin generalisations. Critics of the Usage-based approach to language acquisition say theories need to be more precise about what findings would and would not be expected. One kind of approach that seems particularly successful in generating this kind of rigour is combining corpora (transcripts of child speech and child directed speech) and experimental methods to answer a focused question about learning (e.g., Bannard & Matthews 2010; Dąbrowska, 2008; Goldberg, Casenhiser, Sethuramen 2004). Children's errors are the one area in which Usage-based theory does make clear predictions: errors in children's data are predicted to occur when children start to go beyond tried and tested slot-and-frames, and should occur on low frequency items. However, there is evidence that this isn't the whole story (Ambridge & Rowland 2009). Plus there may be areas where we might expect more errors to occur but which children seem to master pretty quickly. Finally, there are still surprisingly few studies that have attempted to characterise the input children hear in dense enough detail and at the level of linguistic representation that is plausible in Usage-based theory (Cameron-Faulkner et al. 2003, being a notable exception). Studies of this type are essential if we are to achieve a better grip on the frequencies and distributions of items that will give Usage-based theories more chance of predicting in detail the specific developmental trajectories of linguistic items.

6. Summary and future challenges

Human language acquisition is a remarkable achievement. Despite the fact that the input to this process (child directed speech) and the output (adult language) is all around us we still haven't got a complete description of how this process works. The challenge is immense. Complex networks of interactions between genes, brains, behaviour and culture with multiple feedback loops at every level prevent any straightforward cause-effect explanation. Theories need to be flexible enough to accommodate the diversity of 6000 plus languages, restrictive enough to predict commonalities across languages and identify those factors that predict individual developmental pathways for language learning – it's a tall order! But, in recent years some difficult syntactic problems have started to yield to the Cognitive-Functionalist approach (Goldberg 2006; Croft & Crowle 2004). For developmental psycholinguistics one of the future challenges will be pinning down the exact cognitive processes that are operating in comprehension and production, as they happen. One of the big open questions for theorists and experimentalists alike is whether there are any purely linguistic representations or whether all linguistic categories be traced back into the communicative roles they play. This need not mean, as some critics say, 'reducing' language to cognition any more than biology is being reduced to chemistry or chemistry is being reduced to physics. What it does mean is that it is a cognitive-science approach that is also concerned with the social foundations of human communication. This framework for studying the acquisition of language has come a long way from Chomsky, but is perhaps no less radical: it suggests linguistic categories emerge from a handful of cognitive skills (for example, perception, attention, pattern-finding, memory) interacting in complex ways with a species-specific set of social skills (for example, shared intentionality, cooperative reasoning, cultural intelligence).

7. Key ideas for to consider and further reading

7.1 Key ideas

- Children don't just repeat what they've heard; they find patterns in the input that allow them to generate what they want to say.
- Researchers are trying to understand exactly what allows humans (but not our closest evolutionary cousins) to find those patterns.
- Different languages have reached different solutions to the problem of communication.
- Children have to learn how their language organises sound (phonology), sentence structure (syntax) and meaning (semantics).
- Cognitive-Functionalism says that many of things that make language work – pattern finding, analogy, reading people's intentions, cultural imitation – are based on cognitive principles (not a dedicated genetic adaptation).

7.2 Further reading

AMBRIDGE, B. & E. Lieven, 2011. *Child language acquisition: contrasting theoretical approaches.* Cambridge: Cambridge University Press

IBBOTSON, P., 2012. A new kind of language. *The Psychologist*: The British Psychologist Society. February 2012, Vol. 25, no 2.

ROY, D., Available online from http://www.ted.com/talks/deb_roy_the_birth_of_a_word.html.

TOMASELLO, M., 2003. *Constructing a language: a usage-based theory of language acquisition* [online]. Harvard University Press.

References

CARPENTER, M., K. Nagell, & M. Tomasello, 1998. Social cognition, joint attention, and communicative competence from 9 to 15 months of age. *Monographs of the Society for Research in Child Development.* 63/4, Serial No. 255), i-vi, 1-174.

CAMERON-FAULKNER, T., E.V. Lieven and M. Tomasello, 2003. A construction based analysis of child directed speech. *Cognitive Science* 27: 843-873.

CAMERON-FAULKNER, T., E.V. Lieven and A.L. Theakston, 2007. What part of no do children not understand? A usage-based account of multiword negation. *Journal of Child Language*, 34, 251-282.

CHOMSKY, N. 1980. *Rules and representations.* Oxford: Blackwell.

CROFT, W. & D. A. Cruse 2004. *Cognitive linguistics (*Cambridge Textbooks in Linguistics). Cambridge: Cambridge University Press.

FOLEY, R.A. & M.M. Lahr, 2011. The evolution of the diversity of cultures. *Philosophical Transactions of the Royal Society B: Biological Sciences* 366, 1080-1089.

GENTNER, D. & A.B. Markman, 1995. Similarity is like analogy: Structural alignment in comparison. In CACCIARI, C. ed., *Similarity in language, thought and perception*. Brussels, Belgium: BREPOLS, 111–147.

GERKEN, L. A., R. Wilson, & W. Lewis, 2005. 17-month-olds can use distributional cues to form syntactic categories. *Journal of Child Language*, 32, 249-268.

GOLDBERG, A., 2006. *Constructions at work: the nature of generalisations in language.* Oxford: Oxford University Press.

KIRJAVAINEN M., Theakston A.L. & Lieven E.V., 2009. Can input explain children's me-for-I errors? *Journal of Child Language.* 36(5), 1091-1114.

LANGACKER, R., 1987. *Foundations of cognitive grammar,* Volume I. Stanford: Stanford University Press.

MACWHINNEY, B., 2005. The emergence of linguistic form in time. *Connection Science* Vol. 17, No. 3-4, September-December 2005, 191-211.

MARCUS, G., Vijayan, S., S. Bandi Rao, & P. Vishton, 1999. Rule Learning by seven-month-old infants. *Science* 1 January 1999: Vol. 283. no. 5398, 77-80.

ROWLAND, C. F. & J.M. Pine, 2000. Subject-auxiliary inversion errors and wh-question acquisition: what children do know? *Journal of Child Language*, 27, 157-181.

ROWLAND, C. F., J.M. Pine, E.V. Lieven & A.L. Theakston, 2003. Determinants of the order of acquisition of wh- questions: re-evaluating the role of caregiver speech. *Journal of Child Language*, 30, 609-635.

SAFFRAN, J.R. 2001. Words in a sea of sounds: the output of statistical learning. *Cognition*, 81, 149-169.

SAFFRAN, J.R., R.N. Aslin, & E.L. Newport, 1996. Statistical learning by 8-month-old infants. *Science*, 274, 1926-1928.

SAFFRAN, J.R. & D.P. Wilson, 2003. From syllables to syntax: multi-level statistical learning by 12-month-old infants. *Infancy*, 4, 273-284.

THEAKSTON A.L., E.V. Lieven, J. Pine & C. Rowland, 2001. The role of performance limitations in the acquisition of verb argument structure. *Journal of Child Language* 28, 127-152.

TOMASELLO, M., 2003. *Constructing a language: a usage-based theory of language acquisition*. Harvard University Press.

TOMASELLO, M., 2008. *Origins of human communication*. MIT Press.

12 CRITICAL DISCOURSE ANALYSIS

Professor Christopher Hart

1. Introduction: history, theory, agenda

Critical Discourse Analysis (CDA) is an approach to language study which (i) theorises the *power of language* and (ii) analyses *power in language*. It focusses on texts that may be broadly characterised as 'political' (as opposed to 'literary' texts, which are the territory of Stylistics – see Stockwell, this volume, Chapter Thirteen). What counts as political, however, is an open question and CDA researchers have analysed texts relating to a wide range of topics where power is at stake (including immigration, race, gender, civil disorder, war, the environment) and belonging to a wide range of genres (including political speeches, parliamentary debates, news reports, advertisements, policy papers and scientific journals).

Contrary to some misunderstandings, CDA is not a method of discourse analysis. Rather, CDA is a particular area of discourse analysis characterised by a *critical* perspective. As a field of study, CDA has developed and applied a number of methods or analytical frameworks based on models of language found in linguistics. In considering the power of language, CDA draws heavily on other forms of discourse analysis, such as found in the work of Michel Foucault who saw language as an essential means of maintaining social hierarchies and governing social groups. What distinguishes CDA from these more sociological traditions, however, is its application of linguistics in detailed analyses of specific linguistic features. In this respect, the focus of CDA is on the way social structures of power and inequality are reflected in, enacted through, and justified by linguistic structures produced as part of texts.

In adopting a critical perspective, researchers in CDA are inspired by other critical theorists, such as those associated with the Frankfurt School of sociology (e.g., Adorno, Horkheimer and later Habermas). To be critical here means to go beyond the standard academic tasks of describing and explaining to consider data in its social context, adopting an explicit socio-political stance and ultimately changing society. Following in this critical tradition, CDA is problem-oriented and change-focused. This means that researchers in CDA start from a perceived social problem, such as the treatment of migrants. This naturally involves adopting a particular normative or ethical stance in the first place. They would then seek to show, through detailed linguistic analysis, how the language used to talk about migrants and migration might contribute to sustaining their cruel and unfair treatment. For example, by constructing migrants as worthless, inferior or just 'Other', discriminatory actions toward them are justified. By highlighting the discriminatory nature of discourses, such as migration discourses, it is hoped that critically empowered audiences will be better placed to resist those discourses and the actions they call for or lead to.

At this point, a note is needed on the terms **text** and **discourse**. In CDA, discourse is understood as the unfolding activity of producing and consuming language in context. A text is the material 'trace' of that process. A text may be written, as in a newspaper article, or spoken as in a political speech, and written down only for purposes of record or analysis. Texts are not produced in historical vacuums. Rather, every text is connected to and contains traces of previous texts. This is known as **intertextuality**. Intertextuality may be explicit, as in the case of quotation, or implicit, when a text deliberately or otherwise borrows from, alludes to or carries echoes of another text. Increasingly, the term discourse is extended to include communicative activity in modes or channels other than language while text may refer to non-verbal forms of expression. So, for example, a picture can be counted as a text. Many texts are **multimodal** containing both linguistic and aural or visual elements. The term **discourses** refers to ways of talking and thinking about particular topics, such as migration. Hence, we may speak of competing discourses of migration. Discourses are inherently ideological, representing a particular worldview. However, some discourses are so dominant that the worldviews they encode can seem natural or common-sensical. In theorising the power of language, CDA views discourses as both reflected in but also brought into existence by texts.

The question then arises, whose texts and whose discourses should we analyse? CDA tends to target the texts and discourses of social actors and institutions in whom authority is invested and who have the most influence in society. This includes politicians, large multinational corporations, and the national mass media. In other words, CDA is focused on communicative contexts where there is *power behind language*. More recently, however, CDA has begun to explore the language of 'ordinary' citizens in social media settings.

CDA began as **Critical Linguistics**, pioneered by scholars at the University of East Anglia in the 1970s. Those scholars were dissatisfied with the state of linguistics at the time, which, since the Chomskyan revolution, had been dedicated to describing the formal features of language without much consideration for the functions or purposes of actual language usages within the social systems of which they are a part. One theory that began to redress this situation and which came to form the analytical basis of Critical Linguistics,

12. Critical Discourse Analysis

was Halliday's Systemic Functional Grammar (SFG). SFG has since remained an important analytical framework for CDA. However, in the wake of Critical Linguistics, CDA further flourished to become a rich and multifaceted field which draws upon a variety of models of language to analyse a broad range of linguistic (lexical, grammatical and pragmatic) phenomena. This has given rise to a number of distinct programmes or 'approaches' in CDA which are focused on different features, forms and dimensions of discourse.

What all approaches to CDA have in common is (i) a view of language as instrumental in creating and sustaining relations of power and inequality; (ii) a view of texts as embedded in socio-historical and intertextual contexts; (iii) a commitment to lay bare or 'demystify' the ideological properties of texts that encode/enact power and inequality; and (iv) a commitment to using models of language developed in linguistics as the basis for analysis. This last point is important for it is not only what distinguishes CDA from other critical forms of discourse analysis, it is what takes us from impressions of or opinions about a text to more systematic and rigorous forms of analysis. As with CDA's sister discipline in Stylistics, then, CDA is committed, if not to 'objectivity' in the strict scientific sense, to research that is transparent, theoretically informed and, so long as the same model of language is being followed, replicable (see Stockwell, this volume, Chapter Thirteen). Applying linguistic models is also what allows us to make observations that lie beyond the purview of other readers. All readers are capable of critical reading. So CDA needs to bring something extra to the table; its analyses should be illuminatory. In having at one's disposal models of language, as well as other resources including the time, knowhow and materials to conduct research, studies in CDA should either say something about the text that other readers cannot, because the observation is only discernible in light of linguistic theory, or else supply evidence in support of analyses that are more intuitive.

More recently, as with many fields in the arts and humanities, CDA has undergone a number of radical 'turns', including a cognitive turn, a quantitative turn and a multimodal turn. These have occurred partly in response to criticisms of the field, partly due to developments in linguistics and the availability of new methods, and partly to keep up with changing discursive environments. I return to these in the section 'Developments in CDA'. In the section below, I highlight, through short exemplary analyses, just some of the textual practices frequently identified and analysed in CDA. Before we get to the sample analyses, though, two things are worth pointing out. First, although in each case I use data relating to one social topic, this is just for the sake of illustration. The same textual practices will be relevant in analysing discourses relating to other social topics. Second, the same textual practice can serve multiple functions within and across different discourses. Analyses must therefore be sensitive to the data and context in question.

2. CDA in practice: four examples

In the analyses that follow, it is important to recognise that texts are always a product of choices. For every linguistic unit in the text, alternative formulations are available. The choices presented by a text may have been made deliberately by individual writers/speakers or may be a consequence of genre conventions, institutionalised constraints, or just plain laziness. Whether deliberate or not, the choices presented by texts reflect the ideologised discourses of individuals or institutions and invite the reader to share in that worldview. Part of a critical analysis is to consider what other words, grammatical structures, figures of speech etc. could have been used and what the effects are of the selections that are presented.

2.1 Naming people: discourses of migration

When people are mentioned in a text, there are options in how to name them and the choices made have consequences for how the named persons are viewed – which aspects of their identity are foregrounded, which social stereotypes are drawn upon – and the relationship the reader builds with them. In CDA and linguistics, naming is technically a matter of **reference**. Naming choices are therefore sometimes called 'referential strategies'. Scholars in CDA have set out to describe the system of naming options open to speakers/writers in various inventories or typologies for the classification of social actors.

In discourses of migration, people may be referred to as individuals or as groups of people. Newspapers tend to represent powerful people as individuals and disempowered people as groups. By way of example, consider (1):

(1) <u>Immigrants</u> coming to the UK must learn English, <u>Gordon Brown</u> said yesterday. (*The Mirror*, 6 June 2006)

The effect of collectivising people in 'immigrants' is depersonalisation and the perpetuation of social stereotypes – in this case that all immigrants are unable to speak English. When people are represented as groups, they can be assigned numbers and treated merely as statistics, further depersonalising the reader's relationship with them:

(2) Almost <u>90,000 immigrants</u> entered the country in the past year – the highest number since records began. (*The Mirror*, 13 Sept. 2006)

'Immigrant' is a term used in official as well as media discourses of migration where it has a specific legal definition. The media, however, tend to use it interchangeably with other labels that have their own legal definitions, like 'refugee' and 'asylum seeker'. This is important because different labels access different stores of knowledge (known as **frames**) and invite different attitudes

12. Critical Discourse Analysis

and evaluations. For example, the term 'refugee' is suggestive of someone who is perhaps homeless or escaping persecution and in need of help. The use of the term 'migrant' over 'refugee' is more distancing, discourages sympathy and makes it easier to think about repatriation ('sending them home'). Other unofficial terms used to collectivise people in discourses of migration include 'foreigners', 'outsiders' and 'strangers' as in (3)-(5). Such examples not only depersonalise but differentiate. They create a sense of 'the Other' who doesn't belong 'here' or who is somehow different from 'us'.

(3) The latest survey on our attitudes to immigration shows that three quarters of Britons believe there are too many <u>foreigners</u> coming into the country. (*The Express*, 11 Dec. 2004)

(4) The Government is going out of its way to cater to vast numbers of <u>outsiders</u> but isn't looking after our old and ill. (*The Mirror*, 28 May 2002)

(5) The British are not racists. We have a long history of toleration and acceptance of <u>strangers</u>. (*Daily Mail*, 13 April 2000).

When people are identified as individuals, there are further choices in how to refer to them. Any individual has multiple identities and speakers/writers can choose which aspects of their identity to focus on. For example, when powerful people are individualised, they may have their titles or roles within an organisation given, further elevating their authority in a particular context and presenting their opinion as one that matters or which is more valid:

(6) Sir Andrew Green, <u>Chairman of Migrationwatch UK</u>, said the numbers still in Britain could be as high as 340,000 because estimates do not include dependents. (*The Express*, 14 March 2006)

People may be referred to in terms of other identity features, such as their legal status or their family role. In (7), it is the immigration status of the driver that is highlighted while for the victim it is their familial role as a father. There is no reference to whether the driver had a family. The formulation not only encourages sympathy with the bereaved family without affording any sympathy to the family of the driver but it also contains a kind of implicit 'logic' that if we had tougher enforcement of immigration laws, then this tragedy would have been avoided. The formulation thus turns a news report about a road traffic accident into an argument about immigration policy. The immigration status of the driver is otherwise irrelevant to the story. Were the driver not an 'illegal immigrant', their legal status or country of origin would almost certainly not have been mentioned.

167

(7) An illegal immigrant was convicted yesterday of killing a father of two teenagers after speeding with a 'seriously under-inflated' tyre. (*The Daily Telegraph*, 5 June 2004)

In a similar way, discourses of migration can be conflated with discourses of national security as in (8). Immigration and national security are two separate issues but by bringing them together in the same text, links are forged between them leading to the train of thought that if we put a stop to immigration then we put a stop to terrorism. In terms of naming, in (8) the individual is referred to in terms of their job role. This is especially significant in this context because the job in question further heightens the 'threat' posed by immigration as immigrants (who are also terrorists) are presented as able to access jobs in secure areas such as airports.

(8) The Heathrow worker, now in jail, was one of more than a dozen suspected terrorists allowed to enter Britain, it emerged this weekend. (*The Sunday Times*, 14 September 2003)

2.2 Describing actions and events: discourses of disorder

Just as people can be named in different ways, so the same action or event can be labelled differently. For example, whether a political demonstration is referred to as a 'riot' or a 'protest' tells a different version of events. While 'riot' emphasises violence, chaos and criminality, 'protest' suggests an organised expression of political discontent. Right-wing media especially prefer to characterise such instances of civil disorder as riots rather than protests. This is part of what is known as the 'protest paradigm', according to which mainstream media tend to focus on the violent and disruptive consequences of political protests rather than the causes behind them. Consider the contrast in headlines following the demonstrations against student fee increases in 2010:

(9) Student protests: school's out across the UK as children take to the streets (*Guardian*, 24 November 2010)

(10) Burning with anger: London streets in flames again as 25,000 go on rampage in new student fees riot (*Daily Mail*, 24 November 2010)

While contrasting ideological positions are revealed by looking at the nouns used to label events, then, more subtle insights may be gained by looking at the choice of verbs within a text. Different verbs describe different types of process or action. They also specify different types of role within the action. In CDA, this is captured by the term **transitivity** (in CDA, as in SFG, 'transitivity' is a broader concept than the number of complements required by a verb). For example, some verbs describe **verbal processes**, such as 'saying', 'asking', 'complaining'. Others describe **material processes**, such as 'running', 'kicking' or 'stealing'. The main role played in a verbal process is that of a 'sayer' while the main role played in a material process is that of a 'doer'. In discourses of disorder, this matters because if a text contains more verbal process verbs than material process verbs, it is likely to be focused less on the violent and disruptive consequences of the event and more on the message the event is aimed at delivering.

Even more subtle differences, which suggest competing discourses around citizenship and policing, occur in the grammatical choices made around verbs within these categories. For example, two different types of verb are regular transitive verbs and reciprocal verbs. Examples of regular transitive material process verbs are 'attack', 'kick' and 'strike'. **Regular transitive verbs** encode a single agent (the 'doer') who acts upon a patient (the 'done to'). Examples of reciprocal material process verbs include 'fight', 'clash' and 'collide'. **Reciprocal verbs** involve two agents acting equally upon one another (grammatically, reciprocal verbs can by followed by a preposition + reciprocal pronoun structure such as *with each other*). Across a number of studies looking at verb choice in press reports of violence at political protests, it has been found that the right-wing media prefer to use regular transitive verbs while more liberal newspapers prefer to use reciprocal verbs. The different strategies are exemplified in (11) and (12):

> (11) A number of police officers were injured after they came under attack from youths, some wearing scarves to hide their faces. (*The Daily Telegraph*, 10 November 2010)

> (12) Activists who had masked their faces with scarves traded punches with police. (*Guardian*, 10 November 2010)

While both examples focus on instances of violence, and thus conform to the protest paradigm, they configure the violent interaction in subtly different ways. The regular transitive verb in (11) presents the violence as one-sided with protesters the ones doing the attacking. (11) thus adheres to a discourse in which the police are seen only as victims of violence and not as perpetrators. By contrast, the reciprocal verb in (12) presents the violence as two-sided with both the police and the protesters playing their part in acting it out. The example in (12) therefore at least recognises a discourse of state violence in relation to the policing of political protests.

Potential references to violence can be avoided altogether through the use of **intransitive verbs** such as found in (13). Intransitive verbs are those that do not take a direct object and thus the action described does not directly affect a second participant. Examples of intransitive verbs include 'run', 'smile' and 'sleep'.

(13) About 50 riot police moved in just after 5pm as the majority of the protesters began to leave the scene (*The Independent*, 10 November 2010)

In (13), the intransitive verb ignores any resistance put up by the protesters and the response of the police in overcoming that resistance. In this context, then, the intransitive verb glosses over an important aspect of the event and is functionally linked to deletion, which we address in the following section.

2.3 Deletion: discourses of war

One key feature of language frequently commented upon in CDA is the ability that sentences have to omit crucial information while technically still telling the truth and remaining grammatically complete structures. This facility enables speakers/writer to describe actions in such a way that the people responsible for the action or those affected by it are deleted from the representation. One area where this has ideological implications is in the exercise of state power where events that are difficult to accept can be made more palatable either by disconnecting them from human actions or by overlooking their human consequences.

Deletion can be achieved in lots of ways, including verb choice, agentless passivisation and nominalisation. By way of example, consider this tweet issued by the *New York Times* after Israeli soldiers shot and killed a number of Palestinians protesting at the Gaza border:

(14) Dozens of Palestinians have died in protests as the US prepares to open its Jerusalem Embassy (https://twitter.com/nytimesworld/status/996009245853265920)

The verb 'die' in (14) is intransitive and therefore does not involve a second participant. Palestinians are the agents who do the dying themselves. The deaths are presented as just happening with the manner of death left a mystery. This is in contrast to transitive alternatives such as 'kill' where Palestinians would not be the ones doing the killing but the ones who are killed by a second participant. The intransitive verb therefore fails to disclose the cause of Palestinian deaths. The ideological nature of this representation is made clear in replies to the tweet. In the internet phenomenon that has come to be known by the initialism 'ftfy' ('fixed that for you'), critical readers reformulated the tweet in ways that recognise the role of Israeli forces in bringing about the deaths. All of these involve transitive verbs:

(15) WERE KILLED. They didn't all get sudden heart attacks.

(16) 'Dozens of Palestinians were shot to death by Israeli soldiers while protesting the US opening of the Jerusalem Embassy'... There, I fixed it for you'

12. Critical Discourse Analysis

(17) Here, I fixed it for you: Dozens of unarmed Palestinians have been <u>murdered</u> by Israeli forces in protests as the US prepares to open its Jerusalem Embassy.

However, even when transitive verbs are used, responsibility for the actions in not always explicitly spelled out. For example, the headline ran by the *Wall Street Journal*, reproduced in (18), reported the event using the **agentless passive voice**. In agentless passives, the 'by X' phrase containing the agent is left out but a grammatically complete sentence is still presented. The fact that the sentence remains grammatical means the deletion is easily missed by casual readers.

(18) Scores <u>Killed</u> as Palestinians Protest U.S. Embassy Opening in Jerusalem (*Wall Street Journal*, 14 May 2018)

This process of concealing agency goes a stage further in **nominalisation**. Nominalisation occurs when an action process is referred to by means of a noun rather than being described using a verb. English is rife with nominalisations – we all use them all of the time. In political discourse, however, they take on a particular ideological significance. As an example, consider the heading in (19) which the Wall Street Journal published alongside a video of the events on the Gaza border:

(19) <u>Clashes</u> Over New U.S. Embassy in Jerusalem Leave Dozens Dead (*Wall Street Journal*, 14 May 2018)

'Clashes' in this context is egregious because it characterises a brutal show of state power, in which it was only Palestinians who were killed or injured, as a two-sided event. It is also an instance of nominalisation. *Clash* is a verb that would normally occur in sentences of the form *X clashed with Y* or *X and Y clashed with each other*. Collapsing a full clause into a noun means that certain details are lost, such as who was involved as well as what exactly happened where and when (which may be expressed as part of a circumstantial clause attached to a main clause). The nominalisation in (19) thus avoids reference to those responsible for the deaths. It also avoids reference to who it was that died which, together with the indefinite 'dozens' means we don't learn that it was only Palestinians. But more than that, nominalisation means that the new nominalised form can feature as an actor in the process described by another verb. Thus, in (19) it is the event itself, rather than another participant in it, that 'leaves' the Palestinians dead.

What these various forms of deletion do, in this context, is paint over the role of Israeli forces in bringing about the deaths of Palestinian civilians. Faced with reporting actions that don't fit with most ethical standards, by disconnecting them from human actors, deletion allows speakers/writers to protect the reputation and legitimacy of those responsible – in this case the State of Israel.

2.4 Figurative language: discourses of migration

One form of figurative language that is especially significant for CDA is metaphor. A metaphor is a figure of speech that describes or refers to one thing in terms usually associated with another. In doing so, metaphors liken one thing to something else. Metaphors differ from similes, however, in that they don't explicitly signal the comparison being made using 'like' or 'as'. Metaphors are normally associated with literary writing where they often stand out as novel and highly creative forms of language. But they are also prevalent in political discourse where they follow more conventional patterns and thus seem less remarkable. It is precisely this 'unremarkability', however, that makes metaphors in political discourse so ideologically effective because they communicate ideas and values subtly and indirectly. CDA is therefore interested in systematic rather than isolated instances of metaphor. That means metaphors that take different linguistic forms but which repeat a common, underlying semantic association. When metaphors occur systematically in texts they are indicative of particular discourses or worldviews.

Metaphors have different functions in different discursive contexts. In anti-immigration discourses, a frequent function of metaphors is dehumanisation. This can be seen when we read reports of migrants 'flooding' or 'pouring' in or about a 'tidal wave' or even a 'tsunami' of migrants on the way. The metaphors all compare migrants to large and dangerous quantities of water. Another group of metaphors that serve a dehumanising function are those that compare migrants to animals. As a quite salient example, consider the following remarks made by Donald Trump in May 2018:

> (20) We have people coming into the country, or trying to come in – and we're stopping a lot of them – but we're taking people out of the country. You wouldn't believe how bad these people are. These aren't people. <u>These are animals.</u> And we're taking them out of the country at a level and at a rate that's never happened before. And because of the weak laws, they come in fast, we get them, we release them, we get them again, we bring them out. It's crazy.

In (20), Trump describes people as animals. This explicit statement of the form A IS B attracted a lot of attention with some dispute over whether the comment referred to unauthorised migrants in general or whether the President was referring specifically to migrants who belong to a gang known as MS-13. The ambiguity cannot be completely resolved and we may never know Trump's real intentions. But that is in a way beside the point. The issue is whether the metaphor may be taken as talking about migrants more generally and whether

12. Critical Discourse Analysis

or not it is an isolated instance. Here, context is important. The comment was made during a roundtable meeting dedicated to discussing migration to the US. The linguistic context (known as **co-text**) is also important. What is the **antecedent** of the **anaphor** 'these' in 'these are animals'? The nearest candidate is the indefinite noun phrase 'people' which would seem to cover all migrants rather than a specific subset. Co-text and intertextual context are also significant in working out whether this example is a one-off or if it forms part of a pattern of representation. Elsewhere in this text, for example, Trump is recorded as saying:

> (21) In January, the Los Angeles Police Department arrested an illegal immigrant from Mexico for drug possession. Instead of honoring the ICE detainer, they <u>set him free</u>.

'Set free', like 'release' in (20), is a phrase we often associate with captured wild animals. And the referent in this example is clearly identified as 'an illegal immigrant from Mexico' rather than an MS-13 gang member. In another text, this time a tweet, Trump said the following:

> (22) Democrats are the problem. They don't care about crime and want illegal immigrants, no matter how bad they may be, to pour into and <u>infest</u> our Country, like MS-13. They can't win on their terrible policies, so they view them as potential voters! (https://twitter.com/realDonaldTrump/status/1009071403918864385)

Again, the reference is clearly to 'illegal immigrants'. MS-13 is given as an example of the category illegal immigrants but it is the broader category that is the subject of 'infest', a verb normally reserved for talking about insects. In another tweet, Trump spoke of sanctuary cities as 'breeding concepts' for illegal migrants (https://twitter.com/realDonaldTrump/status/986544648477868032).

From these examples, a pattern begins to emerge which suggests a worldview in which migrants are associated with animals. It is also worth pointing out that this textual practice is not unique to Trump but characteristic of right-wing discourses on migration more generally. For example, in Britain the media regularly describe migrants as 'flocking', as exemplified by the following headline:

> (24) Nearly 500,000 refugees and their kids could flock to Britain from EU by 2020 (*Daily Mirror*, 31 May 2016)

In an interview for ITV news at the height of the refugee crisis in Europe, David Cameron is recorded as saying:

> (25) You've got a <u>swarm</u> of people coming across the Mediterranean seeking a better life.

In a notorious text published by *The Sun*, the columnist Katie Hopkins similarly stated that British towns are 'festering sores, plagued by swarms of migrants and asylum seekers' before using the following simile:

(26) Make no mistake, these migrants are like cockroaches (Katie Hopkins, *The Sun*, 17 April 2015)

These forms of language cannot be dismissed as 'mere figures of speech'. Language that dehumanises people is what makes it possible to treat people as less than human. The metaphors strip people of their human qualities making it easier to accept treating them like animals – locking them in cages, separating children from their parents. Moreover, the metaphors we find here don't compare migrants to any type of animal but to animals that are low down in the Great Chain of Being (a mythical hierarchy of all matter and life that serves as a kind of moral guide in western cultures) and which are associated with damage and disease. This kind of language has been shown to have a real, measurable impact in arousing negative feelings like fear and disgust toward migrants. And in history, dehumanising language has preceded the most devastating human actions. The current language around migration carries worrying echoes of, is intertextually related to, the language of the Nazis. A principle concept in the Nazi ideology was that of ***untermenschen*** (subhumans). In 1939, after visiting Jews in the Łodz ghetto, Joseph Goebbels wrote *'Jews are not people; they are animals'*. In the Nazi propaganda film *The Eternal Jew* (1940), Jewish people were likened to rats. For example, at one point the narrator says:

(27) Just as rats are the vermin of the animal kingdom, Jews are the vermin of the human race and similarly spread disease and corruption.

And in *Mein Kampf*, Hitler's (1925) autobiography-come-manifesto outlining his ideology and future plans, Jewish people are variously referred to as 'spiders', 'rats' and (in the example below) 'parasites' consuming Germany:

(28) But his spreading is the typical symptom of all parasites; he always looks for a new feeding soil for his race.

Of course, the actions of the Trump administration, however abhorrent, are not, at the time of writing, comparable to the actions of the Nazis but the obvious parallels in language do have the potential to send us down a similar path.

3. Developments in CDA

CDA has received a number of criticisms over the years. However, these criticisms have spurred a number of innovations in the field. In this last section, I will briefly highlight three key criticisms and the new approaches to CDA that have developed in response.

CDA is too focused on language

CDA developed out of linguistics and thus language has always been of primary concern. However, contemporary texts are rarely monomodal. Instead, texts are multimodal, composed of material belonging to more than one semiotic mode. For example, many texts, such as print and online news articles, are made up of both language and images. And the images in a text are equally significant in supporting specific ideological worldviews.

In response to this issue and in order to study texts that are increasingly visual in nature, CDA has undergone a 'multimodal turn'. Here, CDA has found that many of the textual practices observed in language are also discernible in images. For example, in the visual equivalent of transitivity, social actors can be depicted in different types of process which can be 'transitive' or 'intransitive'. Actors can also be deleted from the representation. By way of example, consider the three images below, taken from the online contents of the *Wall Street Journal* and the *New York Times* and documenting events on the Gaza border. Images are given together with their captions.

a. *Palestinian protesters look up at falling gas cannisters near the border with Israel in the southern Gaza Strip on Tuesday* (*Wall Street Journal,* 14 May 2018) © Said Khatib/ Agence France-Presse/Getty Images

b. *Palestinians carry a man injured during clashes with Israeli forces near the border between the Gaza Strip and Israel on Monday* (*Wall Street Journal*, 14 May 2018)
© Mahmud Hams/Agence france-Presse/Getty Images

c. *Israeli soldiers across the border from the Gaza Strip watched the protestors* (*New York Times*, 14 May 2018) © Jack Guez/Agence France-Presse/Getty Images

12. Critical Discourse Analysis

In multimodal texts, language and image work together in the creation of meaning with representations in each modality often converging on a single narrative; that is, 'telling the same story'. News photographs and their captions are a prime example of this. In each of the examples above, Israeli forces are disconnected from the killing of Palestinians as their role in the violent and fatal attacks is omitted from the representation in both the linguistic and the visual text. For example, in (a), tear gas canisters are described as 'falling' – an intransitive verb – without any reference to who fired them. Correspondingly, in the image, the canisters appear falling from the sky like rain. The image does not show the canisters as being fired by a human agent. In (b), the caption uses the agentless passive 'injured' so that there is no reference to who the man was injured by. Similarly, in the image, we are shown only the injured man and learn nothing of how he came to be injured. Finally, in (c), Israeli soldiers are referred to in the caption and do appear in the image. However, in both the caption and the image they are disconnected from killing Palestinians as the process they are described/depicted as engaged in is a mental process of 'watching', which does not involve any direct contact with or impact on the protesting Palestinians.

Other areas where language and image can converge are metaphor and predication. To illustrate this, consider the headline and accompanying image below published by the *Daily Star* in 2016.

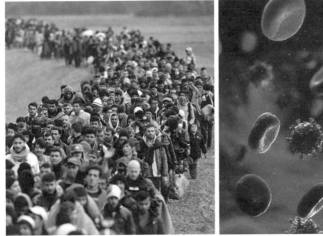
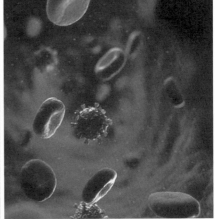

d. *Refugees flocking to Britain are carrying deadly superbugs, warn experts* (Daily Star, 12 April 2016) © Getty

In (d), the headline uses the verb 'flocking' to describe the movement of refugees. When used in relation to human beings, this verb, as we saw in the previous section, produces a metaphor in which people are likened to animals.

The first part of the accompanying image strengthens this association as people are depicted in a herd-like formation. If you search Google Images for the phrase 'flock of animals' you will find images that bear an uncanny resemblance to this picture. The 'syntax' of the headline and image also correspond. Every complete sentence contains two parts: a subject and a predicate. The subject is who or what the sentence is about while the predicate tells us something about the subject. In the headline, the subject is 'refugees flocking to Britain' and the predicate is 'are carrying deadly superbugs'. Now, if we 'read' the image from left to right, as most English speakers will, then the two parts of the image mirror the subject-predicate structure of the headline. The left part of the image shows who the image is about, in this case refugees, while the right part of the image tells us something about them. The right part of the image is a visualisation of red blood cells surrounded by the human immunodeficiency virus (HIV) that causes AIDS. Taken as whole, the image therefore suggests, in harmony with the headline, that refugees are carriers of HIV.

Data in CDA is not representative.

The data selected for analysis in CDA is often only exemplary and fragmentary. Therefore, it may not necessarily be reflective of typical textual practices. There is, instead, a danger that data has been cherry-picked to suit the analyst's political agenda or to illustrate a theoretical point.

To address this issue, quantitative methods based in Corpus Linguistics are now frequently deployed in CDA. Corpora are large bodies of texts which, using computer software, can be automatically searched for repeated patterns of representation (this is more difficult for images). This allows researchers in CDA to check their intuitions that a text or feature is typical of a given discourse as well as discover patterns that they had not intuited. For example, corpus-based analyses confirm that discourses of migration in the British press tend to revolve around a limited number of topics, routinely present migration as a 'problem', and frequently refer to migrants in numerical terms. Corpus-based studies in CDA have also shown that dehumanising metaphors are a salient feature of right-wing discourses about migration.

CDA is too subjective.

Analyses in CDA are necessarily subjective, reliant on the researchers' reading of the text in light of their knowledge about the historical, socio-political context in which it was produced. However, there is a risk that analyses represent only the researcher's interpretation of the text which, biased by their own political point of view, may be an over-interpretation. No evidence is presented that readers respond to texts in the ways predicted by analyses in CDA.

To address this issue, CDA has developed cognitive and experimental methodologies drawing on Cognitive Linguistics and Psycholinguistics. By adopting analytical frameworks based in Cognitive Linguistics, a psychological theory of language, researchers in CDA have been able to consider the mental representations activated by specific textual features. For example, in Cognitive Linguistics, metaphors in texts are not considered incidentals, there for purposes of literary ornamentation. Rather, metaphors in texts are cues for cognitive processes in which one thing is genuinely understood, imagined and reasoned about in terms of another. Approaches to CDA based in Cognitive Linguistics shift the emphasis from the text itself to the cognitive processes involved in text reception but they do not empirically demonstrate the effects of texts on social perceptions, attitudes, inferences etc. This is taken up by approaches inspired by Psycholinguistics which uses experimental methods to empirically investigate the influence of texts. Here, for example, it has been shown that the use of regular transitive versus reciprocal verbs in press reports of violence at political protests affects the way readers assign blame for the violence and the level of aggression they perceive in the social actors involved. It has also been shown that when they are not blocked by incongruent images in the same text, fire metaphors in media reports of political protest, such as 'the protest engulfed the city', conjure mental images of fire which facilitate support for police use of water canon as a means of controlling civil disorder.

4. Key ideas to consider and further reading

- Critical Discourse Analysis sees language as central to the creation and maintenance of power in society and the critical study of language as a way of exploring and challenging such power structures.

- The close analysis of texts, focusing on a range of linguistic features from lexical to grammatical choices and beyond to the role of metaphor and interplay of text and image, can expose the ideologies that lie behind them.

- Critical Discourse Analysis has developed to take account of the changing nature of language in the modern world and to explore the role of language in shaping perceptions of different individuals and groups in society, using methods from cognitive and corpus linguistics to enhance this.

References

BAKER, P., 2006. *Using corpora in discourse analysis.* London: Continuum.

FAIRCLOUGH, N., 2014. *Language and power* (3rd edn.). London: Routledge.

HART, C., 2014. *Discourse, Grammar and ideology: functional and cognitive perspectives.* London: Bloomsbury.

JEFFRIES, L., 2010. *Critical stylistics: the power of language.* Basingstoke: Palgrave.

MACHIN, D. and A. Mayr, 2012. *How to do critical discourse analysis: a multimodal introduction*. London: Sage.

MUSOLFF, A., 2016. *Political metaphor analysis: discourse and scenarios*. London: Bloomsbury.

RICHARDSON, J.E., 2007. *Analysing newspapers: an approach from critical discourse analysis*. Basingstoke: Palgrave.

WODAK, R. and M. Meyer, 2009. *Methods of critical discourse studies*. London: Sage.

13 TEXTUAL ANALYSIS & STYLISTICS

Professor Peter Stockwell

1. From impression to analysis

Everyone who can speak and read can say something interesting and analytical about any piece of language. Every text in the world that you come across is the product of choices made by someone: which words to select, which order to put them in, where and when to say or write them; who is implicitly addressed, what effect or purpose seems to be intended, and so on. For most people, such observations tend to be highly intuitive and impressionistic. People observe things about texts and utterances like *that sounded rude; that makes me laugh; the language there sounds flowery and fancy*. Sometimes, such impressions can also be a little more technical: *that instruction was too direct; there was no 'please' or 'thanks'; that joke sends you in one direction, and then fools you with a double-meaning; there are too many flowery and overly-poetic adjectives*. These impressions can begin to be considered as being analytical, though we might say they are examples of sensitive language-awareness, or close-reading. If the person making the comments also possessed a little technical knowledge of how language *really* works, then their observations are likely to be far less impressionistic: *the politeness markers there are entirely self-oriented; the ambivalence of that word at the beginning of the joke triggers the release; the frequent pre-modification with archaic lexis creates a self-consciously poetic effect*. These sorts of analytical comments are more precise; they draw on a systematic description of language from the discipline of linguistics; they account for an initial intuitive response: they are examples of **stylistics**.

Stylistics is the application of language study to the choices that are made in texts. Stylisticians tend to explore the language of literary and highly creative texts such as interesting advertising, song lyrics, poetry, prose and drama, though there is also a strong tradition of the stylistic analysis of non-literary texts (political speeches and documents, media articles, television and web broadcasting, and so on). This latter form tends to be called **critical discourse analysis** or even simply **text analysis**, with **stylistics** now largely being reserved for what is also sometimes called **literary linguistics**. It ought to be obvious and self-evident that, since literature is composed of language, it makes sense that its primary form of study should involve some proper understanding of linguistics. However, much literary criticism in the world foregrounds literary history, literary biography, or cultural studies over the textual reality of the literary work. While such studies are interesting, I would argue that only stylistics is directly aimed at the literary text itself.

The beauty of stylistics is that you only need to know a little of how language works in order to begin to explore how literary texts work. You can start to see how a piece of literature creates its particular effects in a reader, because you can see the workings of those features of language in yourself. You don't need a particular sensitivity, or inexplicable moment of magical revelation. You don't have to become adept in the mysterious practices of a private club: you simply need a little training in language study. Then you will pretty much understand the workings of any literary text from any historical period by any writer, within a very short period of time. In other words, stylistics offers you a toolkit for textual analysis, which is open to anyone who cares to take it up, and it is always enormously empowering.

Stylistics is a discipline: this means that it has particular principles and customary methods that you need to understand from the beginning. Its foundational principles are:

- Systematic: the stylistic method involves the application of a particular linguistic framework or exploration of a defined set of features, in a way that is rational and logical.

- Rigorous: the analysis of the literary text has to be precise and accurate.

- Transparent: the account or explanation of the analysis should be as full, clear and open as possible.

- Replicable: it should be possible to understand how the account of the text and its reading could also be held by another reader of the same text.

These principles owe more to the scientific method than to the usual chatter of art criticism, though it is important to recognise that stylistics cannot be a natural science, like physics or biology. This is because even the language features of a fixed text can change their significance over time, and readers bring their social experiences and their individual subjectivities with them. Stylistics is a bit more like a social science (such as psychology or sociology), but I think it is best described as an artful science.

Opinions and judgements in stylistics are always based on evidence from the text. There are several types of evidence that stylisticians use in order to justify their literary critical judgements. Firstly, **introspection** is a very powerful form of evidence: asking yourself whether your systematic stylistic analysis corresponds with your intuitive sense of your own reading is usually the first form of validation. The transparent and replicable feature of stylistic description ensures that this introspection is then available for clear comparison with other readers' intuitions.

Secondly, stylistics uses **linguistic models** that have been generated by linguistics to account for the language system in general. This means that they already have a prior form of validity: we don't have a separate bit of our brains that 'does' literature, so our general language capacity must be the basis for our literary readings, with some obvious adjustments. If a linguistic framework or model seems to work in a literary context, that in itself is a form of evidence.

Thirdly, stylisticians often invoke other **readers' responses** as evidence for a particular explanation. These readers can include other literary critics throughout history, who have usefully recorded their own readings in books and articles if they are professional academic scholars, or in magazines and blogs if they are non-professional readers. Many book-groups of people who read and discuss literature record their observations online, or can be recorded by a stylistic researcher. All of these types of readers offer a comparison for the stylistic analysis of the text.

Fourthly, a stylistician can exercise more control over such responses by setting up **a designed experimental situation**, for example by devising questionnaires or protocols to ask readers for their responses to a literary text. Even more objective methods can be used, such as eye-tracking machines that measure reading times, sensors that measure the physical skin effects of literary reading, and so on. These can also be set against the stylistic analysis of the text under investigation.

Finally, stylisticians can now use large collections of texts in digital form, and computer software to find patterns across a large body (**a corpus**) of texts. This **corpus stylistics** allows us to see features that would have been very difficult to find with an old-fashioned pencil and book. The software can find stylistic evidence across a whole novel, collection of stories or poems, or across an author's lifetime of writing.

2. A brief family history of stylistics

The discipline of stylistics has several forebears, cousins and relatives, since its interdisciplinarity means that it draws on many other fields. These include obvious close siblings in literary criticism and critical theory, theoretical and applied linguistics, psychology and sociology. However, it also has more distant relations in neuroscience and cognitive science, politics and economics, and some surprising long-lost relatives in bible translation and interpretation (**hermeneutics**), and in ancient Greek, Roman, Arabic and Indian rhetoric.

For example, Aristotle set out in his books *Rhetoric* and *Poetics* some of the key features of language that are significant in textual analysis, just under 2500 years ago.

More recently, stylistics in its current form emerged alongside the development of modern linguistics across the twentieth century. In searching for similarities across the language families of the world, the philologists of the previous century had discovered that language could be accounted for in terms of rules, patterns and principles that went far beyond and deeper than the traditional study of grammar that had been part of the education of boys and some wealthy girls in Britain for the previous millennium. Modern linguistics separated out the underlying principles and structures of language (our **competence**) from the actual surface utterance coming out of your mouth or the writing appearing on paper or screen (our **performance**). One branch of theoretical linguistics set out to discover the deep structure principles of competence, and another branch of linguistics aimed to explore the functional, dialectal and idiosyncratic uses of performance in the world – stylistics developed from this latter direction.

At the same time, literary criticism in Britain in the 1920s and 30s, and in the US in the 1940s and 50s, was reacting against the sort of cosy gentlemen's club atmosphere of biographical criticism that had prevailed at the time. Instead, a **New Criticism** was coming into being that rejected all talk either of authors and literary history on the one hand, and readers and their psychology on the other. The text itself and the form of the words themselves became the focus of discussion, and this **formalism** required a close and systematic reading of literary texts. Simultaneously in Eastern Europe, a formalist tradition was emerging that set itself the goal of explaining what literary language was and what was the essence of literariness. And in Western Europe, especially in France, a **structuralist** movement set out to find universal and common patterns across different literary works and across different literary cultures and languages.

All of this forms the ancestry of the discipline, which emerged more or less simultaneously as **stylistique** in France, **stilistik** in Germany and Austria, and **stylistics** in Britain in the 1960s. At first, the relatively simple tools of linguistics allowed stylisticians only to explore the sounds of poetry (from phonetics), the forms of word-building (morphology and lexicology), the structure of clauses (syntax) and their meanings (semantics). Nevertheless, this allowed us to produce detailed and evidenced literary appreciations of some of the great works of English poetry. Attention shifted to the analysis of prose fiction and wider issues of poetic addressivity and dialogue during the 1970s as developments in language study created more tools for analysis. For example, the expansion in the field of pragmatics meant that issues of contextual meaning, the force of literary works, and the impact of drama could be explored systematically: studies included explorations of political messages underlying the fictional viewpoint of characters, or the politeness and power relations in plays.

Over the next few years, stylistics grew its capacity for going beyond the level of clause and sentence in order to explore whole texts and discourses, and the relationships between narrators and characters on the page and the stage. Sociolinguistic work allowed us to explore the power-relations encoded in language in prose fiction and in plays. The ideologies of writers and of readers became a crucial element in many stylistic analyses, signalling a significant shift away from the formalism of the early years. While the stylistics of the 1980s and early 90s remained shy of engaging in systematic discussion of authors and historical context, the New Critical bar on bringing readers' responses, felt effects and psychologies into the discussion was often discarded.

The turn of the century was marked in stylistics by two general innovations that have transformed the field. Firstly, the development of digitisation and computer programs to search large swathes of literary text has created **corpus stylistics**. These techniques have allowed us to explore entire novels, for example, with as much attention to detail and systematicity as we were able to manage with short poetry texts or prose excerpts. Corpus stylistics also has a strong historical dimension, since most examples of digitised literary works occur within larger bodies of digitised texts of various other non-literary sorts. This allows precise and rigorous claims to be made about the historical context and culture of literature on the basis of firm evidence.

Secondly, most fields in arts, humanities and social science have developed a 'cognitive turn' over the last few years, as research into mind, brain and cognition (collectively a cognitive science) has created a **cognitive poetics** as a form of stylistics. This draws in insights from **cognitive psychology** (such as how we picture fictional worlds or draw on our own memories and experience) and **cognitive linguistics** (how we pay more or less attention to different parts of a sentence and text). It allows us to discuss the relationships between different people – whether they are authors, narrators, characters or readers – along consistent principles, even though some of those people simply happen to be fictional. It allows us to explore the choices that authors made within their language systems, and account for emotional and striking effects in readers. With the tools now at our disposal, in fact, stylisticians are able to do most of the things that literary criticism regards as its own domain, but with the advantage of system, rigour, clarity and openness. Indeed, stylistics by now is almost unrecognisable from its forebears, resembling them only as a distant cousin or great-grandchild might.

Of course, stylistics has attracted criticism from several sides. From the perspective of pure linguistics, the analysis of literature and literary reading involves too much subjective interpretation for comfort. From the perspective of literary criticism, the analysis of literary texts as data feels uncomfortable.

However, these are matters which can be addressed by paying attention to the careful methods involved in stylistics: dealing directly with interpretation as a matter of language processing; dealing directly with literary value as a consequence of prestigious styles.

Stylistics has been criticised for being too formalist – for focusing on particular linguistic features while ignoring the essential elements of cultural value, or higher level matters such as theme, interpretation or significance. This might have been true in the past, though even the so-called Russian Formalists of the 1920s were never completely blind to context and setting. However, contemporary stylisticians now have the means of discussing these matters of culture, value and interpretation, as outlined above. Stylistics is nowhere near as formalist as literary critics in general think.

Stylistics has also been criticised for being ahistorical, so the stylistic choices explored in a text are measured against our own meanings, rather than against historically contemporaneous meanings. Again, this was possibly true in the past, but recent stylistic work has also explored the choices that are apparent in archived versions of manuscripts. So stylistics is perfectly capable of operating in the service of historicism, when appropriate.

Stylistics has been criticised for focusing on meaning, rather than feeling, value or significance. It is probably true that the tools of linguistic analysis from phonetics to syntax and semantics encourage an emphasis on **denotation** rather than sensation, local meaning rather than social and cultural meaning. However, literary stylistics has benefitted a great deal from the analysis of ideology and politics in **critical discourse analysis**, and much of our work concerns value and significance. Recent advances in **cognitive poetics** are allowing us to explore feeling and emotional effects in principled ways which are a great improvement on the impressionism and inarticulacy of much literary theorising. To give a single example, we now have a good understanding of how a reader can empathise or not with particular characters as if they were real people, and this offers us a powerful means of accounting for emotional involvement (absorption) in a literary world.

Stylistic analysis has been criticised for being too reductive: aiming to discover general patterns and principles across literature without sufficient regard being given to the particularity of the literary text at hand. Certainly, early stylistics often looked at texts that were linguistically deviant or odd in some way, partly because they are the easiest and most exciting for a stylistician. However, you will find a greater range of literature amongst the work of contemporary stylisticians. While it is true that common patterns are of interest across literary works, the discovery of such patterns is a consequence of pretty much all human investigation of anything, so this criticism seems to me simply a recognition that stylistics is a systematic discipline rather than an artistic enterprise in itself. Sometimes work in narrative or cognitive universals can risk losing sight of the literary text altogether, but it is precisely the demand from stylistics that evidence should be rooted in texts and textuality that saves the discipline from losing the individual singularity of a literary work.

Lastly, a criticism levelled at stylistics is that the process of analysis produces the very features that the field claims to be describing. In other words, if you look hard enough for a thing, you will convince yourself that it is there. It seems to me there are two forms of this criticism. Firstly, the notion that the application of a stylistic framework creates the feature under analysis can be easily refuted by pointing out that any reader is invited to agree with the analysis or not, that evidence cannot be produced where none exists, and that often stylistic analysis accords with pre-analytical intuition.

A stronger form of the criticism would say that some of the tiny details produced under analysis cannot possibly be noticed by a casual reader, since the level of detail in the stylistic analysis is far richer than any possible conscious awareness. There are a couple of responses to this. Firstly, it can be argued that sub-conscious or subliminal effects have a significant general consequence for a sense of tone or atmosphere, and a detailed stylistic analysis can make these textual mechanics visible. Secondly, if it is true that detailed analysis can be productive of new insight, then this seems to me not so much a problem as a positive advantage in rendering a literary reading even richer than at first glance. This argument places stylistics as a form of appreciation, both in the approving sense and also in the sense that the literary work grows in richness as a result.

3. A simple stylistic analysis

3.1 A simple practical example

As will be clear by now, stylistics is a multi-faceted discipline that operates on several levels, so presenting an exemplary analysis here that captures all or even most of that is not going to be possible. However, by way of illustration, here is a very short poem that is worth exploring for several reasons. Firstly, it is by Shelley and is quite famous, and it is always interesting to see what stylistics can find that is new, even in well-worn texts. Secondly, even though it is short, it is amazingly rich in texture, so there is plenty to discover. Lastly, I have produced a very full analysis of the poem elsewhere, so an interested reader can look up the same text under a more detailed and advanced analysis (Stockwell 2009: 68-78). Here is the complete poem:

> **To ———**
> Music, when soft voices die,
> Vibrates in the memory—
> Odours, when sweet violets sicken,
> Live within the sense they quicken.

> Rose leaves, when the rose is dead,
> Are heaped for the belovèd's bed;
> And so thy thoughts, when thou art gone,
> Love itself shall slumber on.
>
> *Percy Shelley (1970: 639, publ. 1824)*

To start with a bit of historical context, the poem is labelled as having been written in Pisa in 1821. Percy Shelley died the following year, and the text was edited by his wife Mary and published in 1824. The blank in the title is usually taken to refer to her, though Shelley has a reputation that suggests this might not be an entirely safe assumption.

Now a simple analysis of the poem's syntax, because intuitively there seems to be several examples of repetition in the structure of the text:

NP	[conj	NP (pre-mod+N)	VP]	VP	prep	NP
Music	when	soft voices	die	Vibrates	in	the memory
Odours	when	sweet violets	sicken	Live	within	the sense they quicken
Rose leaves	when	the rose	is dead	Are heaped	for	the belovèd's bed

Table 1

It is immediately apparent that the first three sentences here are closely parallel. Each consists of a noun-phrase (NP), followed by an embedded clause (indicated here by the square brackets), then a verb-phrase (VP), and a final prepositional phrase consisting of a preposition and a final noun-phrase. The embedded clause has a repeated structure, with an identical conjunction *when*, followed by a noun-phrase that always consists of a pre-modifier (*soft, sweet, the*) and a noun (*voices, violets, rose*).

There are further repeated patterns on even closer inspection, when we also consider the meanings of the words in each syntactic position. For example, the initial noun-phrase comes from the relative clause: *music* comes from *soft voices*, *odours* arise from *sweet violets*, and *Rose leaves* fall from the *rose*. The verb-phrases within each of these relative clauses are also all from the same semantic domain: *die, sicken, is dead*. The semantic progression of each sentence moves from sound (*Music*) to smell (*Odours*) to a combined sight and touch (*Rose leaves*) – from most intangible to most material. And there is even a nice matching of form and sense (we call this **iconicity**) where each single sense is realised by a single word, but the doubled sense is realised by two words, *Rose leaves*.

Further details reveal themselves on even closer analysis. Within the relative clauses, the noun-phrases consist of a pre-modifier and a noun. The first two (*soft voices*, *sweet violets*) are closely echoic and the pre-modifiers *soft* and *sweet* are semantically related, and conventionally suggestive of feminine qualities, perhaps. This encourages a reading of *the rose* as a metaphor or symbol for the (male) speaker's female lover. The movement also goes from music placed inside the mind (*in the memory*), to fragrance within the body's senses, to rose leaves placed *on the belovèd's bed*. This goes from interior to exterior, and from perceptual to sensual, gradually. Even in the final prepositions, there is a similar movement from past (***in*** *... memory*), through present immediacy (***within***, meaning 'alongside' the senses), to a prospective future (***for*** *... the belovèd's bed*).

So what we have is an attractive surface repetition and appealing regularity, but with quite a lot of movement and variation beneath. The effect seems to me to be pleasant and seductive, but there are hints of disruption even in these first six lines. The final noun-phrase of each sentence is only roughly repeated, but each is internally variable from the others. The confusing doubled phrase (*Rose leaves*), unlike the previous two nouns (*Music* and *Odours*) also has a potential alternative meaning ('rose' as the past form of 'rise', and 'leaves' as the third person verb-form of 'to leave') that the other words do not have. In the context of a dead female lover, rise and leave are desirable but not realised here.

Overall, there is a subtle sense that the woman is being effaced: she is blanked in the title, reduced to her perceptions and senses only, metaphorised as a rose, and passivised (*Are heaped*) out of the scene. This initial sense, evident even in the apparently affectionate first six lines, is further developed by the disruption in the final sentence. Having trained the reader in a particular pattern three times, the poem upsets this comforting form:

NP	[conj	NP (pre-mod+N)	VP]	VP	prep	NP
And so thy thoughts	when	thou	art gone			
Love						itself
				shall slumber	on	

Table 2

Whenever I get anyone to read this poem aloud to someone who has never seen it before, they always trip up over these final two lines. They are expecting the same pattern, and the poem almost provides it, but deviates away in a particularly tricky manner. It begins as customary with a noun-phrase (*And so thy thoughts*), but this is complex compared with the previous three examples: the *And* suggests it is picking up a prior line of thought; but the *so* points forward to some as-yet-unrealised logical completion. In spite of this initial deviance, the next part of the poem looks at first like another relative clause introduced by a 'when' conjunction, but it turns out to be a single noun noun-phrase (*thou*) and a complex verb-phrase (*art gone*). Even with this signal that things have been disrupted, many readers still try to keep to the established pattern by reading *Love* (just like *Vibrates*, *Live*, and *Are heaped*) as a verb, but the reflexive *itself* quickly makes you realise it is a noun. The verb-phrase that follows is a complex mix-up of the established verb-phrase plus prepositional phrase: *shall slumber on*. The temptation is to read *Love* as a transitive verb as in 'thy thoughts love X', even in spite of the recursion of *itself*, and so readers often go looking for a main verb for the subject *thy thoughts*. However, the verb *shall slumber on* has been deflected to collocate with *Love itself*, and so *thy thoughts* are left hanging, verbless, moodless, and dissatisfyingly incomplete.

The poem holds out your mental faculties and consciousness, through the metaphors of echoing music, persisting fragrance or symbolic roses, as a potential comfort against death, only to whip that possibility away so that it really means what it says *when thou art gone*. The poem ends by replacing the sensual with the abstract *Love*, capitalised as a quality rather than actualised as a verb.

So far, I have restricted myself almost entirely simply to a description of the text, mainly focusing on syntax but noticing when other dimensions of the poem (semantics or iconicity) align themselves with the syntactic analysis. Of course, so far this is a linguistic account, not a stylistic one, because we have more or less simply labelled the text rather than said anything about the significance of the patterns we have noticed. The linguistic description of features above is mainly unarguable, it seems to me: I have not imagined the patterns I have outlined – they are there, plainly described for all to see. However, lining up this descriptive account with a thematic interpretation is where stylistics moves from something roughly scientific to something more artful.

3.2. From stylistic description to significance

What is the significance of the poem's disjunction? It is possible to read the poem not as a love-lyric that conventionally asserts the persistence of love beyond death, but as a more general statement of the spiritual over the material. This could be religious, but isn't, not only because you might import Shelley's famous atheism into the poetic voice but also because the poem had a chance at Christian redemption (*rose* as the past participle of 'risen') and chose not to take it. Alternatively, you could focus on the symbolic aspects of the poem and read it as a text about the persistence of art (the word *art* occurs, and is about *itself*). The seductive echoic sound-patterns of the poem represent art for art's sake, in this reading.

Alternatively again, you could place the poem back into its moment in history and notice that the choice of fragrant flowers sets Napoleon (known as 'Corporal violet') of France against the rose of England. Napoleon also collected violets from the tomb of Josephine to take into exile with him, and his supporters wore violet as a symbol of their loyalty. The falling rhythm of the poem's syntax, ending in dissatisfaction (a form of bathos) then represents the promise of the political revolutionary who became a despot, in Shelley's radical political view. Another poem in the same collection is a withering condemnation of Napoleon.

Or by contrast you could remove the poem from its moment of history and from Shelley's own voice, and read it as a dramatic monologue in which a general poetic voice contemplates art. The title's blank becomes universal, the present tense propositions then appear proverbial and generic, and the movement towards abstraction becomes a commitment to the sublime and idealised beyond the material life of the world.

All of these possible frames are consistent with the initial stylistic analysis, and so all are reasonable and evidenced possibilities. If anyone arrived with another interpretation, it would be a requirement within the discipline of stylistics for them to show in similar terms how their reading could be substantiated from the text as well. It should be clear, even from this simple and brief analysis, that stylistics in itself is a method rather than a critical approach. It can be used in the service of a range of different ideological and personal readings, but in itself it is essentially a toolkit and a technique, and it can be used by anyone who cares to spend the time learning a little linguistics and working out what you are looking at, thinking and feeling.

4. Some key ideas to consider and further reading

How disciplined can you be?

Take a short literary text almost at random, and try to decide which key feature or aspect strikes you the most (it could be its syntax, its sound-patterning, its odd form of address, a startling metaphor, an odd arrangement on the page, and so on). Restricting yourself only to this single feature, try to sketch out the most detailed linguistic description that you can. Only when you have finished, try to line up your descriptive account with a sense of your reading and evaluation of the literary work.

How good a stylistician are you?

The journey from beginning stylistics to becoming proficient is actually very short. Take a stylistic feature (such as a sound-pattern, metaphor, point of view, speech presentation, and so on) and think of a literary text that you know in which it is a key feature. Try to account as systematically as you can for the workings of the text.

How can you do literary criticism better?
Find a piece of published literary criticism and see how you can improve it by adding a close stylistic analysis of the literary work that it is discussing. Try to discern whether there are any claims made in the essay or article that cannot be substantiated at all, and then decide what the status of such claims can be.

Where can you find out more?
There are several very good introductions to stylistics, such as Gregoriou (2008), Simpson (2004), Toolan (2001), and Verdonk (2002); some key overviews, such as Leech and Short (2007) and Leech (2008); and a dictionary by Wales (2011). There are also good collections of short stylistic analyses: for a historical anthology, see Carter and Stockwell (2008); for contemporary stylistics, see Lambrou and Stockwell (2007), and McIntyre and Busse (2010).

References

CARTER, R. & P. Stockwell, eds., 2008. *The language and literature reader*. London: Routledge.

GREGORIOU, C., 2008. *English literary stylistics*. London: Macmillan.

LAMBROU, M. & P. Stockwell, eds. 2007. *Contemporary Stylistics*. London: Continuum.

LEECH, G.N., 2008. *Language in literature*. Harlow: Longman.

LEECH, G.N. & M.H. Short, 2007. *Style in fiction* (2nd edition). Harlow: Longman.

MCINTYRE, D. & B. Busse, eds., 2010. *Language and style*. Houndmills, Basingstoke: Palgrave Macmillan.

SHELLEY, P.B., 1970. *Poetical works*, ed. Thomas Hutchinson (2nd edition). ed. G.M. Matthews. Oxford: Oxford University Press.

SIMPSON, P., 2004. *Stylistics: a resource book for students*. London: Routledge.

STOCKWELL, P., 2009. *Texture: a cognitive aesthetics of reading*. Edinburgh: Edinburgh University Press.

TOOLAN, M., 2001. *Narrative: a critical linguistic introduction* (2nd edition). London: Routledge.

VERDONK, P., 2002. *Stylistics*. Oxford: Oxford University Press.

WALES, K., 2011. *A dictionary of stylistics* (3rd edition). Harlow: Longman.

14. FORENSIC LINGUISTICS

Dr Nicci MacLeod

1. Introduction

Forensic linguistics as it is broadly defined refers to any interface between language and the law. It is useful to think of work within the field as falling into three main categories: (1) studies of the language of legal texts, (2) analyses of the discourse of spoken legal practices, and (3) the use of linguistic analyses of forensically relevant texts for investigative and/or evidential purposes.

Within the first category, studies of legal texts, scholars have concerned themselves variously with:

- The language of police cautions, i.e. the words police officers must utter to suspects when an arrest is made (Rock, 2007; 2012), known in the US as Miranda warnings (e.g., Ainsworth, 2012);
- The instructions given by judges to juries before they are sent to deliberate on a verdict at the end of a criminal trial (e.g., Dumas, 2012; Tiersma, 2010);
- The warning labels that appear on certain products (e.g., Shuy, 1990);
- A whole array of **performative** written documents, i.e. documents whose wording consummates an action or creates another state of being, such as contracts, statutes, and wills (Tiersma, 2001).

One outcome of such research has been the rewriting of legal texts in order to improve their comprehensibility. For example, following the high-profile acquittal of OJ Simpson for murdering his wife and her friend in 1995, the late Professor Peter Tiersma became involved in the redrafting of the instructions provided to juries in California. Noting that the existing instructions were often criticised for not being easy for jurors to understand, a task force was formed of judges, lawyers, members of the public, and Tiersma himself, in order to draft new ones that were more comprehensible. Among the problems that were identified with the old instructions were that the term 'reasonable doubt' – a central tenet of adversarial criminal justice – was not defined. Jurors were told what it *was not*, but not what it *was*. The committee rearranged the wording and rephrased the instruction as a positive statement, defining *proof beyond a reasonable doubt* as *proof that leaves you with an abiding conviction that the charge is true* (Tiersma, 2010:260). Since the reason for instructing jurors is to promote the rule of law, activity of the kind described here demonstrates real potential for forensic linguistics scholars to contribute to the delivery of social justice.

Work that might be considered to fall into the second category described above, i.e. analyses of spoken legal discourse, covers the nature of interactions within legal contexts, including the discourse of the courtroom (e.g., Ehrlich, 2001) and that of investigative interviews (e.g., Haworth, 2017; Heydon, 2005). Scholars have also taken interest in how a bilingual context affects the dynamics of these interactions (e.g., Berk-Seligson, 2002) and in the experiences of lay participants whose linguistic and/or cultural background differs to that of the legal system in which they find themselves (e.g., Eades, 2002). The role of the interpreter in legal interactions has proved a further focal point for research in this area (e.g., Hale, 2004), as has the linguistic experiences of particular categories of vulnerable witnesses within the judicial system, such as children or those with communicative disabilities (e.g., Aldridge, 2010), or victims of sexual crimes (e.g., MacLeod, 2016). The application of work in these areas has included the publication of handbooks for legal practitioners to assist in communicating with clients of particular backgrounds (e.g., Eades, 1992) and the delivery of research-based training packages to institutional agents such as police interviewers (MacLeod and Haworth, 2016), representing a direct and mutually beneficial engagement between professionals and researchers, and undeniable societal impact.

MacLeod and Haworth's activity (reported in MacLeod and Haworth, 2016), involved the successful development of a police interviewer training package grounded in discourse analyses of interview interactions. The earlier work had demonstrated that police-negotiated 'final versions' often fall quite wide of the mark in terms of fully and accurately reporting interviewees' stated position, and that there was a need to increase awareness of the many linguistic factors affecting interview evidence.

The third and final category to come under the umbrella of forensic linguistics is the provision of investigative assistance and/or evidence based on linguistic analysis. Linguists are consulted by both sides in both civil and criminal matters on an increasing scale, and often called upon to present their findings in court. In so doing, they put their skills to the best possible use in the pursuit of justice. The work undertaken by forensic linguists in this vein is diverse, ranging from commenting on linguistic aspects of trademarks (e.g., Butters, 2008) through to providing opinion on a suspect's linguistic competence and ability to participate in an interview (e.g., Pavlenko, 2008), to ascertaining meaning in forensic contexts (e.g., Grant, 2017). In the case reported by Grant (2017) he exploited a number of different methods for determining the meaning of particular Multicultural London English terms in an instant messaging conversation between two friends, both heavily involved in the

14. Forensic Linguistics

Grime music scene, who stood accused of conspiring to murder the fifteen-year-old pregnant girlfriend of one of them. One phrase in the chat was *I'll get the fiend to duppy her den*, and through compiling a Grime Music Corpus from online sources, Grant was able to determine the meaning as 'I'll get the drug addict to kill her then' – a clear conspiracy to murder. Both the men were jailed.

Perhaps the most common task that a forensic linguist is asked to engage in, at least in the UK context, is commenting on the possibility that two or more texts share an author, or who is most likely author of a disputed text from a candidate pool of suspects ('comparative authorship analysis' – see Grant, 2010), or whether one text was derived from another (e.g., Coulthard, 2004). At the early stages of an investigation, police may wish to employ the services of a forensic linguist to comment on the social background of the author of an anonymous text, in order to narrow down the pool of suspects or provide intelligence for media appeals, and there is a body of research aiming to refine techniques for doing so (e.g., Nini, 2015). A famous early example of this kind of work was a case in which Roger Shuy considered an anonymous ransom note that had been received in connection with the abduction of a teenage girl in Illinois, USA (reported on in Leonard, 2005). The note read:

> Do you ever want to see your precious little girl
>
> again? Put $10,000 cash in a diaper bag. Put it
>
> in the green trash kan on
>
> the devil strip at corner 18th and Carlson.
>
> Don't bring anybody along.
>
> No kops!! Come alone! I'll be watching you
>
> all the time. Anyone with you,
>
> deal is off and dautter is dead!!!

There were two valuable pieces of information that Shuy was able to glean from this text to enable the police to narrow their pool of suspects quite substantially. Firstly, he drew attention to the author's apparent inability to spell simple words like 'can' [*kan*] and 'cops' [*kops*], while simultaneously being capable of relatively more complicated words such as 'precious'. This, claimed Shuy, pointed to an intelligent person 'playing dumb'. Secondly, Shuy was able to identify the author as hailing from Akron, Ohio – based on the use of the term ***devil strip***, meaning the patch of grass between the pavement and the road. This was a phrase unique to that town, and, sure enough, one of the police's suspects came from Akron. The suspect was arrested, confessed, and was convicted.

Forensic linguists of all persuasions subscribe in some way to the notion of an **idiolect**, which is to say the idea that 'every native speaker has their own distinct and individual version of the language they speak and write' (Coulthard, 2004: 432). While some refer to this as a 'linguistic fingerprint', that term is frowned upon by most, who would question the evidence supporting the idea that an idiolect is unique to an individual, like their physical fingerprint. The point of departure for sociolinguistic profiling and comparative authorship analysis as described above is an understanding of the causes of consistency and variation in language production. This understanding also underpins the new forensic linguistic task of **authorship synthesis**. We return to this task later in the chapter, but for now consider this scenario: a child has been identified by a parent as being at risk from an online would-be sex offender. The child and the perpetrator have been engaging in sexualised conversation for some time, and the child believes she is in a relationship with the adult man with whom she has been chatting. The parent alerts the police, and the child is removed to a place of safety. Clearly the police wish to identify the perpetrator and secure an arrest, but for obvious reasons the child cannot be placed back in the dangerous situation, even if she was willing to be. Instead, an officer must operate undercover online, posing as the child, *synthesising* her identity, to arrange a meeting where the police can close in and make their arrest. Linguists have become involved in assisting investigators with this kind of identity assumption (see MacLeod and Grant, 2017), providing a clear evidence base for covert policing methods.

2. Forensic linguistics: a brief history

Although the first use of the term **Forensic English** can be traced back to 1949 and **Forensic Linguistics** to 1967 (see Coulthard and Johnson, 2007:5), attempts to establish a cohesive discipline of forensic linguistics arguably began in the early 1990s. Developing simultaneously yet independently in Europe, the US and Australia, examples of forensic linguistic work prior to this were isolated and sporadic.

As far back as 1979 in the United States, Roger Shuy, widely considered to be the pioneer of forensic linguistics in that part of the world, received his first instruction as an expert witness as the result of a chance meeting with a lawyer on an aeroplane. Professor Shuy testified for the defence in the trial of Cullen Davis, an oil baron accused of soliciting the murders of his estranged wife and a judge involved in their divorce proceedings. Shuy gave his opinion that supposedly incriminating recordings of the defendant and the alleged hitman did not in fact implicate Davis in the way the state claimed – rather than being indicators of assent to the hitman's suggestions, Davis' responses were in fact discourse markers relating to entirely different topics in the conversation, and he was acquitted (see Shuy, 2014).

On this side of the Atlantic, forensic linguistics had an important part to play in overturning one of the most notorious miscarriages of justice in UK history. Despite being under arrest at the time his companion shot a police officer dead during a thwarted burglary, Derek Bentley was tried and convicted of murder in 1952, received the death sentence and was subsequently hanged in 1953. The evidence against Bentley, who had severe learning difficulties, comprised largely of a statement he allegedly dictated shortly after his arrest. The statement indicated that he knew his accomplice on the night in question was in possession of a gun – a crucial incriminating point upon which the original trial judge placed great importance. There was much public unrest about the conviction, and Bentley's family launched a campaign to clear his name, resulting in an appeal more than forty years later.

Professor Malcolm Coulthard's analysis of the statement, which was presented as part of the appeal, demonstrated that the statement was much more reminiscent of one half of a dialogue than of a dictated monologue. The presence of negative statements with no narrative justification, such as *Up to then Chris had not said anything*, was suggestive of a series of answers to yes-no questions rather than a continuous account. Furthermore, there were lexical and grammatical choices in the text that did not appear to be consistent with Bentley's language. One particular feature that Coulthard focused on was the use of **post-positioned** 'then' – that is, 'then' positioned after a subject, e.g., *Chris then jumped*. You or I might be more inclined to express it as *'Then Chris jumped'*, and Coulthard was able to demonstrate with the use of corpora – large collections of electronic texts – that this use of 'then' was overwhelmingly more consistent with police language than with Bentley's, or indeed with general English. Coulthard's analysis showed that what the police had claimed to be a monologue from Bentley had in fact been edited with the questions removed. The Court of Appeal quashed Derek Bentley's conviction in 1998, following the granting of a posthumous royal pardon in 1993.

In Australia forensic linguistic evidence began to be heard, albeit very rarely at first, in courts from the late 1970s onwards (see Eades, 1994). Much of this has focused on the nuances of Aboriginal English, and cultural differences in the communicative practices of Aboriginal speakers as compared to non-Aboriginal people. For example, one tendency of Aboriginal people is to seemingly assent to every proposition that is put to them. Known as 'gratuitous concurrence', this phenomenon is used to build a relationship between conversationalists in Aboriginal contexts. It is easy to see how it might have quite negative consequences within the Anglo-Australian justice system. Likewise, silence is an important part of Aboriginal communicative norms, while lengthy periods of silence are generally avoided in mainstream Australian interaction. Without knowledge of these differences on the part of the representatives of the justice system, it is easy to see how Aboriginal defendants and witnesses can be severely disadvantaged by this gap. Research in this area came to be more widely recognised within the legal system after the publication of Eades' (1992) handbook for lawyers, and there has been a corresponding increase in the number of forensic linguists called upon to provide their expertise.

All over the world, in fact, there are now an ever-increasing number of cases in which linguists are called upon by either side in both criminal and civil matters in order to provide their opinions through linguistic analyses in the form of a report, sometimes going on to testify as an expert witness in court.

As the discipline has increased in visibility, more attention has been paid to refining the methods forensic linguists use to address their questions (e.g., Wright, 2013; 2017). The research forensic linguists carry out as part of their full-time academic day jobs underpins the casework and consultancy they take on outside of that role.

3. Current trends in forensic linguistics

As discussed earlier, there have been increased attempts to refine methods within forensic linguistics and to establish a cohesive discipline with a common code of practice (IAFL, 2013), and to deepening our understanding of the ethical implications of the work of the forensic linguist (see Butters, 2012).

Forensic linguists are now included on the National Crime Agency's Expert Adviser Database, allowing for investigators to get their contact details at the click of a mouse – although they obviously need to know what it is they are looking for.

A case reported by Grant (2013) concerns SMS text messages sent from a woman's mobile phone hours before her apparently accidental death in a house fire. The woman's husband, Christopher Birks, claimed that his wife Amanda had been at home during the day, had gone to bed early, and subsequently became trapped in an attic bedroom by the flames. A number of details provided by Christopher were not consistent with evidence the police had collected, such as the lack of smoke in Amanda's lungs, the fact she was wearing outside clothes in bed, and the fact the home burglar alarm had not recorded her movements during that day. On this basis Christopher was charged with Amanda's murder.

SMS text messages had been sent from Amanda's phone to Christopher and other family members during the afternoon when Christopher was out, and the content of these messages indicated that she was at home and carrying out ordinary everyday tasks. Grant was tasked with analysing these messages and providing an opinion on whether or not they were more consistent with her usual texting style or with Christopher's. Focussing on 28 features across 368 messages – such as the spelling of *had* as 'ad', *jst* for 'just' and *'wiv'* for 'with' – Grant concluded that the questioned texts were in fact more consistent

14. Forensic Linguistics

with Christopher's style than Amanda's. This supported the police's theory that Christopher had sent the messages from her phone in order to disguise the timing of Amanda's death, and the fact he had murdered her prior to setting the fire to cover his tracks. Before trial, Birks changed his plea to guilty, and was sentenced to life imprisonment.

In 2016 I was approached by Gloucestershire Police in the course of their investigation into the murder of 21-year-old Dolton Powell outside a party in Gloucester. The force's largest operation since the arrest of serial killer Fred West in 1994, the case had involved 100 witnesses, 60 identity parades, and the arrest of eleven suspects, eight of whom eventually stood trial at Bristol Crown Court for Dolton's murder. My task was to listen carefully to recordings that had been made covertly in the back of a police van as the suspects were being transported to the magistrate's court in order for the police to request extensions to their custody time. In the recordings, the suspects could be heard conversing with each other, some of the time in Standard English, and other times in what the police referred to as 'code'. My first job was to transcribe the recordings. An extract of my transcript appears below.

1   JB: So when I first put (*inaudible*) Remember, First come to the feygus keyga peygark .... yeh
2   ES: Yeh
3   […]
4   ES: He got it?
5   JB: Yeh. He had it. (His) steygab preygoof eygon
6   […]
7   ES: Was leygeeven, (*lip suck*) and then (*inaudible*) done that and then you (*inaudible*) Now you see
8   in my mind that was the last thing that happened before we left.
9   JB: Thats what I'm saying dee in my mind, I just really remember fucking, geygetting meyg in the
10 weygip. Wavey told me to geyget in the weygip, I've geygot in the weygip.
11 These times, Meygar and meygar meygit de weygin deygo. Opened the deygo, meygar and
12 steygar got in the keygar

What struck me first was the repetition of the 'eyg' sound, placed between the onset and rime of certain stressed syllables. It may put you in mind of language games played in the playground – Pig Latin, for example, where the first consonant is placed at the end of the word and the 'ay' sound is tagged onto it, rendering 'Pig Latin' as ['Igpay Atinlay']. These games tend to be played by children when they are discussing matters whose meaning they wish to obscure from overhearing authority figures. Here, it appears a similar process is happening, but with the straightforward insertion of 'eyg' – a speech game known variously as 'Egg Latin', 'Egg English' or 'Eggy Peggy'. My first step, then, was to remove all the occurrences of 'eyg' and see what was left:

199

1   JB: So when I first put (*inaudible*) Remember, First come to the fus ka park .... yeh
2   ES: Yeh
3   [...]
4   ES: He got it?
5   JB: Yeh. He had it. (His) stab proof on
6   [...]
7   ES: Was leeven, (*lip suck*) and then (*inaudible*) done that and then you (*inaudible*) Now you see
8   in my mind that was the last thing that happened before we left.
9   JB: Thats what I'm saying dee in my mind, I just really remember fucking, getting m in the wip.
10 Wavey told me to get in the wip, I've got in the wip.
11 These times, Mar and mar mit de win do. Opened the do , mar and star got in the kar

The conversation now becomes much easier to follow. Read aloud, the *fus ka park* on line 1 sounds like 'first car park', and subsequent background reading on the case revealed that there were in fact two car parks at the location where the fatal stabbing took place. Reference is then made on line 5 to someone having their *stab proof on* – rather incriminating information given that the group had apparently gone out to have a good night at a party. Lines 9-10 make a number of references to a *wip*, and a glance at a slang dictionary tells us that a 'whip' is a slang term for a car, which makes sense in this context. Finally, line 11 appears to show discussion of some individuals who *mit* (meet) at *de win do* (the window), opened the *do* (door) and got in the *kar* (car). I testified for the prosecution at the murder trial of Jordan Barclay and others, and Barclay was convicted of Dolton's murder and sentenced to life imprisonment.

4. Future developments in forensic linguistics

Forensic linguists continue to work on developing theory to underpin the methods employed in casework (see Grant and MacLeod, 2018) and new forensic problems continue to present themselves. As police work moves onto the heavily-encrypted Dark Web to track online sharers of abusive imagery, traditional methods of identifying users, such as tracing IP addresses are rendered useless. Operatives are therefore increasingly looking to methods such as forensic linguistics to help them infiltrate these spaces, and to identify and draw out offenders.

Linguistic training for the task of what has been termed 'authorship synthesis' (Grant and MacLeod, 2018) consists of sensitising officers to a target persona's linguistic choices at all levels of language analysis – not simply at the structural level and choices of spelling, punctuation, capitalisation etc., but also at higher levels such as pragmatics – what does this individual *do* with language? Operatives are encouraged also to look at choices at the level of interaction, such as what topics the individual introduces, which they maintain, and which they reject. Completing detailed analyses of an individual's historical chat log with these categories in mind has been shown to improve operatives' linguistic performance of identity (see MacLeod and Grant, 2017), such that their true identity is less likely to be uncovered by the perpetrator(s).

Forensic linguists' continued involvement with training is one method by which the visibility of the discipline is maintained within law enforcement. The upkeep of such awareness is certainly one challenge the future poses for the field, and aside from training initiatives (e.g., MacLeod and Grant, 2017; MacLeod and Haworth, 2016) and articles in publications more likely to be seen by law enforcement (e.g., MacLeod, 2011), forensic linguistics practitioners are heavily reliant on word of mouth for attracting requests for help.

Debate will continue about what 'counts' as forensic linguistics. For example, can comments on social media relating to reports of crimes be considered 'forensically relevant'? I would say so – many types of data in which forensic linguists are interested are, owing to legal and ethical restrictions, inaccessible to the general public, yet there is untapped potential in publicly accessible types of data, such as media reports, below-the-line comments, and other public discourse around crime and criminality (e.g., Tabbert, 2016). Given the media's role in the formation of public opinion, which in turn has implications for jury decision making and institutional responses, it would be remiss of us to ignore these sources.

I turn finally to the question of *who* 'counts' as a forensic linguist. What qualifications should be required of someone who carries out the types of work outlined above? Many short courses and summer schools in forensic linguistic analysis are run worldwide and online, but we would be loath to call anyone a 'forensic linguist' after merely completing one of these. Students often approach me with requests for work experience or advice about how to achieve a career in forensic linguistics. The truth of the matter is this – 99% of forensic linguists are full-time academics, researching, teaching and completing associated administrative tasks in universities, taking on the occasional case, consultancy task, or training course as a sideline. This does not lend itself particularly well to work-shadowing opportunities. The second point to keep in mind is that the forensic arena is simply one of many where you can apply the skills and techniques you pick up from studying descriptive linguistics. Honing one's analytical skills and keeping abreast of the latest methodological developments must always take priority over the specific type of text to which you want to apply these techniques.

5. What's useful for the forensic linguist?

Many aspects of language study have potential application to the field of forensic linguistics. For example, we know from research in areas such as linguistic variation, language attitudes and language ideology that people tend to form opinions about others based on their interactions with them. What might be the implications of this within the legal system, the treatment of particular individuals within it, and the right to a fair trial?

Child language acquisition research gives us an understanding of children's linguistic abilities at particular ages. This might lead us to ask whether the questioning of child witnesses within the legal system is entirely appropriate, and to making suggestions about how we can help alleviate any problems we might perceive. For example, a case discussed by Aldridge and Luchjenbroers (2008) illustrates that the account provided by a child victim of sexual abuse being interviewed by the police may be left open to manipulation by the child's inability to structure narrative answers. The police interview process can therefore be seen as not sufficiently effective in presenting the child as a victim, since children below a certain age may not have the requisite experience to focus their narrative accounts in ways that support their position. Similarly, studying language disorders might provide us with a starting point for investigating the treatment of individuals with specific communicative impairments within the justice system.

A sound grasp of critical discourse analysis and institutional talk might lead us to examine the respective roles of police interviewers versus interviewees, of barristers versus witnesses, or of the status of an expert witness versus a 'lay' witness (i.e. a non-specialist), and to explore the mechanics of interactions with these roles in mind. Studying intercultural communication might further allow us to comment on the experiences of individuals with other cultural backgrounds in their encounters with the police and courts.

A knowledge of computer-mediated communication, the constraints it imposes and the resources for linguistic creativity it provides, equips us with all the right tools to approach a piece of forensically relevant text, such as a series of social media messages, and comment on the patterns therein.

Familiarity with corpus approaches to linguistics and competence with using corpus software could allow for an in-depth examination of particular forensic genres, for example suicide notes, which in turn could prove beneficial for answering questions around what we expect of a genuine versus a fabricated suicide note.

Even studying descriptive grammar has its uses in the forensic sphere. Without a grasp of the terminology for describing sentence structure one would certainly struggle to produce a useful expert report for the police when the question arises about which individual is the more likely author of a particular suspect text.

Only once you are a good linguist can you become a good forensic linguist.

6. Looking to the future

- Although no longer in its infancy, forensic linguistics continues the struggle for recognition amongst law enforcement and legal professionals.
- The work of the forensic linguist is extensive and varied, and may draw on multiple sub-fields of linguistics.
- Work continues to refine the methods underpinning the work of the forensic linguist.

Arguably the most comprehensive introduction to the field is Coulthard, Johnson & Wright (2017). The second edition of Coulthard and Johnson's 2007 title, this textbook is essential reading for anyone hoping to pursue forensic linguistics further, or who has simply a passing interest in this particular application of linguistic analysis. Dealing with all three of the categories discussed at the start of this chapter, the book uses real-life examples to illustrate the wide-ranging work of the forensic linguist, including legal registers, the language of lay-legal interactions, the discourse of the courtroom, authorship analysis, and forensic phonetics. Each chapter concludes with a research task which the reader is encouraged to attempt for some hands-on experience.

References

AINSWORTH, J., 2012. The meaning of silence in the right to remain silent. In L. Solan and P. Tiersma (eds) *The Oxford handbook of language and law*. Oxford: Oxford University Press.

ALDRIDGE, M., 2010. Vulnerable witnesses in the criminal justice system. In M. Coulthard and A. Johnson (eds) *The Routledge handbook of forensic linguistics*. Abingdon: Routledge, 296-314.

ALDRIDGE, M. and Luchjenbroers, J., 2008. Vulnerable witnesses and problems of portrayal: a consideration of videotaped interviews in child rape cases. *Journal of English Linguistics* 36:3, 266-284.

BERK-SELIGSON, S., 2002. *The bilingual courtroom: court interpreters in the judicial process*. Chicago: University of Chicago Press.

BUTTERS, R., 2008. A linguistic look at trademark dilution. *Santa Clara High Technology Journal* 24:3.

BUTTERS, R., 2012. Retiring President's closing address: ethics, best practices, and standards. Proceedings of The International Association of Forensic Linguists' Tenth Biennial Conference.

COULTHARD, M., 2004. Author identification, idiolect and linguistic uniqueness. *Applied Linguistics* 25:4, 431-447.

COULTHARD, M. and Johnson, A., 2007. *An introduction to forensic linguistics: language in evidence*. Abingdon: Routledge.

COULTHARD, M., Johnson, A. and Wright, D. 2017. *An introduction to forensic linguistics: language in evidence*. 2nd Edition. Abingdon: Routledge

COULTHARD, M., Johnson, A. and Wright, D., 2017. *An introduction to forensic linguistics: language in evidence*. Second Edition. Abingdon: Routledge.

DUMAS, B. 2012., Language of jury instructions. In C. Chappelle (ed.) *The encyclopedia of applied linguistics*. Chichester: Wiley.

EADES, D., 1992. *Aboriginal English and the law: communicating with Aboriginal English speaking clients: a handbook for legal practitioners*. Brisbane: Queensland Law Society.

EADES, D., 1994. Forensic linguistics in Australia: an overview. *International Journal of Speech, Language and the Law* 1:2, 113-132.

EADES, D., 2002. Evidence given in unequivocal terms: Gaining consent of Aboriginal young people in court. In J. Cotterill (ed.), *Language in the Legal Process*. London: Palgrave, 161-196.

EHRLICH, S. 2001. *Representing rape: language and sexual consent*. London: Routledge.

GRANT, T. 2010., Text messaging forensics: Txt 4n6: idiolect free authorship analysis? in COULTHARD, M & A Johnson (eds), *The Routledge handbook of forensic linguistics*. Abingdon: Routledge, 508-522.

GRANT, T. 2013.,TXT 4N6: Method, consistency, and distinctiveness in the analysis of SMS text messages. *Journal of Law and Policy* 21:2, Article 9.

GRANT, T. 2017. 'Duppying yoots in a dog eat dog world, kmt': determining the senses of slang terms for the Courts' *Semiotica* 2017: 216, 479-495.

GRANT, T. and MacLeod, N., 2016. Assuming identities online: linguistics applied to the policing of online paedophile activity. *Applied Linguistics* 37:1, 50-70.

GRANT, T. and MacLeod, N., 2018. Resources and constraints in linguistic identity performance: a theory of authorship. *Language and Law/Linguagem e Direito* 5:1.

HALE, S., 2004. *The discourse of court interpreting*. Amsterdam: John Benjamins.

HAWORTH, K., 2017. The discursive construction of evidence in police interviews: case study of a rape suspect. *Applied Linguistics*, 38: 2, 194-214.

HEYDON, G., 2005. *The language of police interviewing: a critical analysis*. Basingstoke: Palgrave.

IAFL, 2013. International Association of Forensic Linguists Code of Practice http://www.iafl.org/uploads/IAFL_Code_of_Practice_1.pdf

LEONARD, R., 2005. Forensic linguistics: applying the scientific principles of language analysis to issues of the law. *International Journal of the Humanities* 3:7, 65-70.

MACLEOD, N., 2016. 'I thought I'd be safe there': pre-empting blame in the talk of women reporting rape. *Journal of Pragmatics* 96, 96-109.

MACLEOD, N. and Grant, T., 2017. 'go on cam but dnt be dirty': linguistic levels of identity assumption in undercover online operations against child sex abusers. *Language and Law/ Linguagem e Direito* 4:2, 157-175

MACLEOD, N. and Haworth, K., 2016. Developing a linguistically Informed approach to police interviewing. In LAWSON, R. & D. Sayers (eds) *Sociolinguistic Research: Application and Impact*. Abingdon: Routledge.

NINI, A., 2015. *Authorship profiling in a forensic context*. PhD dissertation. Aston University, Birmingham, UK.

PAVLENKO, A., 2008. Non-native speakers of English and the Miranda warnings. *TESOL Quarterly*, 42: 1, 1-30

ROCK, F., 2007. *Communicating rights: the language of arrest and detention*. Basingstoke: Palgrave Macmillan

ROCK, F., 2012. The caution in England and Wales. In L. Solan and P. Tiersma (eds) *The Oxford handbook of language and law*. Oxford: Oxford Press, 312-325.

SHUY, R., 1990. Warning labels: language, law and comprehensibility. *American Speech* 65: 4, 291-303.

SHUY, R., 2014. *The language of murder cases: intentionality, predisposition and voluntariness*. Oxford: Oxford University Press.

TABBERT, U., 2016. *Language and crime: constructing offenders and victims in newspaper reports*. Basingstoke: Palgrave

TIERSMA, P., 2001. Textualising the law. *International Journal of Speech, Language and the Law* 8:2, 73-92.

TIERSMA, P., 2010. *Parchment, paper, pixels: law and the technologies of communication*. Chicago: University of Chicago Press.

WRIGHT, D., 2013. Stylistic variation within genre conventions in the Enron email corpus: developing a text-sensitive methodology for authorship research. *International Journal of Speech, Language and the Law 20*: 1, 45-75.

WRIGHT, D., 2017. Using word n-grams to identify authors and idiolects: a corpus approach to a forensic linguistic problem. *International Journal of Corpus Linguistics* 22:2, 212-241.

GLOSSARY

A

Abstract noun: A noun referring to a concept, idea or feeling

Accent: A way of pronouncing sounds differently, usually linked to the region a speaker is from

Accommodation: A term applied to the ways in which different speakers' language styles move closer (converge) towards or move apart (diverge) from each other

Acrolect: The variety of a language that is closest to the standard form (especially when discussing different varieties linked to regional and world Englishes)

Active voice: See **voice**

Adjective: A word class used to modify nouns

Adverb: A word class used for a number of functions, including modifying adjectives and verbs. Adverbs often tell us about time, manner and place. These are called adverbs of manner. They can also modify adjectives and verbs by telling us to what degree (how much or how little) a verb is operating or an adjective is modifying

Affordances: In discussing Computer-mediated Communication (CMC), these are the what the technology or platform offers the user in terms of benefits (e.g., the potential to address multiple recipients, communicate instantly over a large distance, or imbed video links). See also **limitations**

Anaphora: A form of reference that relates to a previously established referent e.g., a pronoun referring back to a person or thing that has previously been introduced in the text. The antecedent is the 'thing' that has been previously established (e.g., In the sentence 'The protesters carried on until they were forced back by police', the antecedent is *the protesters* and the pronoun *they* makes an anaphoric reference back to *the protesters*

Analogy: A mechanism of language change in which a speaker 'regularises' a language feature that appears to break a regular pattern

Aspect: A grammatical term that refers to whether an action or process is ongoing (progressive aspect) or completed (perfective aspect)

Authorship synthesis: Using linguistic techniques to mimic the style of another person and artificially assume their language identity

Auxiliary verb: A verb that operates alongside another verb in a verb phrase, often to specify tense or modality

B

Borrowing: A linguistic process in which a word from one language is taken and used in another

C

Child-directed speech (CDS): A way of speaking to a child that uses simplified lexis and grammar and more exaggerated pronunciation patterns

Clause: A grammatical unit generally used to express a single idea, usually consisting of a verb phrase and a noun phrase

Code-switching: The way in which a speaker moves between one register, style or variety of a language into another

Codification: Part of the standardisation process of a language in which the standard is written down in dictionaries or grammars

Collocation: A word or phrase that is often linked to another word

Community of practice: An approach to language variation which takes account of the groups of people speakers associate with and the forms of language they use in these groups

Complex sentence: A sentence consisting of at least two clauses, one of which is subordinate to (or dependent on) a main clause

Compound sentence: A sentence consisting of two or more main clauses linked with one of the conjunctions *or*, *but* or *and*

Computer-mediated communication (CMC): A mode of communication that combines elements of written and spoken forms and is produced using a computer or digital device (e.g., text messaging, email or social media posts)

Conjunctions: Words that are used to connect words, phrases and clauses, e.g., *and*, *because*, *so*

Connotation: The wider, associated meanings of a word

Convergence: See **accommodation**

Conversational floor: The term used to refer to who is speaking at a given time or 'holding the conversational floor'

Conversational historic present: A term used to describe a speaker's use of the present tense when recounting a narrative that has already taken place

Conversational turn: The basic unit of structure in a conversation, generally seen as being a single contribution made by one speaker before another speaker takes their turn

Corpus (corpora): A body of language data, often in the form of a digital database

Corpus stylistics: An approach to stylistics which uses corpus data

Language Handbook – Key Thinkers on Key Topics

Covert prestige:	A linguistic term used to describe a type of status or value placed upon the language style of a speaker or group of speakers. In this case, the status is seen as outside, or opposing, mainstream values (c.f. overt prestige)
Creole:	A form of language that develops from a contact language (pidgin) through subsequent generations
Critical Discourse Analysis (CDA):	A linguistic approach that uses textual analysis to unpick underlying attitudes and ideologies

D

Declarative clause:	A clause expressing a statement (usually with a subject verb word order)
Declinism:	A belief that language standards are in decline
Deictic expression:	A term that 'points' towards a person, an object, a time or a place, often used in speech where participants share the same physical context
Descriptivism:	An approach to language that attempts to describe rather than judge usage
Determiner:	A word class consisting of words which help specify and determine which noun or noun phrase is being identified (e.g., *an* extremely long time and *the* one on the right)
Dialect:	A variety of a language, usually linked to a geographical area, that is different from the standard in its lexis, semantics, grammar and/or phonology
Dialect levelling:	A reduction in the spread, range and features of local dialects, often associated with greater contact and movement of peoples in the 20th and 21st centuries. Also referred to as **levelling**
Dialectology:	The study of dialects
Direct address:	Talking or writing to a text receiver directly, using their name or a second person pronoun
Direct speech:	Using the exact words spoken by someone in an account of what they said (c.f. indirect speech)
Discourse:	When used in the field of ideology and interpretation, a discourse is a way in which an ideology or argument is expressed through language
Discourse markers:	Words or phrases that indicate a change in topic, or a return to a previous topic
Discourse pragmatic features:	Features of spoken language which help to manage interaction rather than convey specific lexical or semantic meanings
Divergence:	See **accommodation**

Dynamic verb:	A verb used to describe a physical process

E

Elaboration:	Part of the standardisation process of a language in which having been selected and codified, the standard is used for a wide variety of purposes in various genres
Elliptical constructions:	Constructions that omit certain words, often for economical reasons in speech
Emoji:	A small image file used to express emotions and represent ideas and objects in **Computer-mediated Communication (CMC)**
Emoticon:	A symbol used to express emotion or attitude, like a smiley
Ethnolect:	A variety of language related to an ethnic group (See also **multiethnolect**)
Exclamative clause:	A clause used to exclaim or express shock or surprise (usually with a specific word order), usually starting with a wh- word (e.g., *What a tragedy!* or *What a fool he is!*)
Expressive punctuation:	Using punctuation in a non-standard fashion to express or exaggerate a feeling (e.g., *!!!* rather than just *!*)

F

Face theory:	A theory that suggests that all speakers have 'face needs' that we are aware of when we engage in conversation (e.g., the need to be liked and/or given freedom to have options)
Filler:	A short, often non-lexical utterance that acts like a pause in conversation
Fixed expression:	A word or phrase that has generally become established in its accepted meaning and no longer necessarily conveys its literal meaning

G

Genre:	The particular category a text is placed into on the basis of an agreed set of conventions, for example advertising, poetry, text messaging
Grammar:	The structure of a language in terms of its word order and morphology

H

Hedging device:	A word or phrase used to avoid being direct when a participant expresses an opinion

I

Ideology:	A set of beliefs or values which form a way of thinking about the world

Idiolect:	A distinct and individual language style
Idiom/idiomatic expression:	A word or expression that might be non-literal or metaphorical, but be generally understood through context or culture
Imperative clause:	A clause used to command or direct (usually starting with a verb)
Implementation:	A stage in the standardisation of a language in which the standard is applied as widely as possible and alternative, non-standard usages are treated as incorrect
Inclusive address:	Addressing a text receiver as part of a group that also includes the text producer, often using the first person plural pronoun
Indirect speech:	A way of reporting what someone has said but without using their exact words (c.f. direct speech)
Intensifier:	An adverb of degree, adding strength to an adjective that it premodifies
Intonation:	The way in which vocal pitch is used in speech
Interactional features:	Language features that are primarily interactional (most commonly used in speech)
Interactional language:	Language where the primary concern is to maintain personal and social relationships
Interrogative clause:	A clause used to ask a question
Intertextuality:	The process whereby one text refers to or borrows from another text or genre for effect
Intransitive verb:	A verb that doesn't take an object
Invariant tag:	A question tag that doesn't change to match in agreement with the person of the subject (e.g., *I've got bare skills at football **innit***)

L

Latched talk:	A term used in spoken language analysis which relates to when one speaker 'latches on' and immediately speaks after another speaker's turn, with no obvious gap between the turns
Letter homophone:	A letter name that is used because it sounds the same as a part of a word (e.g., *U* = you, *B* = be)
Levelling:	See **Dialect levelling**
Lexis:	Vocabulary, individual words in a language

Glossary

Limitations: In discussing Computer-mediated Communication (CMC), these are the restrictions that a technology or platform might impose on a user (e.g., removing facial expressions or the human voice for communication, relying on very basic visual design). See also **affordances**

Lingua franca: A form of language used to communicate between speakers who have no shared language

Linguistic variable: A linguistic feature that is likely to change or vary and that can be used to measure differences between speakers (e.g., two different ways of pronouncing the word *path*)

M

Metaphor: A way of describing or structuring one thing in terms of another

Minimal responses: Short, often non-lexical responses

Minor sentence: A grammatically incomplete sentence punctuated as a complete sentence, often making use of ellipsis

Mode: The way in which a text is produced and received, depending on the channel used (eyes or ears), whether it is spoken, written, or created through the medium of a keyboard or touchscreen. The three modes are generally referred to as spoken, written and blended/mixed. Some broader definitions of mode refer to different meaning-making systems e.g. images or gesture might be viewed as modes as well

Modifier: A word (usually an adjective or adverb) that attributes a quality to another word

Morphology: The structure of words, usually with specific focus on their prefixes (beginnings) or suffixes (endings)

Multiethnolect: A pool of linguistic resources combining elements of different languages and varieties of English, influenced by multi-ethnic and multicultural identities (see also **ethnoloect**)

Multicultural London English (MLE): A form of language used by young multi-ethnic speakers, primarily in London

Multimodal: Texts that make use of more than one mode (e.g., a children's book that incorporates written language and images, or a webpage that makes use of video clips along with written text)

N

Nominalisation: A term used to describe how a process normally described using a verb becomes a noun (e.g., an *attack* is a nominalisation of a verb process *to attack*)

Non-lexicalised speech: Sounds made in speech which are not recognised words

Non-standard usage:	A way of describing language usage that deviates in some way – in grammar, punctuation, spelling, lexis – from the normal conventions of Standard English. Linguists tend to prefer non-standard rather than incorrect because the former makes no judgement about the acceptability or otherwise of the usage
Noun:	A word class used to label objects, people, places and concepts. Can normally have an -s added to make the plural, and often has a determiner like *a* or *the* somewhere in front
Number homophone:	A number symbol that is used because it sounds the same as a part of a word (e.g., 8 = *ate*, 2 = *to*)

O

Open and closed questions:	Closed questions are interrogatives which can only be answered with a yes or no (e.g., *Did you eat your breakfast this morning?*), while open questions offer a larger range of possible responses and often start with a *wh-* structure (e.g., *Why are you looking at me?* or *What is the matter with you?*)
Orthography:	A broad term to refer to the ways in which language is represented by writing and including aspects of letter formation, spelling and type
Overgeneralisation:	A pattern in children's language where regular grammatical rules are applied to irregular words (e.g., *runned* instead of 'ran', *mouses* instead of 'mice')
Overt prestige:	A linguistic term used to describe a type of status or value placed upon the language style of a speaker or group of speakers. In this case, the status is seen as conforming to mainstream values (c.f. covert prestige)

P

Paralinguistic features:	Non-verbal behaviour such as the use of stress, intonation and volume to add effect and meaning to verbal utterances
Passive voice:	See **Voice**
Patois:	A variety of a language often derived from creole forms and using non-standard features
Performative language:	Language that not only communicates straightforward meaning but also performs a function by being uttered e.g., a promise, a declaration, an apology
Philology:	The study of language histories and origins
Phoneme:	The smallest meaningful unit of sound in a language
Phonetic:	Relating to sounds of speech
Phonology:	The study of speech sounds

Glossary

Phrase: A unit of language made up of anything from one word on its own to several words acting together, but usually smaller than a clause. Phrases take their identity from their head word i.e. the most important word in the phrase

Pidgin: A contact language that is formed when speakers who do not share a common language create a means of communication, often using simplified forms

Post-positioning: The process of moving an element of a clause (e.g., a word or phrase) to later in that clause

Preposition: A word that helps tell you where things are and how they are positioned relative to other things (e.g., *under, on*)

Prescriptivism: An approach to language use that argues that there are correct and incorrect ways of speaking and writing and that certain preferred forms should be encouraged

Pronoun: A word class that is sometimes treated as a subclass of nouns. Pronouns are words which usually take the place of nouns or noun phrases. First person: I (singular), we or us (first person plural). Second person: you (singular) or you (plural)

Prosody: Patterns of rhythm and/or sound in speech

Q

Question tags: See **tag questions**

Quotative (expression): An expression used to introduce reported or direct speech

R

Reanalysis: A mechanism of language change in which a word, phrase or sound is looked at again in a way that changes how it is perceived (e.g., a compound word's origins as two separate words is forgotten and it is simply viewed as a single word)

Received Pronunciation (RP): An accent that came to be viewed as a prestige form in English during the early part of the 20th century

Register: A term applied to language choices based on the level of formality and sophistication of the word choices, often linked to the field being discussed (e.g., a person may choose to speak in an academic register because that's what expected in a seminar at university)

Reported thought: A means of conveying what a person was thinking

S

Selection: An early stage in the standardisation process where a variety is chosen to act as the standard

Language Handbook – Key Thinkers on Key Topics

Semantic fields:	Groups of word meanings that are related by theme (e.g., words that have meanings linked to warmth, family or warfare)
Semantics:	Word meanings
Sentence fragments:	Another way of describing minor sentences
Simple sentence:	A sentence consisting of one main clause
Sociolect:	A type of language, usually linked to a social or occupational group, that is different from the standard in its lexis, semantics, grammar and/or phonology
Sociolinguistics:	The branch of language study that explores the relationships between language and society
Standard English:	The variety of English that is generally accepted to be the norm and generally held up to be what users of the language should be taught and become competent in
Standardisation:	The process through which a standard form of a language emerges
Stative verbs:	Verbs that describe a state of being
Stylistics:	A branch of language study that applies linguistic techniques to mainly literary texts
Subject ellipsis:	A form of grammatical compression that features clauses without subjects (e.g., *Hope you are doing OK*, rather than *I hope you are doing OK*)
Synchronic variation:	Differences or variations within a language at a given time
Syntax:	Part of grammar: the structures used when words are put together to create meaning
Synthetic personalisation:	A technique that addresses a text receiver directly as if there is an actual relationship between them and text producer

T

Tag question:	A group of words containing an auxiliary verb and a pronoun, sometimes with 'not' added. Tags are used to prompt an answer from a participant e.g., *isn't it?* Sometimes referred to as **question tags**
Tense:	A grammatical term applied to how verbs are altered to indicate whether an event or process is in the present or took place in the past. It's very closely linked to the concept of time
Terms of address:	How names and titles are used to identify speakers or characters

Glossary

Transitional probability:	The chance that one thing will be followed by another
Transitive verb:	A verb that takes an object

U

Universal Grammar:	A set of innate linguistic principles behind all languages

V

Verb:	Verbs are used to describe states, actions and processes, and are a vital part of clauses. Verb types have often been broken down into **stative** (describing a state of being e.g., she *is*) and **dynamic** (describing an action or process e.g., she *watched* or they *moved*). Cognitive linguistics has also introduced other categories: **verbal** verbs (related to speech), **mental** verbs (related to thought processes), **material** verbs (related to actions and processes), **reciprocal** verbs (related to those processes that are seen as involving two participants engaged in the same process or action)
Verb stem:	Part of a verb which suffixes are usually added to
Vernacular:	The generally used forms of a language, often colloquial or non-standard
Voice:	A grammatical concept that relates to whether the subject of the sentence is doing the verb (**active** voice) or having the verb done to it (**passive** voice)

THE CONTRIBUTORS

Professor Deborah Cameron

Deborah Cameron is Professor of Language and Communication at Oxford University. She has written extensively about language, gender and sexuality: her book-length publications on the subject include *The Myth of Mars and Venus: Do Men and Women Really Speak Different Languages?* (OUP 2007) and *Gender, Power and Political Speech* (with Sylvia Shaw, Palgrave 2016). She is also the author of *The Teacher's Guide to Grammar* (OUP 2007), and a regular speaker, broadcaster and blogger on a range of linguistic topics.

Dan Clayton

Dan Clayton is an Education Consultant at the English and Media Centre and an experienced A Level English Language teacher who has worked at St Francis Xavier College, London and The Sixth Form College, Colchester with a period as a Research Fellow at UCL in the middle. He is a senior examiner and moderator for A Level English Language at a major awarding body and has written and edited a number of English Language publications for Oxford University Press, Cambridge University Press, Routledge and the EMC. His A level English Language blog can be found at http://englishlangsfx.blogspot.co.uk/ and he tweets at @EngLangBlog.

Dr Rob Drummond

Rob Drummond is a Senior Lecturer in Linguistics at Manchester Metropolitan University, and Head of Youth Language at the Manchester Centre for Youth Studies. He works in sociolinguistics, specialising in the study of language variation and its role in the performance of identity, with a particular focus on the language of young people. Recent publications include *Researching Urban Youth Language and Identity* (Palgrave 2018) and *Language Diversity and World Englishes* (with Dan Clayton, CUP 2018).

Dr Sue Fox

Sue Fox is a Senior Lecturer at the University of Bern, Switzerland. She is a sociolinguist whose primary research interest is in contemporary language variation and change in English. Her research has focused on the social and historical contexts that have led to the variety of English that is spoken today in London, particularly among young people. She works on documenting, analysing and accounting for variation in pronunciation as well as variation in discourse and grammatical features, among speakers of various social and ethnic backgrounds. She is interested in tracking changes in progress and the processes that bring about language change, particularly in a multicultural urban environment such as London.

Professor Angela Goddard

Angela Goddard is a Professor of English Language and a UK Higher Education Academy National Teaching Fellow. She has taught English in schools and universities both in the UK and abroad. Angela is Chair of Examiners for English Language A Level at a major UK exam board; she also chairs an international equivalent. She has written many books and articles on language, particularly with an interdisciplinary focus. Her most recent publication is *Discourse: the Basics*, for Routledge.

Professor Christopher Hart

Christopher Hart is Professor of Linguistics at Lancaster University. His research investigates the link between language use, cognition and the legitimation of social and political action. He has been particularly interested in the language of migration in the news and the way the media reports civil disorder in the form of riots, strikes and political protests. Chris is author of *Critical Discourse Analysis and Cognitive Science: New Perspectives on Immigration Discourse* (Palgrave, 2010) and *Discourse, Grammar and Ideology: Functional and Cognitive Perspectives* (Bloomsbury, 2014).

Dr Paul Ibbotson

Paul Ibbotson studied physical geography for three years and then linguistics for a further year. After several more unwise and eccentric decisions he gained his PhD in developmental psychology from the University of Manchester, UK. He currently works at the Open University – continuing to research the learning processes that drive language acquisition and continuing to make unwise and eccentric decisions.

Professor Paul Kerswill

Paul Kerswill is Professor of Sociolinguistics at the University of York. His first research was on dialects in Norway, where he studied changes in the speech of rural dialect speakers who had moved to the city of Bergen. This started his fascination with how dialects change as a result of migration. His first major study, which he conducted with Ann Williams, was of the new accent of Milton Keynes. He is perhaps best known for his ground-breaking study of Multicultural London English (MLE), on which he has worked with colleagues from Queen Mary, University of London. The research covered topics from linguistic changes in MLE, through young Londoners' identities, to the representation of MLE in the media. He is currently researching the origins of MLE, as well as the history of English dialects in the Industrial Revolution. At the same time, he is carrying out joint research on language use in Ghana.

Dr Nicci MacLeod

Nicci MacLeod gained her PhD in Forensic Linguistics from Aston University in 2010, on the topic of police interviews with women reporting rape. Since then she has been employed on various research projects, focussing on 17th-century legal discourse, authorship analysis of tweets, and assuming identities online in the context of undercover online operations against child sex offenders. She is now a Lecturer in English Language and Linguistics at Northumbria University, an Honorary Research Associate at the Centre for Forensic Linguistics at Aston, and a self-employed forensic linguist.

Professor Lynne Murphy

Lynne Murphy is Professor of Linguistics at the University of Sussex. As @lynneguist, she writes the blog *Separated by a Common Language*. Her latest book is *The Prodigal Tongue: the love-hate relationship between British and American English* (Oneworld March 2018).

Professor Jane Setter
Jane Setter is Professor of Phonetics in the Department of English Language and Applied Linguistics at the University of Reading, and a National Teaching Fellow. She specialises in research on the phonology of Hong Kong English (*Hong Kong English*, with Cathy Wong and Brian Chan, Edinburgh University Press 2010) and other South East Asian varieties, and on intonation among children with speech and language deficits. Jane is a co-editor of the *Cambridge English Pronouncing Dictionary* (CUP, 18th edition 2011), and a multi-award-winning academic teacher who lectures on phonetics, phonology and world Englishes. In her spare time, she is a rock vocalist. Follow her on Twitter (@JaneSetter) and read her blog (http://aworldofenglishes.blogspot.com/).

Professor Peter Stockwell
Peter Stockwell is Professor of Literary Linguistics at the University of Nottingham. He has published 15 books and over 50 articles in English language studies, including textbooks for A Level and university students. He edits the Routledge English Language Introductions series, and is a Fellow of the English Association.

The Contributors

Dr Graeme Trousdale
Graeme Trousdale is a senior lecturer in English Language at the University of Edinburgh. He teaches courses on sociolinguistics, figurative language, language change and grammar. His main research interests are in areas of historical linguistics, but he has also written an textbook for beginning undergraduate students, on English sociolinguistics (*An Introduction to English Sociolinguistics*, Edinburgh University Press, 2010). He is keen to work with teachers and school students to promote knowledge about language in schools, and is involved in the organisation of the United Kingdom Linguistics Olympiad (www.uklo.org), a competition for school students in which they have to solve linguistics puzzles.

Dr Kevin Watson
Kevin Watson is a senior lecturer in sociolinguistics at the University of Canterbury, in Christchurch, New Zealand. Originally from Liverpool, Kevin has carried out research on Liverpool English, and also on other accents in north-west England, such as Skelmersdale and St Helens. He runs the Origins of Liverpool English Corpus (OLIVE), based at the University of Canterbury, which has language data spanning one hundred years and so can be used to track linguistic change. He also works on New Zealand English. His research interests focus primarily on phonological variation, in particular on the factors at work in the convergence and divergence between accents, and also on the co-variation of phonological variables across space and over time.

INDEX

A

Accent 17, 23-24, 30-31, 36-37, 42-43, 47-48, 50, 52-54, 56-57, 62, 70, 71-72, 118-119, 124, 140
African urban youth languages 88
African-American English 75-77
American English 70-82
Analogy 115-116, 153-154, 159
Authorship Synthesis 196, 200
Attitudes to language 23, 32, 45, 64, 77-79, 81, 84, 90, 92, 99, 122-134

B

Backchannels 98-101
Borrowing 80, 115-117, 120

C

Case studies 128-129 (Coventry – language change 'texting' study); 86 (Detroit 'Jocks and Burnouts'); 90 (Manchester – urban youth language); 36-37, 39 (Milton Keynes – language change); 26-27, 47-49 (Norwich – language variation); 28-30 (Dudley – language variation); 31-32 (Teesside – language variation); 26, 44-47 (New York – language variation); 44-46 (Martha's Vineyard – language variation); 49-50 (Newcastle – language variation); 17, 51 (Bolton – language variation); 52 (Fife – language variation); 52, 53 (Liverpool – language variation); 87 (San Francisco)

Chicano English 77
Child directed speech (CDS) 155-156, 157, 159
Child language acquisition 136, 148-162, 202
Circles Model 57-59
Code-switching 30, 65
Cognitive functionalism 152-156
Colonisation 73-74, 66-67
Community of practice 18-19, 51-52
Computer-mediated communication 137-138, 141-144
Conversational historic present 103-105
Corpus stylistics 183-185
Creole 28, 76, 118-119
Critical discourse analysis 163-178, 181, 186
Critical linguistics 164

D

Declinism 129
Deixis 104-105
Descriptivism 130-132
Dialect 11, 23-24, 31-32, 37-38, 42-44, 46-47, 52, 61-63, 71, 74-77, 79-81, 87, 89, 91, 113-115, 118-119, 123, 125, 126, 129, 184

Index

Dialect levelling 37, 50-54, 57, 74-77, 119
Discourse-pragmatic features 98, 105-108
Divergence 52-54
Dynamic Model of the Evolution of Postcolonial Englishes 60-61

E

Electronic language 141
Emoji 142
Ethnicity 16, 21, 22-41, 197
Expanding Circle 57-59, 62

F

Face theory 142
Feminism and language change 11, 14
Forensic Linguistics 193-205

G

Gender 10-22, 26-28, 31, 37, 38, 42, 43, 83, 86, 122, 140, 145, 163
General extenders (spoken language) 106
Generalisations 149-150, 154-155, 159
Geographical diffusion 48

H

Hedging devices 13, 15, 106
Hierarchical geographical diffusion 48-49

I

Identity 17, 18-20, 24, 61, 66-67, 73, 77, 81, 83-85, 87-88, 91-92, 95, 122, 124-125, 127, 139-140, 166-167, 196, 199, 201
Idiolect 196
Immigration 24-26, 33-34, 36, 38, 60, 67, 73-75, 87-88, 91, 167-168, 172- 174, 178
Inner circle 57-59, 62-64, 65
Innovation 107, 115, 117, 118
Intensifiers 107

K

Kachru's Circles Model 57-59

L

Language acquisition – see child language acquisition
Language change 11, 48, 71, 85, 91, 108, 112-121, 122-134, 136
Language variation 10-11, 16, 22-41, 42-55, 70-71, 72-77, 81, 83-84, 86, 90, 113-114, 116-118, 120, 122, 127, 143-144, 151-153, 189, 196, 202
Lingua franca 56, 62-64, 66-67

221

Linguistic accommodation 48, 50
Literary linguistics 181

M

Multicultural London English (MLE) 25-26, 33, 38-39, 88-89, 91-92, 194-195
Multicultural Urban British English (MUBE) 88-89
Music 92-93

N

New technologies 11, 124, 128, 132, 136, 137, 144-146
New varieties of English 56, 58-59
Nominalisation 170-171
Norm-dependent, norm-developing, norm-providing 58-59

O

Older Varieties of English 59
Online communication 139
Outer circle 57-59
Overgeneralisations 150, 155

P

Patois 28-30, 36-38, 123-124
Performance 17, 18-19, 20, 84, 86, 90-91, 201
Pidgin 118-119
'Political Correctness' 123, 132
Prescriptivism 130-131
Proficiency model 61
Pronunciation 25-26, 29-37, 42-44, 50-53, 56, 62-66, 70, 72, 75-79, 86-87, 89, 91-92, 112, 115-116
Punctuation 72

Q

Quotative constructions & expressions 108-110

R

Reanalysis (language change) 135
Received pronunciation 11, 24, 29, 43, 56
Regional variation 10-11, 23-24, 37-38, 43, 47, 50, 52-54, 70, 74-81, 89, 108, 110, 119, 122, 126-127, 140
Representation 20, 24, 136-137, 160, 170, 173, 175, 177-179, 216

S

Schneider's Dynamic Model of the Evolution of Postcolonial Englishes 60-61
Slang 84, 94-95, 127, 199-200
Slavery and English 75-77
Social networking 138-141, 194

Index

Sociolinguistic interview 26, 36, 45, 100
Sociolinguistics 10, 22, 31, 44-47, 50-51, 95, 117
Speaker variables 118
Speech communities 10-11, 31, 51, 66, 118
Spelling 70, 72, 73, 79, 128, 195
Spoken language 23, 31, 36, 37, 47-48, 56, 61-62, 65, 70, 73, 75-77, 97-111, 120, 127, 130, 141, 144, 160, 193-194
Standard English 125-126
Standardisation 125-126
Stylistics 181-192, a practical analysis 187-191

T

Tag questions 18, 65, 108, 124, 134
Text analysis 181

U

Universal grammar 151-152, 158-159
Usage-based model and CLA 153, 155, 156, 159-160

V

Variationist sociolinguistics 44, 46, 50, 117

W

Web 2.0 138, 140
Web 3.0 140, 145
World Englishes 56-69
World Standard Spoken English 62

Y

Yiddish 77

223